Collecting Fluorescent Minerals

Stuart Schneider

Schiffer Publishing Ltd

4880 Lower Valley Road, Atglen, PA 19310 USA

About the Value Guide

I have included a value guide to help collectors. It is often said that a price guide is out of date the moment that it is published. Do not let that affect your use of a value guide. A value guide is comparative. It allows you to compare two items to determine if they are of comparable value. It is useful in buying and trading and it can help give you a feel for the rarity of a piece.

The items in this book are valued by people who sell fluorescent minerals and collectors who buy them. Values are given in ranges and I have tried to give values that dealers can sell at and collectors will buy at. The dealers have not set "top dollar" prices and the buyers are not paying "through the nose." It is believed that these are the fair ranges that the minerals usually trade in. Note the size of the piece that is valued. Some are small pieces. It they were larger pieces, they would be worth more.

People who make their living selling minerals usually charge more than the hobbyist who collects and sells off his duplicates or excess material at a mineral show. The person that you deal with may not follow these "rules." Many fluorescent minerals are bought and sold on eBay. If two people want the same piece, the price that is paid may not come close to the values set in this book. Value ultimately is the price agreed upon by a willing seller and a willing buyer. If a collector needs a piece for his or her collection, the collector will pay more than if they already have an example of that mineral in their collection. Also, when a book comes out and interest in that field of collecting picks up, the prices usually rise. The buyer must ultimately decide if the price of a mineral offered is a good deal for him. Just keep in mind that occasionally you will overpay for a rock and occasionally you will underpay. In the end, it probably evens out.

Remember, two is a coincidence, three is a collection. Happy hunting!

Library of Congress Cataloging-in-Publication Data

Schneider, Stuart L.
  Collecting fluorescent minerals / by Stuart Schneider.
     p. cm.
    ISBN 0-7643-2091-2 (pbk.)
1. Fluorescent minerals—Collection and preservation.
2. Large type books—Specimens.   I. Title.
QE364.2.F5S36 2004
549'.125—dc22
                                    2004004164

Designed by Ellen J. (Sue) Taltoan
Type set inDomBold BT/Dutch801 Rm BT

ISBN: 0-7643-2091-2
Printed in China
1 2 3 4

Published by Schiffer Publishing Ltd.
4880 Lower Valley Road
Atglen, PA 19310
Phone: (610) 593-1777; Fax: (610) 593-2002
E-mail: Info@schifferbooks.com

For the largest selection of fine reference books on this and related subjects, please visit our web site at
www.schifferbooks.com
We are always looking for people to write books on new and related subjects. If you have an idea for a book please contact us at the above address.
This book may be purchased from the publisher.
Include $3.95 for shipping.
Please try your bookstore first.
You may write for a free catalog.

In Europe, Schiffer books are distributed by
Bushwood Books
6 Marksbury Ave.
Kew Gardens
Surrey TW9 4JF England
Phone: 44 (0) 20 8392-8585; Fax: 44 (0) 20 8392-9876
E-mail: info@bushwoodbooks.co.uk
Free postage in the U.K., Europe; air mail at cost.

Introduction

My first trip to collect fluorescent minerals was to the mine dump at the Sterling Hill Mine in Ogdensburg, New Jersey. I was a new collector. I had bought all the available books on fluorescent minerals, read them, and thought that I had an idea what I was doing. However, when confronted with tons of rocks to choose from, I was confused. People were cracking rocks open, looking at them and then throwing them back on the pile or into their bucket. I had no idea what I was looking at nor what I should be looking for. Other collectors at the site were kind enough to offer advice and show me what was unusual and interesting. Cracking open the rock gave the collectors a fresh, un-weathered surface to study and oc-

casionally exposed a hidden mineral. After some years of collecting fluorescent minerals and in effect, "learning on the job," I decided that there was a need for a book that showed what the different fluorescent minerals looked like—in daylight and under the mineral UV light. It would have to be useful to beginner collectors, advanced collectors, and everyone in between. It would have to be easy to use, have lots of photographs (since a collection of fluorescent minerals is a visual experience), and it would have to inspire collectors to expand their collecting horizon and get out and collect. This book is the end result of my ongoing study of this fascinating field of mineralogy.

Contents

Acknowledgments

The author would like to acknowledge the many individuals who lent valuable assistance in the creation of this book. By permitting me to view and to photograph pieces from their collections, they can now share their fluorescent minerals with the rest of the world. Thank you to Gar Van Tassel, a good friend, who gave me mining history (his dad was a local miner), an appreciation of what minerals could be found in Franklin, and an opportunity to dig in his backyard. Also thank you to Earl Verbeek, the curator of the Sterling Hill Mineral Museum, and John Cianciulli, the curator of the Franklin Mineral Museum, for their valued input and friendship. Over the years, they have helped to identify rocks and minerals that I could only guess at. Thanks to the FOMS and its members for their monthly meetings where I could hear noted lecturers speak about the mines, learn about their history, learn what it was like to be a miner, and hear about the latest finds and new trends in mineral identification. Many thanks to Mark L. Cole of The Miner Shop for his contribution of material about the minerals of Greenland; Robert and Richard Hauck, the dreamers that made their dreams come true while saving the Sterling Hill Mine in Ogdensburg, New Jersey; Bill Gardner of the Purple Passion Mine for providing information about the mine's history; Bob Jones of Rock and Gem magazine for continuing to write, in an interesting and informative way, about the joys of rock and gem collecting; Benjamin Schneider, who brought home the first of our fluorescent minerals after a scouting trip to the Sterling Hill Mine; Rebecca Schneider, who accompanied me on many trips and enjoyed digging in the rain and mud without complaint; and Manny Robbins, whose books got me started on collecting fluorescent minerals and whose talks on fluorescents at the FMS and FOMS meetings added to my understanding of fluorescent mineral science.

I especially wish to acknowledge the contributions of (in alphabetical order) Richard Bostwick, George Elling and his incredible mineral collection, Nicole Gariepy, Kurt Hennig, Greg Jacobus, Greg Lesinski, Ed Letscher, Peter Lindberg of Greenland, Freddy Lubbers, Don Newsome, George Polman, Joe Vasichko, Francesco Vecchi, Eric Weis, Dru Wilbur, Herb Yeates, and Jack Zektzer (the man for whom Zektzerite is named).

Once again, my thanks to those individuals for their time, their marvelous minerals, and above all their willingness to share so much of their knowledge with me.

Chapter One

Fluorescent Minerals

"Wow! This stuff glows like Kryptonite!" "Did someone paint these?" "Are they radioactive?" Seeing fluorescent minerals up close for the first time is an exciting experience. The colors are so pure and the glow is so seemingly unnatural, that people find it hard to believe they are just natural rocks.

Collecting Fluorescent Minerals

Fluorescent minerals are a relatively new collectible, compared that is, to collecting fossils, crystals, Civil War items, and other long established fields of collecting. Miners have been picking up interesting rocks for hundreds of years, but the lights that allow collectors to see the amazing colors hidden within fluorescent minerals have only been around since after the turn of the century. The beauty of this, from a collector's point of view, is that prices are still reasonable and there are hundreds of old collections of rocks in the hands of collectors and miners' families just waiting for the right person to come along when they are ready to dispose of them. Several pieces in this book came out of a collection from a Sterling Hill miner named John Remyias, the cageman at the mine (elevator attendant who had to remember all the bell signal rings that told him what levels to have the hoistman take him to pick up and drop off miners at the different levels), who lived a few blocks from the mine in Ogdensburg, New Jersey and was a miner there for fifty years. He picked up many unusual rocks at the mine and when he passed away, his family sold off the rocks stored in his basement. My son and I bought about seventy pounds of interesting rocks. We were very pleased with what we bought even though the family had already sold a few hundred pounds to other collectors before we arrived.

Currently, the best place to find fluorescent minerals is at rock and gem shows, on the internet, or at the mines or mine dumps. eBay, the online auction site, has a large section for "Fluorescent Minerals" with ever changing offerings. Whatever the source, the cost of a collection of fluorescent rocks is dramatically less expensive than buying many other collectibles. The largest expenditure is usually the mineral light whose cost will depend upon how big a light you want.

These pages show fluorescent minerals from many collections. Living in New Jersey I first met collectors that concentrated on fluorescent minerals from my state. Many of these fluorescent minerals come from the Franklin and Sterling Hill Zinc Mines in the northern tip of the state. After joining the Fluorescent Mineral Society and then taking a trip to the giant Tucson Gem and Mineral Show, I met collectors from all around the world who had fluorescent mineral collections. There were many beautiful and unusual fluorescent minerals from other places that deserved to be collected including fluorescents from Canada, Mexico, Greenland, Italy, Sweden, and other places. I began working out trades with collectors from other countries and parts of this country.

Getting Started

One of the first questions asked when someone sees fluorescent minerals glow for the first time is "Are they radioactive or dangerous?" The answer is no. Although there is a class of radioactive minerals that glow due to their uranium content, most of those are found in the Southwestern part of the United States and most glow ghostly green. Almost all Eastern United States minerals glow because of an "Activator" such as minute amounts of Manganese or Lead or both. The minerals from the New Jersey mines were so environmentally friendly that the water that accumulated in the mine shafts was safely pumped into local ponds that ran into the public water supply. This is very different from gold or silver mining out west where the water coming from the mine often contains poisons such as arsenic or substantial quantities of lead.

Throughout these pages, the first photo generally shows the mineral under daylight while the subsequent photo shows the mineral under short wave (SW) ultraviolet (UV) light, midwave (MW), and/or long wave (LW) UV light. One of the tricks to great collecting is to see enough variations of what you are collecting so that when you find a good collectible rock, you don't overlook it. The book often shows several examples of a particular fluorescent mineral.

A bit of trivia: Did you know that color television is a direct result of fluorescent minerals? Scientists studying ways to make a color television turned to fluorescent minerals and investigated what made the minerals fluoresce in the different colors. They produced man-made fluorescent materials (called phosphors) that could reproduce certain colors repeatedly and accurately. The materials were applied to television screens and when activated by the electron gun in the picture tube, the different colors appeared on the face of the screen. Additionally, the study of DNA was made easier by the tagging of chromosomes with fluorescent dyes.

What You Need To Take With You To Dig In Mine Dumps Or On Field Trips

Now that your appetite is whetted for going on an adventure to a mine or rock hunting area, there are several different kinds of rock hunting "digs" you can experience. One kind involves going to a mine dump where all the rocks are on the surface or at least just under the surface and close to major roads, mines, or museums. Another kind of dig requires you to dig and break rock. A sledge hammer, chisels, pry bar, protective glasses, etc. are needed. A third kind requires you to actually go into an old mine or mining area, far from the beaten path. You may need maps, a global (or ground) positioning satellite (GPS) device, a four-wheel drive vehicle, overnight shelter, food, etc. It pays to understand what kind of dig you are going on to bring just the right amount of tools and supplies that allow you to carry out as much rock as you can rather than just carrying out all of your unused tools and supplies.

Bring a bucket to carry your rocks. Ask your local building contractor for an empty five gallon plaster bucket and put some closed cell padding around the handle. If you have to carry out fifty pounds of rock, you will appreciate all the padding you can get. Some of the diggers at the Sterling Hill and Franklin mine dumps have a two wheel dolly that hold their buckets. They strap a piece of PVC tubing to the sides and their sledge hammer slides down and is held by the tube. The ground is fairly even here so the dolly helps move the weight of a full bucket. Another nice touch is a heavy duty backpack that can hold an extra fifty pounds of rock or your mineral light, hammer, etc. as you struggle to carry out your heavy bucket. You should wear solid shoes (no sneakers! When a rock falls on your foot, the shoe should offer some protection) and bring a blanket or other light tight cover (I like six mil. black plastic, ten feet by ten feet, obtainable at Home Depot), a rock hammer (or sledge hammer if you like to break rock), heavy duty gloves (leather palms are good and will protect your hands from the sharp edges of freshly cracked rocks), a hat, insect repellent (nothing like a tick bite or lots of mosquito bites to ruin your dig), your SW (and maybe a LW) UV light with a charged battery (a spare electric cord—that goes from the battery to the light—and a spare fuse is nice to have), and protective glasses (these are required since you will need your eyes for the rest of your life). Some people add a screen to cover their UV light's filter and add some closed cell

foam around the outside edges. If you fall or a rock breaks the UV filter, the light bulb, or both, you will appreciate the inconvenience of the extra protection to your light.

A camera is also useful for documenting your dig and showing your friends what you went through to get all these great rocks. If you are going to be working in a hole in damp ground, long wool underwear will keep your lower half warm even if the ground is wet. A closed cell foam product that is made for sitting on when you work in a garden is nice to sit upon. A simple cloth surgical mask or dust mask will help keep dust out of your nose if the ground is dry and dusty.

If you are digging in an area with rocks overhead, wear a hard hat. If you are digging in "diggable" mine dumps, bring a sturdy shovel. (Some pay-to-collect dumps only allow you to pick over the surface. They do the digging with a back hoe to expose new areas.) It is amazing how many broken shovels can be found at a mine dump. Sometimes a pickax is useful while other times a rake is all you need. If you dig at night, you will need a flashlight or better yet, the new hiker or climber's hands-free light that straps on to your head and uses LED (light emitting diode) bulbs. These LED lights cost more than standard bulb lights, but they will burn for twenty hours straight on a single set of batteries and the LEDs never burn out, nor do they break if you drop them.

If you are digging out in the dessert or the back country, you need to bring gear that will keep you warm and comfortable over night when the temperature can drop forty degrees. A backpacker tent, a sleeping bag, food, water, a fire starting kit, a cook stove, rain gear, toilet paper, a first aid kit, sunglasses, a knife, a snake bite kit, cooking utensils, walkie talkies, and trash bags are things that you should have packed up and kept near where you are digging. If you have to hike back a few miles to your car in the dark, you will appreciate having everything nearby. A hand-held GPS device will allow you to find the site you are looking for and make sense out of the maps that you will bring with you. If you are traveling away from civilization, you may need a four-wheel drive vehicle with an extra spare tire. If you are hitching a ride along with other rock collectors, don't assume that they will want to leave when you need to leave or that they will have food and bedding for you.

It is best to make a written check list and have too much stuff with you rather than not enough (the trick, of course, is to have all the unnecessary stuff in the car rather than on your back). Each trip will be a bit different and you will quickly learn what you need and what you don't need. Wherever you go, make sure to tell someone where you went and approximately when you will return. If you are alone and injured, you can take some consolation in knowing that someone will come after you if you have told others where you will be digging.

A word of caution: night time in unfamiliar territory can be full of dangerous traps. While the sun is shining, you can mark out danger spots with fluorescent tape or streamers so that you don't fall into them when moving about. Also note that dessert scorpions (those bugs with stingers) are fluorescent. Wear your gloves or poke something that glows with a stick before picking it up when in scorpion territory. Bees, wasps, and snakes also make nests in the ground or in ground openings. Check before you move rocks. Bears live in the woods and don't appreciate visitors. Crossing streams with a pack full of rocks lashed to your back can be a death trap. Make sure the pack is easy to slip off in an emergency. Pay attention to your surroundings and try not to make stupid mistakes.

In the resources section at the end of the book, you will find addresses for internet fluorescent sites, history, books on the subject, suggestions for lights and other helpful information.

One of the funniest things you can see at a rock and mineral show or on the mine dumps are the people who carry their mineral lights and a blanket. When they check out a rock, they cover their heads with the blanket and shine the light on the material in the darkened space. If you see people crouching under a blanket at a rock show, go over and see what kind of fluorescents they are looking at.

MINE DUMP DIGGING: Two photos showing Gar Van Tassel standing in a pit that he and the author dug in a Franklin, New Jersey Parker Shaft mine dump. The first photo shows the hole at the beginning of the summer after several weeks of digging. The second photo shows the hole six months later. Thousands of pounds of rock were moved while seeking rare Franklin fluorescent minerals. Most everything that you see glows under SW UV. It is mostly Calcite, some with Willemite, Andradite, and Franklinite. A small percentage contained Hardystonite or Fluorapatite, and two stones contained Xonotlite. There were some nice Clinohedrites, green Amazonites, NF Rhodonites and Bustamites, a small amount of Barite, two stones with Scheelite, a few pieces of Cleiophane/Sphalerite, two stones with a bit of Esperite, some gem red Willemite, and one stone containing yellow Willemite. Over all it was a successful dig, but we did not find the elusive Margarosanite, Manganaxinte, nor Roeblingite.

THE ROCK COLLECTOR'S HOLE: Once you find a mine dump, you start to dig a hole in a likely area. As you find each rock, you crack off a piece with your hand sledge or hammer so you can see the inside of it. This is done since each rock is covered with dirt and all look the same. The rocks are piled around the edge of your hole with the clean inside showing. You then either wait until dark or throw a light proof cover over your head and your rocks and look at them with your SW or LW UV light. Good stuff goes in the bucket and the Leaverite gets thrown away from the hole. Leaverite is the stuff that you "leave her right" there.

Fluorescence

The discovery of fluorescence might be traced back to the mineral Fluorite from which the word "fluorescence" is derived. Not all Fluorite fluoresces, but some of it actually glows and changes its color in bright sunlight. About 1850, a scientist, Sir George Stokes, experimenting with a piece of Fluorite from England was amazed to discover that it would exhibit a green color in the shade and a strong blue color in direct sunlight. He is credited with giving this ability to glow and change color under a different light source the name "fluorescence" in honor of his study material—Fluorite.

Fluorescence is a physical (as opposed to a chemical) process. For a mineral to fluoresce, light (which is electromagnetic radiation) of one wavelength, strikes a fluorescent mineral and causes light to come out of that mineral at another, longer wavelength. When those wavelengths reach the visible spectrum, we see the different wavelengths as different colors. The light emitted is confined to a narrow band and it yields a pure intense color that is startlingly beautiful.

The discovery that led to the portable ultraviolet long wave and short wave lights that make these mineral fluoresce or "glow," appears to have been an accidental spark in a mine. Mines were early users of electricity. When electricity was introduced to the mines and a motor was switched on or off, the switch would give off a spark. In a mine with fluorescent minerals, that spark caused the rocks in the mine to glow. Geologists at the mine soon created an electric arc machine that gave off a similar spark. This spark turned out to contain substantial short wave ultraviolet light. G.F. Kuntz and C. Baskerville were among the first to write about the effect in 1903. Unfortunately, their early spark machine cast a visible blue light on the rocks that they examined and many of their observations assumed that the rocks and not their machine was the source of the blue color. It was not until the 1920s that filters were added to the spark machine to reduce the amount of blue light and more accurate reports of color were prepared. It was still about ten years more until the lights became portable.

The New Jersey Zinc mines were early users of these ultraviolet lights. It was found that the rocks containing high Zinc ore content glowed a very bright green and the rocks that contained calcite, which had no Zinc ore content, glowed bright red-orange. By using the "Picking Table," sorters at the New Jersey Zinc mines could push all the Zinc ore into one chute and all the Calcite containing rocks into another chute. (The picking table was a circular table fed by a conveyor belt, that moved the ore and gave workers time to remove wood and metal debris that could clog the rock crushing machines. The sorted material would then go to other conveyor belts that took it to the crushers and eventually the re-finery or into the cars headed for the mine dump.) This system enabled the Zinc mines of New Jersey to produce high grade ore that contained about 20% recoverable Zinc.

Tenebrescence, Triboluminescence, and Thermoluminescence

As you study your fluorescent minerals, you may notice that some of them have interesting properties. Some stones change color, usually turning darker—violet, pink, purple, or raspberry color—or losing their color when exposed to SW UV, LW UV, darkness, or sunlight. This color change is called tenebrescence. The best known example is Hackmanite which is a color changing Sodalite. Tenebrescence also occurs in some other stones. Hackmanite can be found as masses, opaque crystals, and clear crystals. Most Hackmanite turns a raspberry color when exposed to SW UV. The color fades over time or in direct sunlight. Some Hackmanite from Greenland fades in sunlight but regains its color over time in darkness. There is a Hackmanite from Afghanistan that will turn bright violet when left in direct sunlight or exposed to SW UV.

Scientists have determined that the color is actually composed of tiny grains in the mineral turning blue and red, giving the impression that the color is violet or raspberry. One reason for the change is that in tenebrescence, the SW UV causes electrons in the stone to become unstable and the stone darkens. As long as the stone stays in the dark, the electrons stay the same. If the stone is exposed to sunlight, energy is added to the electrons, they become stable, and the color disappears.

Although not really considered to be tenebrescent, some Tugtupite loses its red color when exposed to sunlight and regains it again when exposed to SW UV. Green Willemite from Franklin will get brighter green when left in direct sunlight or under SW UV for an hour.

Triboluminescence is another interesting property. It was first observed in Sphalerite. When a metal object scratched the rock or the rock was crushed, orange sparks appeared. Some examples were found that were so sensitive that the scratch of a fingernail across them will cause the sparks to appear. Surprisingly, wintergreen Lifesavers exhibit this property when they are crushed by your teeth.

Thermoluminescence, another interesting property, was noticed in Chlorophane, a Fluorite. When Chlorophane was heated, it gave off light. It glowed. Some Chlorophane was so sensitive that the heat of a person's hand was enough to cause it to glow. Although the tenebrescence effect is usually able to be repeated many times, thermoluminescence is usually a one shot affair. These are just a few of the amazing things that fluorescent minerals do in addition to glowing in intensely beautiful colors.

Activators

Fluorescent rocks are obviously different from other rocks. The typical rock does not glow under UV light. The fluorescence is usually caused by minute amounts of other minerals called "activators" (although there are at least four other methods that cause fluorescence in minerals). Some "impurity" has invaded the rock during its creation and that impurity activates the fluorescent quality of the rock. Calcite is a particularly good example to study since Calcite is found worldwide and the standard piece of Calcite does not fluoresce. With the right activators, it will fluoresce red, blue, white, pink, green, or some other color under SW or LW UV light. The brightness of the fluorescence also varies with the type or quantity of the activator. Fluorescent Calcite from the Franklin, New Jersey area may or may not fluoresce. The pieces with the brightest fluorescence are found closest to the ore body. The further from the Zinc ore body, the less brightly the pieces fluoresce. The most common activator in the Franklin area is Manganese. It is responsible for the glow of many of the Franklin-Sterling Hill minerals. In the Franklin Calcite, Manganese gives it its red-orange color and a second activator, Lead, allows it to make use of the SW UV light and fluoresce.

Two well known mineral exceptions that do not need activators are Tungsten's source mineral—Scheelite—that fluoresces without any activators and Uranium-type minerals, which glow (usually green) with variable degrees of radioactivity. The study of activators is fairly technical and without a laboratory to assay your minerals, you will just have to rely upon what the more scientific articles tell you about the activators. Earl Verbeek, curator of the Thomas S. Warren Museum of Fluorescence at Sterling Hill, has covered the subject nicely in the book *Ultraviolet Light and Fluorescent Minerals* (see bibliography).

As there are activators, there are also "quenchers" of fluorescence. If they are present, in often the tiniest amount, the rock will not fluoresce. Iron is a known quencher. However, with an exception to every rule, a few rocks that contain iron, such as Albite and some Sphalerite, do fluoresce.

Crystals Versus Massive Form

Fluorescent minerals can be found in crystal form or in massive form. The massive form shows no crystals in its structure. Typically Hardystonite, Esperite, and many Willemites are found in their massive state. Crystalline forms of a fluorescent mineral are generally more valuable when there are two forms to choose from. Large fluorescing crystals are rare and highly sought after. Collectors pay more for choice crystals that fluoresce. For example, a one inch rock with a few nice crys-

tals of Sodalite are worth much more than several pounds of the massive form. Fluorapatite from New Jersey can be found in both forms. Most of the Franklin Fluorapatite seems to be massive and much of the Sterling Hill Fluorapatite appears in crystalline form. Most Fluorapatite crystals are solidly bedded in the host rock—Calcite or Amphibole—and are very tough to extract without breaking. Clinohedrite is especially sought after in its crystalline form which sells for a high premium over the non-crystalline form. Crystals can take many shapes and often the crystals are so small that you will need a magnifying glass to see them. When in the field, be on the lookout for vugs with crystals that fluoresce.

Important Things to Consider

Buy the best—In comparing fluorescent mineral collecting to other collecting fields, it is expected that prices on items will continue to rise. Higher prices may be a blessing in disguise. Some people have no incentive to sell a piece for only a few dollars, but if they can get "a lot of money" they will sell a piece. You will pay more but you will get a mineral that you may never have another chance to own. Collections can be put together for very little money, but, as has been proven true in every field of collecting, the best pieces in the best condition have held or increased in value at a greater rate than the more common pieces. Buy the best that you can afford. Upgrade your collection where possible. Remember, you will rarely regret having paid too much for an item, but you will always regret the good pieces that got away.

Cost—A fluorescent mineral collection need not cost a great deal of money. Some people collect fluorescents from around the world. Joining a local mineral club can provide leads to items. Using your imagination, a nice collection can be put together within your budget. Exhibiting your collection at a local library can generate new leads to the type of material that you collect. Tell friends what you collect. You may be amazed to find that they know some old time collector who is no longer active and lives in your area.

Buy books on minerals—Learn from others' experience. The more you know about minerals, the more likely you will be able to spot a good piece for your collection or to trade or sell. Many collectors put their local minerals on eBay, sell them, and then use that money to buy minerals from other places.

Go to local mineral shows—eBay is a great boon to fluorescent mineral collectors, but there is a lot to be said for having the piece in your hand for a careful exam. A local mineral show may turn up pieces from old collections that may not be available from other sources.

Availability or "Will I ever find another?"—Some items are always available at mineral shows or on the internet. Ask yourself if it is just a matter of dollars to acquire an example or is this a once in a lifetime chance to find that item? With a once in a lifetime item, you may never get another chance to buy one and another person may be waiting for you to put it down so that he or she can buy it. Don't hesitate to buy it.

Investment—I discourage people from "investing" in minerals. Collecting should be for fun and not just for profit. Profits will be come if you collect the items that you enjoy and at some later time decide to sell.

Specialize?—Some people specialize in one type or kind of mineral. Buying, selling, and trading items can help you hone a collection to those items that bring you the most pleasure. A bigger collection is not always a better collection. On the other hand, having a broad collection of many different types of fluorescent minerals can be very satisfying.

Be courageous, buck the trend—You don't have to collect the most popular (and often most pricey) Franklin minerals. There are numerous places in the world that produce fluorescent minerals. They still can be had for less money and are often just as enjoyable. Minerals from the former USSR are starting to trickle into the United States. Some are rather expensive, but are unique to the location.

Think small—Micro minerals are getting more popular each year. They take up little space, often cost only a few dollars, and the variety can be incredible. They don't appeal to all collectors. A small piece of stone with a few Clinohedrite crystals will delight a micro collector and can easily be overlooked by a larger stone collector. Micro collectors seem to have such fun on digs as they gaze through their magnifying lenses at tiny crystals that other collectors have passed without seeing.

Mineral Lights

The black light that is widely sold in party stores and that lights up fluorescent paints and posters so nicely, will not bring out the colors in most of these stones. You must use a specially filtered short wave (SW) or long wave (LW) ultraviolet (UV) mineral light to obtain this effect. These are sold as mineral lights and are available in SW, MW (midwave), and LW frequencies. Sometimes they are labeled as UV-C, UV-B, and UV-A, respectively. The Sources section of this book lists several sources for lights. Mineral lights cost anywhere from $30 to $400 or more. The cost difference is in the power of the light. The lower end UV mineral lights have less output and the higher end have greater output. I have used several different powered lights over the years. If you can afford it, buy a powerful light. I currently use a SuperBright™ 2000 SW UV light in the field and to take my photographs. Once you use the more powerful light, you will be spoiled and rarely go back to the lower powered lights.

Light wave length can be measured in Nanometers (nm). *Short wave* mineral lights emit light at approximately 254nm. SW UV is the most widely used light source for displaying fluorescent minerals since more minerals fluoresce under SW than under LW or MW. The biggest cost of the SW mineral light is the filter which is only made by one or two companies. The filters are expensive pieces of coated phosphate glass or quartz that will transmit SW UV light but absorb visible light. The UV light emitted by SW lamps is invisible but they also emit a wavelength of visible light. The filter allows the UV light to pass through but holds back most of the visible light. Since SW light is almost completely stopped by regular glass or plastic you can use this as a test of fluorescence. If you shine a UV light at a light colored stone and see a blue color, you may think you have a stone that glows blue. However, the blue color may be a reflection of the light. To find out if the stone glows blue or is merely reflecting the light source, one can place a piece of ordinary glass between the light source and the stone. If the blue color is only caused by a reflection on the stone, the light areas of the stone will still look blue. If the blue color disappears, then the plain glass is stopping the SW UV from reaching the stone and the color you are seeing is the stone's fluorescent color.

The SW mineral light lamps (the bulbs) are also more expensive than typical, inexpensive fluorescent light tubes. Quartz or erythemal glass must be used in the tubes of a mineral light and the light must give out a substantial amount of SW UV. Low pressure mercury-vapor lamps are high in SW UV output and they are the lamps of choice in most mineral lights.

SW rays can, over time, cloud the filter causing it to lose output after many hours of use. This is caused by the filter material absorbing moisture. The moisture reacts with the filter material and causes a coating on the surface. This was more of a problem in the past, than it is today. Since the 1990s, superior filters have been created that resist clouding much better than before. Turning the light on and off can reduce the life of the lamps. If you are working on cataloging your rocks, leave the light on, rather than shutting it on and off to try to save the life of the filter. Short Wave UV light can also cause sunburn and burn the eyes. Plastic glasses should be worn when using the SW light for more than a few minutes and you should never look directly into a SW lights without eye protection.

Long wave mineral lights emit light at about 360nm. There are actually two wavelength lamps with one emitting light at 350nm and the other emitting light at 370nm (some minerals fluoresce better under one while others fluoresce better under the other). About 15% of fluorescent minerals fluoresce under LW (Fluorites and Sodalites typically fluoresce better under LW). Sometimes a mineral will fluoresce in both LW and SW. Sometimes the LW color is different from the SW color (Terlingua Calcite is one of the best examples—it fluoresces blue under SW and pink under LW). LW UV is closest to visible light and unlike SW light, will pass through most glass and plastic. LW lamps and their filters are less expensive than SW lamps and filters. The black light bulbs sold at party stores are a LW source, but they usually give out too much visible light to be of much use to fluorescent mineral collectors. There are incandescent bulbs (regular screw-in type bulbs) that are sold as "black light" bulbs. Their UV output is minimal and they burn very hot so that they can actually output some UV light. You should avoid using them since they emit very little usable LW light.

Midwave mineral lights emit light at about 302nm. MW lights are beginning to become more popular. Collectors want to see what minerals are excited by MW light. Some minerals will glow brighter under MW or will show a different color than either LW or SW. MW ultraviolet lies in between LW and SW. It is has similar properties to SW, (it is blocked by glass and passed by the special filters). The downsides of MW is the cost of an additional expensive UV light and the smaller group of fluorescents that react differently to MW UV light than they do to SW or LW UV light.

The study of fluorescent minerals under different wave lengths of light is evolving. Graphs are being created that show the best wave length for different fluorescing minerals. If a small portable, variable wave length UV light is ever created, you could look up the best wave-length for your particular mineral, dial that into your light, and get the best response available. This would also aid in identifying different minerals in a rock that is composed of several minerals. If one part fluoresced best at a certain wavelength, you could exclude other minerals that you knew did not fluoresce at that wave length. Currently these machines are large and very expensive. Hopefully the demand for a variable wave length mineral light is great enough for some manufacturer to someday create a smaller, less expensive model.

BE WARNED, SW and MW UV light can cause sunburn and burn the eyes. Fluorescent collectors know that you aim the light away from your face and when you must use the light for extended periods of time, wear protective eye shields or glasses that block UV rays.

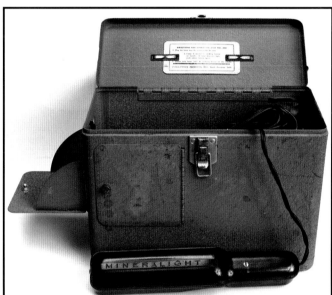

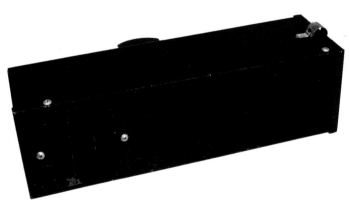

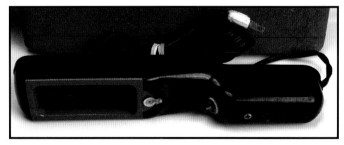

MINERAL LIGHT: A 1940s UV Products of California, Model 12 short wave, battery powered UV light. This was one of the most popular portable short wave lights on the market in the 1940s. It had a relatively small UV filter (about 2" square) and used a 6 volt lantern battery to give off light with a very purple tint. It is about 10" long. Value $30-45.

MINERAL LIGHT: A 1940s UV Products, Model 404 portable prospecting box that would hold a Mineralight™ wand in either SW or LW (or both). It used two 45 volt batteries to power the wand, or the wand itself could be plugged into a regular AC outlet. This was a popular portable SW/LW light that was used to look for Scheelite and Uranium. There is a compartment door that let the prospector load the sample into the box. He would then open the small door on the front to see if the sample glowed. The box is about 12" long. These were real prospector's working tools and are usually found in beat up condition. They can be made to work off a battery if you built the battery yourself. Wire up five 9 volt batteries to make up each 45 volt battery pack. When wired together, they will give 90 volts of electricity for a short time. Value (working condition) $60-75.

MINERAL LIGHT: A late 1940s, early 1950s UV Products of California, Model G short wave and long wave AC powered UV light. This was a popular portable short wave/long wave light used in schools and labs. The small SW UV filter was a bit bigger than the Model 12's. It is about 8" long. Value (working condition) $50-65.

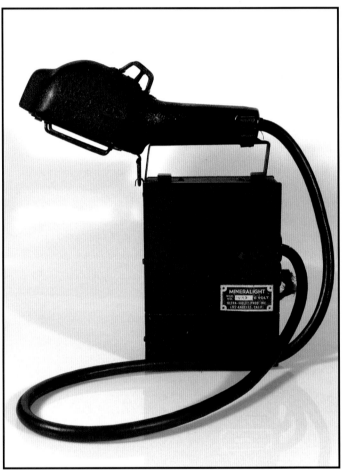

MINERAL LIGHT: A late 1940s-50 UV Products Model V43, 6 volt portable Mineralight™ in SW. It used a large 6 volt battery to power the light and could be plugged into a regular AC outlet. It is 11.5" tall. Value (working condition), $50-60.

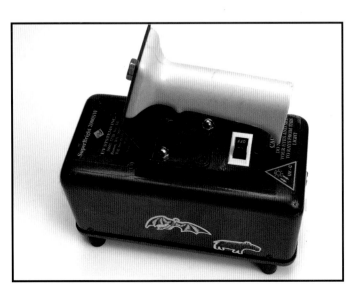

MINERAL LIGHT: One of the best portable UV lights on the market. It is the SuperBright 2000 SW™ by UV Systems. It can run off the included 120 volt to 12 volt power supply or a battery pack for portable use. It is expensive, but gives off a tremendous amount of very clean UV light. It can light up an area of ground in the Franklin NJ area to about a twelve foot diameter circle. The SuperBright™ is available as a short wave or long wave light and is the light used to take all the photographs in this book. It is about 9" long.

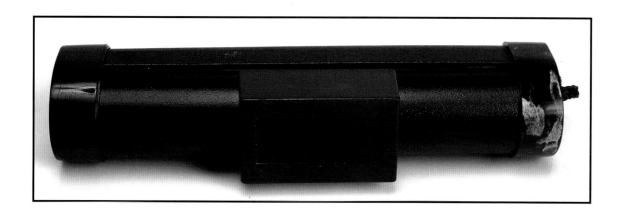

MINERAL LIGHT: A nice beginner's portable UV SW light. It must be used in a very dark room and the filter is only about 1" by 2". This was our first light and got us started collecting. It is only about 6" long and is great to throw in your pocket when going to a show. Its shortcoming is that it is not very strong and if you display your minerals, it can only light up one rock at a time. The cost was about $30.

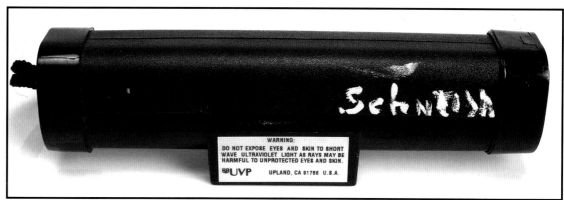

MINERAL LIGHT: An all around good portable UV light. Similar lights are made by Raytech or by UV Products. This model has a 6 watt long wave and a 6 watt short wave light that can be run independently or together. It can be configured with two LW or two SW lights also. It uses a lead/acid built in battery for portable use. It is moderately expensive ($150 to $270), but about half the price of the SuperBright™ UV light. It is about 11" tall.

Chapter Two

Finding Fluorescent Minerals

There are a few places that you should try to visit every so often. These are the mines or areas that are known for their fluorescent minerals. Collectors from other places can only imagine digging in a mine dump where the ground glows multiple bright colors and where the collector can find a rare fluorescent mineral to add to their collection. There are many mines that are better known for their non-fluorescent minerals but that also contain fluorescents. If you have access to any mine dump, it is worthwhile to check out the rocks at night or under a light proof tarp. You never know what you will find.

History of the Area

Two mines in New Jersey—Sterling Hill and Franklin—are so important to fluorescent mineral collectors that a brief history must be included.

In the Beginning

The exact way that the grouping of minerals came to be in this place is a matter of scientific conjecture. What is generally agreed is that millions of years ago, the area was covered by a sea. Under the sea, volcanic fissures ran deep into the earth. These fissures acted like geysers (think of Old Faithful in Yellowstone Park) that would bring up hot material from deep in the earth. The hot material contained heavy metals that settled down around the fissure and built up a tube of metal material, in this case the metal was mostly Zinc. Over time and as the earth's surface shifted, most of these metal tubes tipped over and were covered up by carbonate mud and early plankton-like creatures. As the plates of the earth moved, these tubes were forced under the earth and then eventually back up towards the surface. This caused the ore body to metamorphize under heat in the 700 to 800 degrees Celsius range resulting in the ore body melting and solidifying and then being surrounded by limestone and marble. As the plates of the earth continued to move, faults were created in the material and fluids entered these cracks and voids in the material. These fluids brought in new materials and reconfigured or altered the materials that were already in place. This added to the complexity and combinations of minerals. Eventually, as the surface partially wore away, these minerals began to be exposed on the surface.

Man and the Minerals

The earliest Dutch settlers in New Jersey, during the 1600s, included men sent out to discover what mineral wealth could be found in the "New World." They discovered the outcroppings of ore in the Franklin area. Thinking that this was a form of iron, samples were sent back to Holland and assayed. The ore did not contain iron, it contained Zinc. Unfortunately, Zinc, at that time could not be extracted from the ore and the mineral hunters were told to abandon the area. The area's ore body was unlike any other known deposit in the world. It contained Zinc, Manganese, and Iron, but in complex oxides such as Franklinite, silicates such as Willemite, and simple oxides such as Zincite. There were almost no lead and copper ores that were usually found with Zinc deposits. Copper and lead had great value to the early settlers. Zinc did not. Since Zinc can only be smelted in a complex method that was years away from discovery, there was little interest in the area other than minor iron mining.

About 1760, William Alexander, the Earl of Stirling, inherited his father's estate that included all of this area of New Jersey. His father had been given the property by the King of England. The Earl mined the iron in surrounding areas and provided that iron to the new American colonies. For his efforts, he attained the position of a Major General in George Washington's army. The Sterling Hill Mine's name was changed slightly, but was adopted in honor of the Earl's ownership. In later years, Dr. Samuel Fowler bought the property from the Stirlings and then transferred it to his son, Samuel Fowler. Sam Fowler brought in mining experts to figure out how to take advantage of the minerals in the area. In 1848 he formed The Sussex Zinc and Copper Mining and Manufacturing Company. The company built a Zinc processing plant in Newark, New Jersey.

At first the powdered Zinc ore was roasted and the smoke burned to create Zinc oxide which had commercial use in making paint. A smelting technique, called the Belgian Process, was discovered that would turn the Zinc oxide into Zinc metal. It involved mixing powdered Zinc ore with carbon, heating the mixture in a horizontal retort (distilled in a reducing atmosphere) and waiting for the metal to flow out. Although Zinc metal was produced, this process was fuel inefficient, so the company concentrated on making Zinc oxide which was cheaper to create. In 1852 the company changed its name to the New Jersey Zinc Company. It began to produce a product called Spiegeleisen which was an Iron-Manganese alloy that was separated from the Zinc ore. It was a very hard material and was found to increase the hardness and wear ability of steel. Train wheels profited from the addition of Spiegeleisen. It made them last longer. The American Civil War helped to push America into the industrial age. New Jersey Zinc Company was now making Zinc oxide that was used in making paint, tires, and cosmetics. Zinc oxide made the paint's colors brighter and made the paint longer lasting. They also produced Zinc metal. Zinc became a very useful material. Iron and steel could be coated with Zinc to give them corrosion resistant properties. Battery casings were made of Zinc. The portable battery that we know today was invented about 1888. Try to imagine how many Zinc cased batteries have been made over the years.

In 1890, Thomas Edison, through his New Jersey and Pennsylvania Concentrating Company, bought mines to Sussex County to mine iron. His mines were ultimately unsuccessful due to the fact that there was not enough iron ore to recover the costs of all of his equipment. However, he invented methods of mining —using electromagnets to separate iron from the crushed ore, cable systems and motors to move ore, crushers that concentrated ore into bricks that were easily smelted, etc. These methods were adopted by the nearby Zinc mines to improve their efficiency.

As more uses for Zinc were discovered, the high grade ore from Franklin and Sterling was now in great demand. New Jersey Zinc Company began to acquire more mines (all of the local companies were consolidated in 1897 into one company) and all mine output was directed to Palmerton, Pennsylvania for processing. Palmerton was chosen because it was in the middle of the Pennsylvania coal fields. The coal was needed to feed the furnaces that transformed the ore into metal.

Franklin and Ogdensburg became successful communities that supported many mining families. Miners arrived from Poland, grew successful and moved on to other jobs. Miners were then brought in from Mexico. After World War II, environmental awareness began to increase the costs of mining—the ground contained Tremolite, a form of Asbestos—and the mine had to provide more safety measures. A battle ensued with the town of Franklin about the real estate taxes. The town valued the land high due to the high Zinc ore content. The mines valued it low, based upon the increasing cost of recovering the ore. Tax appeals on the mine properties deprived the town of revenue. The town had to increase real estate taxes on the miner's homes and local businesses to make up the lost revenue. People began to move away from the area. Eventually by the 1950s in Franklin and by the 1980s in Sterling Hill, the mines closed. The reasons given were that the recovery of the ore involved digging deeper and deeper, there was a qualified manpower

shortage, and the cost of mining the ore became too expensive to continue. There are still millions of tons of ore remaining in the ground.

Collectors and museums today are very fortunate. During the life of these mines, miners were able to take out ore samples in their lunch buckets. Most other mines in the country discouraged taking samples. Those mines determined that the miners were there to dig ore for the company and anyone taking samples was not concentrating on his job. The Franklin area mines were very different and the miners who did take samples out in their lunch buckets would sell a bushel basket full of interesting rocks for a few dollars to early collectors. These examples now reside in museum collections and occasionally remain in the basements of the miner's family homes.

There are still many minerals to discover from the Franklin-Sterling mines. Most of the new discoveries are being made by the "micro-mineral" collectors. These collectors look for microscopic samples of rare minerals in the rocks that they find. There is an active micro group at Franklin. Since the collecting of micro-minerals has begun, it has become more and more popular each year. All a collector needs is a suitcase full of tiny plastic boxes, lots of labels, and a microscope. Some minerals that cost thousands of dollars if they weigh a few ounces, cost only a few dollars in samples that weigh a few grams. This is great if you are on a budget or live in a small apartment.

The Franklin Mine

The "Fluorescent Capital of the World" is an area of northern New Jersey in Sussex County. It is the town of Franklin, although most collectors think of it as the adjoining towns of Franklin and Ogdensburg. Franklin is the home of the Franklin Zinc Mine that was an operating mine from the 1700s to 1954. When the Franklin Mine closed in 1954, over 22,000,000 tons of Zinc ore had been removed. Ogdensburg is the home of the Sterling Hill Mine, operating from 1848 and closed in 1986. It produced about 11,000,000 tons of Zinc ore over its lifetime.

The reason that this area is called the Fluorescent Capital of the World is that more fluorescent minerals have been found here than in any other place in the World. There are about eighty-six different fluorescing minerals that have come out of these two mines and surrounding marble quarries. The next nearest quantity of fluorescent minerals comes from Mont Saint-Hilaire, Quebec, Canada which has about forty-five different fluorescents. Another reason the Franklin area is known as the Mineral Capital of the World is that more varieties of mineral (approximately 360) are found here than in any other place in the World.

Collectors of fluorescent minerals can still go to the two mines and for a fee, prospect on the mine dumps. A "dump" is where the rock that was mined, but not used, was dumped. Bring your UV light and a blanket to cover your head for daylight digs (see the section on What To Bring With You). Night time digs are also held for mineral society groups, so it pays to join a mineral society such as the Franklin-Ogdensburg Mineral Society or the Fluorescent Mineral Society. (Mine contact information, collectors groups, internet links, and places to buy lights are listed in the Source section at the back of the book.) The dumps are generally composed of low grade Zinc ore and other minerals that were removed from the mine and dumped in areas near the mine site. After years of mining, the waste material was no longer hauled out of the mine (an expensive process). It was just moved sideways and used to fill in shafts that were mined out. This rich-in-minerals waste rock that was dumped in adjoining shafts is now under water. What treasures they must hold. The tunnels connected to the Parker Shaft of the Franklin Zinc Mine at the 400 to 600 foot levels produced some of the rarest fluorescent minerals. These rare and popular collectible minerals have names such as Clinohedrite, Esperite, Margarosanite, Johnbaumite, Roeblingite, and Hardystonite. One of the above ground dumps next to this shaft was prospected by collectors for years until the local firehouse was built on the site and the whole dump area was paved over for a parking lot. The Buckwheat dump is operated by the Franklin Mineral Museum, and is down a steep hill behind the museum. Some collectors remember the 1960s when the pit known as the Buckwheat was actually a hill. Collectors take thousands of pounds of rock out each year. Regular collector access can be arranged when the museum is open. On special occasions the privately-owned nearby Franklin Trotter dump is also open to collectors.

The Parker Shaft

The Parker Shaft name attached to fluorescent minerals is an indication that the minerals are the best and rarest in the world. The Shaft was sunk in limestone, next to the ore body in 1891 by the operators of the Parker Mine. It was not until 1895 that the ore body was actually reached. Two years later, the New Jersey Zinc Company bought or combined all the mines in the area and the Parker Mine became the Parker Shaft of the Franklin Mine. The Shaft was connected with the other shafts in the area in 1902 and became the main entrance into the mine and the main exit out of the mine for the ore. In 1910 the Parker Shaft was closed when the Palmer Shaft became the main shaft.

Certain minerals are associated with the Parker Shaft. That shaft was either the only source of the minerals or the source of the best examples of the minerals. Several of these are the most sought after and most expensive minerals that fluorescent collectors can own. At the top of the list are Roeblingite and Margarosanite. Others are Pectolite, Prehnite, Xonotlite, Clinohedrite, Esperite, Hardystonite, Cuspidine, Minehillite and two are so hard to get that few collectors will ever own a piece—Charlesite

(aqua blue SW) and Nasonite (greenish yellow SW). The real beauties of the Parker Shaft are assemblages of several of these minerals. There is also a group of non-fluorescent minerals that have come out of the Parker Shaft that are very rare and collectible. The mine operators dumped unwanted rock in several areas in the town of Franklin, New Jersey. Most of this material is on private property that is fenced and off-limits to collectors. The dump material was also used as a base for the roads in the area and as fill for some of the older buildings. Recently a collector found a small quantity of Cuspidine in the ruins of a Franklin building. The rock had been used in making the walls of the foundation.

Sterling Hill Mine

One town over from Franklin, in Ogdensburg, at the Sterling Hill Mine, you can take a tour through the upper mine shaft (the lower ones are flooded). Be warned that the temperature is about 54 degrees year-round and you may need a jacket. (My first time was a hot summer day and I was wearing a tee shirt and shorts.) A trip through the mine is a real eye opener. You begin to realize that you are under a mountain of solid stone and yet, water is dripping into the tunnel cut through this mountain. The solid stone has loads of cracks and fissures that allow the water to percolate down through the rock. This water has carried dissolved minerals through the cracks for millions of years and in the process, created new minerals. During mining, the water was removed by gigantic pumps that expelled thousands of gallons a day. Luckily, the Franklin-Sterling Hill Mines were composed of non-poisonous rocks (few arsenics, sulfurs, and other minerals that form acids or poisons when mixed with water). This allowed them to direct the water into ponds below the mines without harming the wildlife and people who get their water from wells in the area. Unfortunately, when the mines were no longer profitable, the pumps were not maintained. When the pumps broke down, the water began to fill the mines. In 1989 the water flooded up to the 1200 foot level; in 1990 it flooded the 1000 foot level. That year, an area in the 800 foot level collapsed sending the water up hundreds of feet. The 340 foot level contained a great find of bright yellow-orange Wollastonite that was extensively mined in 1989. The water kept moving up so that by about 1996 only the top few levels were not under water. The cost to pump all this water out again is prohibitive and the owners of the Sterling Hill Mine have no intention of spending millions of dollars to reopen the mine's lower levels to tourists. Additionally, as the water rose, it loosened the early fill material that supported the shafts and many of the lower shafts collapsed, forever closing them off to rock collectors.

There are many fluorescent minerals that are only found at Sterling Hill and not Franklin. Genthelvite is one. Also, there are many non-fluorescent minerals that are associated with the fluorescent ones. They deserve a place in any collection. There are some differences that are apparent between the Franklin version of a mineral and the Sterling Hill versions. The photographs in the book will hopefully give you a feel for some of the differences. Christmas Calcite/Willemite can still be found at Sterling Hill. One of the most attractive and nearly impossible-to-find Sterling Hill rocks is mylonitized Calcite and Willemite. The term mylonitized refers to the deformation of the rock resulting from the application of heat and pressure in a definite direction without any appreciable chemical alteration of the materials. These rocks have great swirls and look as if two or more thick liquids were gently swirled together and hardened in that form. They are really incredible looking under SW UV.

The Sterling Hill Mine dump is open on the last Sunday of each month during the season. This area contains minerals dug from other areas on the property and dumped in piles near the southeast side of the parking lot. Some great examples of Norbergite, Wollastonite, Willemite, Calcite, drill cores, and other interesting fluorescents can be found. The collector pays $10 and is entitled to 10 pounds of material. Usually other diggers will help educate you on what to look for. If you belong to a collecting group, you can dig in the Sterling Hill Mine's Passaic Pit area, the Noble Pit area, the hump between these areas (a great place to look for large Franklinite crystals, Scapolite, and Wollastonite), or the fill

quarry where a deep surface mining pit was filled in with sand, limestone, and miscellaneous minerals and whose walls contain interesting minerals. All of these areas are southwest of the parking lot and access is through and beyond the Sterling Hill Mine dump.

WELCOME TO FRANKLIN BOROUGH: The sign proclaims Franklin as the Fluorescent Mineral Capital of the World.

FRANKLIN MINERAL MUSEUM: The Franklin Mineral Museum shows a history of the Zinc mining activities in the area. It has a world class mineral museum that includes cases of minerals that have been found in the area, an excellent representation of fluorescent mineral, gift shop, Buckwheat mine dump, and a small replica of the mine which was closed in 1954. The Franklin-Ogdensburg Mineral Society meets at the Museum once a month. There is a mineral museum at the Sterling Hill Mine. It is called the Thomas S. Warren Museum of Fluorescence. It, too, is definitely worth a visit when you are in the area.

STERLING HILL CONVEYOR TOWER: An exterior view at the Sterling Hill Mine of the conveyor that would take the pulverized Zinc ore powder from the crushers to the storage hoppers.

STERLING HILL: A view from inside the conveyor of the Sterling Hill Mine looking over the parking lot. You are looking south. To the left, just outside the picture, is the mine run dump. To the right is the mountain, the mine is beneath the area, and the entrance to the mine is in the rock face. On top of the mountain is the mine head (opening where the miners entered the mine and the ore was removed). Going southward past the rock face and a little to the right is the Passaic Pit and a bit further beyond it is the Noble Pit.

STERLING HILL ZINC POWDER DRYER: An interior view at the Sterling Hill Mine of the drying oven that took the wet pulverized Zinc ore powder from the crushers to the conveyor.

STERLING HILL CONVEYOR: An interior view at the Sterling Hill Mine of the conveyor belt that would take the pulverized Zinc ore powder from the crushers to the storage hoppers. Trucks or trains could roll in under the chutes and the ore powder loaded so that it could be taken to Palmerton, Pennsylvania for processing into Zinc metal or Zinc oxide.

STERLING HILL MINE HEAD: The mine head (opening where the miners entered the mine and the ore was removed) at Sterling Hill. Miners would ride down on the inclined rails deep into the mine. As the miners descended, the ore would be coming up, using the weight of one to help ease the power needed to lift the other.

THE BUCKWHEAT DUMP: The Buckwheat Dump is behind the Franklin Mineral Museum of Franklin. It has been attracting collectors for about fifty years and yet there are still interesting minerals to find at the site. The site provides a shed where you can check the fluorescence of your finds. Upon getting to the site, you are immediately overwhelmed by the amount of seemingly indistinguishable gray and tan rocks. As you begin to examine and crack a few rocks, you start to see interesting minerals. Some incredible finds still come out of this dump.

STERLING HILL MINE PASSAIC PIT: The Passaic Pit of the Sterling Hill Mine of Ogdensburg is continually being explored and excavated. New finds of minerals are reported each year. Fluorescent Genthelvite was found there in late 2002. The area is several football fields in size and the area has been mined since the 1700s. Lots of "Christmas" Calcite and Willemite comes out of here. A bit further up the hill is the "saddle" leading to the Noble Pit.

STERLING HILL MINE NOBLE PIT: The Passaic Pit is connected to the "saddle" leading to the Noble Pit. Fluorescent Wollastonite, Barite (very rare), and Scapolite can be found there as well as larger Franklinite crystals, Apatite crystals, Jeffersonite (a weathered Augite), and numerous other minerals–fluorescent and non-fluorescent.

STERLING HILL MINE DUMP: Each month, minerals are hauled out of the Passaic and Noble pits along with material from the nearby Limecrest Quarry. These are dumped into an area that collectors can pick over on the last Sunday of each month and for about a dollar a pound, they can take home some incredible material. There is also a World Mineral dump where old collections of minerals are dumped. Occasionally you can find the original collection tags attached to the rocks.

Franklin-Sterling Mine Fluorescence Table

Some of these minerals are found only at Sterling, some only at Franklin, and some are found at both sites.

Mineral	SW	LW
Albite	velvety purple-red	
Analcime	weak blue-white	yellow
Apophyllite	green, yellow	green, yellow
Aragonite	white, yellow, green	cream
Barite	cream, yellow, or white	
Barylite	violet, red	
Bassanite	violet	
Beta-Willemite	weak yellow, yellow-orange	
Bustamite	occasionally cherry red	cherry red
Cahnite	cream	weak yellow
Calcite	orange-red or many other colors	
Canavesite		violet
Celestine		cream
Celestite	weak yellow white	weak yellow white
Celsian	light purple-blue	
Cerussite		yellow
Chabazite	green	
Charlesite	pale blue	
Chlorophane	teal blue	teal blue
Chondrodite	yellow, yellow-orange	
Clinohedrite	pumpkin orange	
Corundum		cherry red
Cuspidine	orange-yellow	
Datolite	cream, yellow-green	weak yellow
Diopside	blue-white	
Dolomite	red	
Dundasite	weak yellow	weak yellow
Dypingite	gray-blue	blue
Epsomite		cream
Esperite	lemon yellow	weak yellow
Ettringite	yellow-white	yellow-white
Feldspar	red	blue
Fluoborite	cream	
Fluorapatite	burnt orange, gold, or blue	
Fluorapophyllite	white	
Fluorite	blue-green	violet-blue, blue-green
Genthelvite	weak green	green
Guerinite	white	yellow-white
Gypsum	cream, pale blue, pale violet	
Hardystonite	purple-blue	weaker purple-blue
Hedyphane	cream, orange	weak red
Hemimorphite	pale yellow	white
Hodgkinsonite		cherry red
Humite	pale yellow	
Hyalophane	weak red-purple	
Hydrotalcite		cream
Hydroxyapophyllite	weak white	
Hydrozincite	bright sky blue	weak yellow
Johnbaumite	orange	
Junitoite		weak yellow
Magnesiohornblende	greenish blue	
Magnesioreibeckite	grayish blue	
Manganaxinite	red	
Margarite	weak white	weak white
Margarosanite	sky blue or pink-red	
Marialite	yellow	pink
Mcallisterite	cream	
Meionite	orange, pinkish red	no res. or orange, yellow, cream
Meta-ankoleite	green	
Metalodevite	green	
Microcline	weak blue or red	weak blue
Minehillite	violet	weak yellow
Monohydrocalcite	green	green
Nasonite	pale yellow	
Newberyite	cream	
Norbergite	yellow	
Pargasite	greenish blue	
Pectolite	orange, purple	
Pharmacolite	white	
Phlogopite	yellow	
Picropharmacolite		white
Powellite	yellow	cream yellow
Prehnite	orange-pink, peach	
Quartz	yellow or green	
Roeblingite	red	
Samfowlerite	weak red	
Scapolite	medium red, blue	weak yellow
Schleelite	yellow white	cream yellow
Smithsonite	weak yellow	weak yellow
Sphalerite	weaker orange or blue	orange, pink, blue
Spinel		cherry red
Strontianite	violet	violet
Svabite	orange	
Talc	cream yellow	
Thomsonite	cream yellow	
Tilasite	yellow	
Titanite	yellow-orange	
Tremolite	blue	yellow
Turneaureite	orange	
Uranospinite	green	
Uvite	yellow	
Willemite	green	gen. weaker green
Wollastonite	orange or yellow	
Xonotlite	violet	
Zincite	weaker creamy yellow-white	creamy yellow-white
Zircon	yellow-orange	
Znucalite	green	

Mont Saint-Hilaire

Mont Saint-Hilaire (MSH) in the province of Quebec, Canada is an important source of minerals. The count stands at over two hundred seventy-five different minerals. Some collectors say that the whole quarry glows at night under UV light. Other collectors refer to MSH as crystal micro heaven. Many examples are only found as tiny mineral groups, under an inch in size, with beautiful crystals. MSH is located about twenty-five miles east of Montreal. It stands about 1150 feet above the surrounding area and is a bit less than two miles wide. Just west of the mountain is the Richelieu river. Volcanic magma intrusions formed the East side of the mountain.

The quarries at MSH are not old. They began in the 1950s and produced ground-up rock to make asphalt roofing shingles, road fill, and concrete filler. Originally there were two quarries—the Poudrette on the east side and the Demix on the west. The Poudrette quarry was named after an operation's manager in the 1950s. The Demix quarry was originally operated by the Uni-Mix company which became the De-Mix Company in 1966 (later shortened to Demix). The two quarries came together in the 1980s and kept the Poudrette name. The quarries were physically joined when the part of the mountain separating them was excavated away. Each side had its differences and certain minerals can be found on one side and not the other. The mine is sodium rich and also rich in silicates and carbonates and abounds in crystals—from larger than usual to many smaller micro crystals of rare and unusual minerals. Collecting is by organized field trips arranged through the Montreal Gem and Mineral Club.

Geologically, MSH is an alkaline intrusive complex which is very rare. The two quarries each have distinctly different areas. A common rock in the Poudrette Quarry is Hornfels, a dark, hard, compact, metamorphic rock that was formed from clay, shale, or slate. It breaks into sharp angular pieces when cracked open. It is not often found in the Demix quarry. Hornfels can be silicate rich or carbonate rich.

Pegmatites (a light-colored igneous rock or rock group containing Feldspar and Mica, characterized by coarse grains of interlocking crystals with granitic composition) contain some of the most interesting minerals found at MSH. Pegmatites at MSH can contain Mica, Feldspar, and Quartz. When the pegmatites are altered (heat, pressure, the elements, etc), the collector can find new minerals and mineral combinations.

Sodalite Xenoliths seams are very common in the Poudrette quarry and very uncommon in the Demix quarry. Marble Xenoliths can also be found which contain many interesting mineral combinations. Xenoliths are isolated pillars of rock that broke away from its host rock millions of years ago and now stand unrelated to adjoining rocks. Different types of small crystals can be found in the igneous breccias (coarse rock composed of angular fragments of older rocks that are cemented together in a fine matrix).

Some rocks contain a cavity or opening in the rock (a "vug"), having its interior surface or walls lined with small projecting crystals. Mineral collectors call this microcrystalline coating "druzy" or "drusy." These vugs contain black, biotite mica and analcime which act as a base that other minerals form on (similar to some Chinese examples in the book). Miarolitic cavities were formed by gas bubbles in Nepheline ((Na, K)(Al, Si)$_2$O$_4$) syenite (a crystalline rock group, characterized by granular texture and consisting principally of alkali feldspar and possibly traces of quartz) which has a distinct flow structure with streaks and blobs of darker minerals. Fluorescent minerals such as Sodalite, Albite, Apatite, Microcline, and Zircon are often found in the gas pockets in Sodalite syenites. There is also a group of mildly radioactive minerals that can be found in the Sodalite such as Thorium.

Mont Saint-Hilaire Fluorescence Table

Below are listed fifty-one fluorescent minerals that the collector can try to obtain. Many of the fluorescent minerals fall into the micro class and some have been found in such small quantities that a collector will have a hard time locating them. The beauty of MSH is that members of collectors' groups are permitted to collect at the

site and occasionally, Canadian minerals dealers obtain a group of interesting material and offer them for sale. The easiest material to obtain from this area is Sodalite that glows a strong orange under LW UV. Fluorescent activators are similar to the Franklin area—Manganese and Lead—although it is believed that Sulfur may be involved in the reaction in Sodalite. Some of the fluorescents that you may be able to locate from this area include Polylithionite crystals (Polylithionite is a rare mineral of the Mica group and glows yellow), Willemite (green), Calcite (white or red), Hydrozincite (white), Fluorapatite (blue or orange), Analcime (green), Elpidite (yellow-green), Fluorapophyllite (yellow, yellow-green), Leucophanite (violet or blue), Natrolite (green), Pectolite (pink, orange-pink), Quartz (yellow-orange), Zircon (yellow-orange), and possibly Tugtupite (red).

Mineral	SW	LW
Albite	velvety red	
Analcime	green, yel.-orange(?)	green
Burbankite	pink	
Calcite	white and red	white and red
Catapleiite	green	green
Cerussite	pink-yellow	pink-yellow
Clinoptilolite	light green	
Cryolite	blue-white	
Elpidite	yellow and green	yellow and green
Fluorapatite	blue	pink-blue
Fluorapophyllite	green	yellow
Fluorite	violet blue	violet blue
Franconite	yellow-white	yellow-white
Gaidonnayite	green	green
Gaultite	apple green	
Genthelvite	green	green (tan-midwave)
Griceite	weak yellow	
Gypsum	orange-yellow	orange-yellow
Helvite	deep red	red
Hydrozincite	white	white
Kogarkoite	weak blue	white
Leucophanite	pink-violet	pink-violet
Leucosphenite	yellow-white	
Lorenzenite	weak yellow	
Magadite	yellow-white	yellow-white
Makatite	weak green	yellow-white
Meionite	yellow-white	red
Microcline	cherry-red	
Milarite	blue-white	
Monteregianite	green	
Natrolite	weak green	green-white
Parakeldyshite	orange-white	
Pectolite	weak pink	orange-pink, lavender
Polylithionite	yellow	
Quartz	yellow to orange	yellow to orange
Sabinaite	yellow	(sometimes) pink
Scheelite	blue-white	
Searlesite	blue-green	
Sodalite (blue)	pink-orange	orange
Sodalite	orange	orange
Sphalerite	yellow-orange	yellow-orange
Strontianite	white	white
Terskite	yellow-white	yellow-white
Tetranatrolite	pink-white	pink-white
Thornasite	apple green	apple green
Tugtupite	red	red
Villiaumite	red	
Vuonnemite	green-yellow	weak yellow
Willemite	green	green
Wurtzite		red or orange
Zircon	yellow-orange	

Oka

Another interesting Quebec Province mining area is Oka in Deux-Montagne county. Although not as mineral packed as MSH, Oka produces some interesting fluorescent minerals (Sodalite, Natrolite) and some of them are mildly radioactive (Thorium, Cerium, Lanthanium, Niobium, Uranium, and Yittrium). The Oka area is best known for its radioactive Niobium mining operations.

Purple Passion Mine

The Purple Passion Mine, originally known as the Diamond Joe Mine, is located approximately eight miles northeast of Wickenburg, Arizona. The mine is in the Sonora Desert, about 3,300 feet above sea level. In the mine there is a hydrothermal vein consisting mainly of calcite, but having some quartz, galena, and silver ores. This vein extends intermittently for about 3,000 feet running roughly north and south. The ore vein (silver, lead, and a touch of gold) was discovered by a Mr. A.B. Lovell around 1890. Some time in the early 1900s, several prospecting cuts and short tunnels were made along the vein to determine where it was best to mine. The ore was mined intermittently from 1901 until 1926. In 1926-1927, a mill site was erected and a medium sized operation was started by the Diamond Joe Mining Company Inc. About 135,000 tons of ore were removed and a total of 2,250 feet of tunnels, shafts, and stopes were dug, with levels going down to 225 feet. The mine closed in 1928 due to insufficient water to support the mining operations.

The largest prospect tunnel is located about 1,500 feet south of the Purple Passion Mine up on a hill. The tunnel travels horizontally for about forty feet to access the vein. The walls and ceiling are mostly Calcite and Fluorite.

The Purple Passion claim is located on the southerly slope of a batholith which has been eroded so that no sedimentary rocks are present. The uplift of the batholith has produced numerous fissures as channels for ore deposits. The texture of the rock is granite-like. It contains quartz, soda-lime feldspar, orthoclase, hornblende and biotite. The mineral vein has a banded structure. Lead and silver are spread out across the vein. Coarse-grained Calcite predominates along the footwall, intermingled with veins of Quartz and purple or green Fluorite.

Under SW UV, the Calcite fluoresces a bright fire-orange color or hot pink. The Caliche coating fluoresces a peach color and the Fluorite fluoresces bright blue (equally well under either SW or LW). The Willemite occurs as microscopic sprays of transparent colorless to white or pinkish hexagonal crystals, often on a smoky quartz crystal matrix. The Willemite fluoresces a weak yellow color with spots shading to green. It is also phosphorescent. There is also Hydrozincite, Aragonite, and Wulfenite.

The Wulfenite can be found in many colors and also occurs on a wide variety of matrices, such as Wulfenite on quartz (clear, smoky, milky, and amethyst) and Wulfenite on Fluorite, Calcite or Galena. Some of the Wulfenite fluoresces a dull orange color under SW UV.

The Purple Passion fluorescent material has the following characteristics: the fluorescent reds and red-oranges are Calcite, the blues, violets, and purples are Fluorite; the white, yellow, and greens are Willemite, and the peach color is Caliche; a few specimens have some Aragonite which fluoresces and phosphoresces a weak blue-white. The Fluorite does its best under LW, but will usually show to some extent under SW. Four colored pieces (either with Caliche or Aragonite) are unusual and are priced individually from $16-20 per pound, based on the brightness of the colors and how well the piece shows. The best three colored pieces have been selling for about $16 per pound. General fist sized or larger three colored material sells for $12 per pound, and pieces smaller than fist sized sell for $5 per pound. One or two colored material sells for $1 per pound.

Balmat, St. Lawrence County, New York

This area has been mined for Talc, Zinc, and Manganese since 1915. Two companies were active in the area—the Gouverneur Talc Company and the Zinc Corporation of America (ZCA). The ZCA mined the area from 1930 to 2001. They owned 3,000 acres and had mining rights to another 51,000 acres at their mine in Balmat. The mine produced 35 million tons of Zinc ore and shafts descended 200 to 3,100 feet deep. The mill at the site could process 5,000 tons a day and the Zinc content of the ore was 8 to 18 percent. The ore had a high Tremolite content (Tremolite is an Asbestos material) and the Department of Environmental Protection increased demands for protection from and cleanup of the Tremolite at the mine. The company ceased operations in 2001 and was to be acquired by a Canadian company who would continue the Zinc mining. As of January, 2004, that deal still had not been completed, but it is expected to be finalized soon.

The Gouverneur Talc Company also works the area and mines Talc and associated minerals. Collectors can expect to find nice examples of Tirodite (red or hot pink under LW and less bright red under SW), Tremolite (tangerine orange under SW and less bright orange under LW), Talc (bright to dull yellow under SW), Calcite (bright sky blue SW and yellow LW), Diopside (sky blue SW), Phlogopite (yellow SW), Norbergite or Chondrodite, (lemon to orange-yellow SW), Sphalerite (orange, sky blue, blue-green, or green under LW), Willemite (bright green under SW and LW), Anthophyllite (red under LW and SW), Fluorapatite (yellow SW), Wernerite (var. Scapolite—glows bright orange-yellow under LW).

New York requires "remediation" when a mine is closed. The land must returned to its natural state, as it was before mining began. Unfortunately, the West Pierrepont and Talcville mines are closed and the area, including the dumps, has been covered over with new soil and grass. Field trips to the area are sponsored by the St. Lawrence Rock and Mineral Club. It might be worthwhile to become member of the club so that you can join them on a trip to the remaining dumps that still turn up new and interesting finds.

Yavapai County, Arizona

There are dozens of mines in Arizona. They produce Silver, Gold, Lead, and Copper. Fluorescent collectors can find Scheelite (blue-white SW), Andersonite (bright blue-green or green-white LW and SW), Bayleyite (weak yellow-green LW and SW), Fluorite (violet-blue LW, less intense violet blue SW), Schroeckingerite (bright blue-green or green-white LW and SW), Zunyite (cherry red SW), Swartzite (bright yellow-green LW and SW), Wickenburgite (dull orange to pink SW), Cerrusite (pale yellow LW and SW), Crocoite (brown SW), Mimetite (red-orange SW and LW), Pyromorphite (white or yellow LW), and Eucryptite (cherry red SW).

In addition, in Yuma County, Arizona collectors can expect to find Willemite (green SW), Fluorite (violet-blue LW, less intense violet blue SW), Calcite (orange red SW, also a variety that is white SW and green LW, and a variety that is green SW and white LW), Barite (orange LW),

California and Mexico

California is home to many mines and a group of minerals that fluoresce, such as Trona (blue-gray, blue-green SW and LW), Hanksite (yellow-white SW and LW), Scheelite (blue-white SW), Colmanite (yellow-orange SW), Halite, a sea salt (bright red-orange SW), Dumortierite (blue SW), Calomel (yellow SW), Benitoite (bright blue SW), Calcite (orange, red or white SW), Hyalite Opal (green LW and SW), Caliche (peachy orange SW), Chalcedony (green SW), Hydrozincite (blue SW), and Aragonite (blue-white SW).

Mexico produces Terlingua-type Calcites (blue SW, pink LW), Red Calcite (red SW), Adamite (green SW and LW), Danburite (blue and green SW), Fluorite (red LW), Hydrozincite (bright bluish-white SW and cream MW), and geodes containing Chalcedony (green SW) and Hyalite Opal (green LW and SW).

Collecting Fluorescent Minerals in Greenland
by Mark L. Cole, The Miner Shop

Most fluorescent collectors started out collecting Franklin minerals. They are among the brightest, most var-

ied, and most sought after fluorescent minerals known to the hobby. One can only imagine what it was like fifty years ago to actually be able to search the active mine dumps and come home with a piece of rare Esperite, or even dream of finding a piece with a little Margarosanite. Today, collectors must be content with exploring endless piles of bright red fluorescent calcite and bright green Willemite.

In the past three years a new locality has come to light (pun intended). The Ilimaussaq complex in Southern Greenland has been a famous center for geological exploration for hundreds of years. As early as 1806 mineralogists were exploring the unique geology of the complex. Since then, over two hundred minerals have been identified within the intrusion, many only known from a few areas in the world and ten of which are unique to Ilimaussaq. It is the type locale for dozens of species. Perhaps the most amazing fact is that until three years ago, Greenland's only claim to fame in the "glowhound" world was Tugtupite!

Today there are over fifteen different fluorescent minerals identified, and scores waiting to be identified. The brightness of these pieces, along with the highly sought-after multi-color combinations rivals those from Franklin. Many pieces exhibit dramatic phosphorescence or a remarkable tenebrescence (color change) found in few other minerals. No literature exists describing the fluorescence of the various minerals within the complex. Few people have even brought a UV light to the area! Yet these minerals simply lie there, waiting for the adventurous collector to shine a light on them and find the hobby's next rarity! Fluorescent collecting in Greenland must be akin to collecting in Franklin in the old days—exciting, productive, and simply fascinating.

But, Greenland isn't just a matter of hopping on the interstate and driving a couple of hours. Greenland is located just north of where the Titanic sank. Primarily, it is an island covered in ice (the world's largest island even if it is mostly ice), the coastline actually has strips of green in the summer months (Erik the Red named it Greenland after he was booted out of Iceland). Southern Greenland is "warmed" by the gulf stream and in the short summer months (June to September) temperatures averages in the 50 to 60 degrees Fahrenheit range . But even during these warm spells one is amazed at the majestic icebergs, the glaciers, and the lingering snow covering that elusive piece of Tugtupite.

Greenland was very much a part of Denmark until 1979 when a "Home Rule" Government was established, insuring that the culture and Greenland way of life would not be lost. Denmark still plays a major role in Greenland's government, but the Greenlandic people control their destiny. They are a proud, self-sufficient people living off the land. They are great hunters and fisherman, and very proud of their natural resources. Greenland is one of the few undeveloped natural wonders left on earth that one can visit and still experience nature's beauty and solitude at its finest.

Getting to Greenland can be interesting. In 2003, Air Iceland opened a route to Southern Greenland making things a little easier. They fly twice a week (weather permitting) to Narsarsuaq (the only major airport in South Greenland). The only other way to get there is to fly all the way to Copenhagen (Denmark) and then fly back to Greenland (not a lot of fun). If the Greenland weather interferes, flights might be diverted to Stromsfjord Airbase in northern Greenland (or the plane may just sit in Reykjavik until it clears up). This is the first lesson in travel to Greenland—the weather rules. Thankfully, the summer months are usually quite cooperative.

Once in the country the adventure begins. There are no roads connecting the cities (there really aren't any cities either). The larger settlements have roads in town, mostly so people can drive down to their boats that are the main mode of travel. Flying into Narsarsuaq (a bustling airport town of 200 people) one can travel by ferry or private boat to Narsaq—home for the next week while exploring the Ilimaussaq Complex. After this trip, one has an appreciation for the passengers on the Titanic as it traversed the ice filled waters of the North Atlantic.

Narsaq is a small village located about 16km outside the Ilimaussaq Complex. The Narsaq people are used to geologists traveling there from all over the world. Several excellent guest houses are available. One even has a restaurant and all have cooking facilities where you can cook up your own meals. There are two grocery stores in town stocked with the best shrimp, salmon, trout, lamb, whale, and seal around and all are within easy walking distance. The locals speak Danish and Greenlandic and have a (reluctant) grasp of English. Most of all, the local people are friendly and quick to help in any way they can.

Travel to and from the various areas within the Ilimaussaq complex is by boat or four-wheel drive truck. An old road leads to the famous Kvanefjeld area (Tugtupite mines) and the Tasaq slopes. Other parts of the complex are accessible only by boat. Many of the locals will ferry people to various areas in the summer months for a reasonable fee.

The area is a large sprawling complex spanning several fjords and mountains. A road (or boat) only gets you to the base of the collecting areas. From there one must be prepared to hike up old river beds, climb slopes, and even do some relatively rugged climbing to get to some of the more productive areas. The maximum elevation is around 700 meters and usually easy to traverse. Rocks are everywhere! Everything glows! These two facts are the major impediment to climbing. It simply takes too long to get to the top because the climbers get lost collecting on the way up!

Kvanefjeld

The Ilimaussaq Complex

The Ilimaussaq Complex in Southwestern Greenland is an 8km x 17km intrusion spanning two fjords—Kangerdluarssuk Fjord and Tunulliarfik Fjord. Located near the city of Narsaq, access to certain parts of the complex (Kvanefjeld) can be made by foot, while other areas (Kangerdluarssuk and Tunulliarfik) requires travel by boat. It is without a doubt the most mineral-rich area in Greenland. Due to the rapid weathering of the friable (brittle and easily crumbled) syenites, most of the mountains have no vegetation (no soil). The gray rockscape contrasts sharply with the deep blue fjords and gleaming white icebergs.

The 1.2 million year old intrusion consists of three different rock suites. Nepheline-bearing Augite syenite first formed a shell along the sides and the roof, next a quartz bearing alkali granite and alkali syenite formed two thin sheets near the top, and finally the biggest part and center of the intrusion was formed by a layered series of under-saturated syenites. These three main rock suites represent three pulses of different kinds of magmas. The rocks close to the roof are the oldest. The most common rocks in these areas are a Sodalite-nepheline syenite called Naujaite, an Arfvedsonite-Aegirine bearing nepheline syenite called Lujavrite, and a Eudialyte-bearing nepheline syenite called Kakortokite.

Ilimaussaq is the area with the most minerals in Greenland—more than 200 so far, half of them silicates. Here the silica content is much higher than elsewhere in the world. Numerous pegmatites and hydrothermal veins, streaks, and patches are found all over the intrusion, but are most common in the areas of Kangerdluarssuk and Kvanefjeld.

Atop Kvanefjeld one is greeted with a wonderful view of the valley below, Narsaq in the distance, and the iceberg dotted fjords. It is easy to spend the entire day exploring the relatively flat areas at the top, and digging through the years of tailings that the locals have amassed while searching for gem red Tugtupite. The main Tugtupite mining area is located a short walk to the east and is littered with snow-white pieces of Albite and Analcime. Most pieces glow bright red under SW UV. Occasionally one will meet a local miner pounding away at a white vein in an effort to pry loose some bright red "Tutupit."

Unlike fluorescent collecting in other parts of the world, in Greenland you quickly learn that you have to bring your own "darkness." Waiting for nighttime is not an option. During the summer months it doesn't get dark until 10:30PM, and only stays dark for a couple of hours. (The sun rises again at 2:00AM!) Basically, you need something that you can crawl under with a UV light, seal out all external light, and examine potential specimens. A great strategy is to explore the area during the daytime for likely spots, check out samples and mark good spots for later viewing during the premium dark hours. Atop Kvanefjeld, any white rock is a likely candidate. The odds are that it will glow red with Tugtupite, green with Chkalovite, and possibly yellow with Sorensenite (if you're lucky). The locals are only interested in the gem red variety of Tugtupite, so they mostly ignore the fluorescent material.

Tasaq Slopes

A valley separates Kvanefjeld and the Tasaq Slopes. A glacial stream runs through the valley and there is only one place to cross, a small footbridge in the middle of the complex. The Tasaq Slopes are expansive, running the entire width of the complex. Almost anywhere is a great area to hunt. Towards the bottom of the slopes there are large boulders that have eroded from the cliffs above. Climbing up, pockets of Sodalite, white veins of Albite and Analcime, and outcroppings of a myriad of other minerals can be observed. The goal is to find veins within the Lujavrite rocks containing fluorescent minerals like Sodalite, Ussingite, Tugtupite, Polylithionite, and others. One quickly learns that the outward appearance of weathered rock does not accurately reveal what is inside. For example, Sodalite often weathers to a dirty white, but when cracked open the true beauty is revealed. One interesting note: almost every rock cracked open will initially show a deep purple color, which quickly fades. While similar to tenebrescense, this is a one time occurrence usually. It never happens again unless the mineral is a tenebrescent Sodalite or Tugtupite. It could, however, be a good indicator of fluorescence.

The most productive areas on the slopes can be found in the upper levels (500m). Veins of Sodalite, Tugtupite and Ussingite are quite easily found. Polylithionite is found in vugs and cavities, and other rare minerals are found "where you find 'em." Mother nature is quite helpful in mining these minerals for the collector. Over the winter, rain, ice, and wind very actively expose fresh new material. Boulders, breaking away from the cliffs, roll towards the bottom and can result in some fantastic finds. There are three areas of interest on the Tasaq Slopes: the eastern slopes, middle slopes, and western slopes. This area is noted for the heavy concentrations of beryllium, and produces some fantastic specimens. The middle slopes and eastern slopes both produce great examples of Sodalite and Tugtupite, along with a myriad of unidentified species. It would be easy to spend the entire trip only on the slopes.

The adventurous should consider camping atop the areas on the Tasaq Slopes. The views are spectacular and the area's surprises are endless. It's quite easy to pitch a tent and spend the night prospecting promising veins and outcroppings. The next day the veins showing the most promise can be worked by hand to pull out some fantastic specimens. Water is plentiful as the reservoir for Narsaq is located at the very top of the slopes.

Tunulliarfik

The Tunulliarfik Fjord cuts right through the middle of the Ilimaussaq Complex. Access to the best collecting spots here is only by boat. Traveling from Narsaq, the sights are wondrous; the deep blue water of the fjords broken by massive white and blue icebergs contrasts remarkably to the rocky cliffs and sparse vegetation on either side of the fjord. Upon approaching the transition zone into the complex, the land changes abruptly. There is almost a complete absence of vegetation due to the rapid weathering of the friable syenites—only gray rocks with an occasional white vein high above. Boulders lie at the water's edge and landslide areas offer up exciting sections to prospect.

On the northern side of the fjord are several "dry" river beds (resulting from snow melt over the winters) that offer a convenient avenue to tackle the cliffs high above. This area is perhaps the most demanding. One must climb from sea level to the 500m level at a relatively steep incline. But the rewards are many for those that make the climb. Gem quality Ussingite, massive veins of Sodalite, and brilliant assortments of multi-color Tugtupite specimens can all be found here.

At the water's edge there are also many spots to occupy a collector for days. Tugtup Agtakorfia is a small area right on the water and is the type locality for Tugtupite. The original vein has been worked over quite heavily but there is an area that has been ignored until the summer of 2003 because it just looked like a white Albite. Put it under a UV light and amazing things happen!

At the end of the Tunulliarfik Fjord is a peninsula offering excellent collecting opportunities. Huge Aegirine crystals and massive specimens of Eudialyte abound. Sodalite is quite common in this area. Determined collectors can easily find large, brilliant, and gemmy specimens. In this area and other relatively flat areas, the trick is to find large boulders which have fallen from the cliffs above, or to search for frost heaves where mother nature has worked the rocks out of the ground or broken some open. As in other areas, most rocks must be split open to reveal the minerals inside as the weathering on the surface does a great job of disguising the contents. Night collecting is superb in this area, and there are many places to pitch a tent. Bring along a fishing pole and catch a couple of tasty salmon for dinner right from the fjord.

Kangerluarsuk

The Kangerluarsuk Fjord forms the southeast boundary of the Ilimaussaq Complex. Like Tunulliarfik, the fjord cuts through the complex and steep cliffs rise from each side of the fjord. A large expanse of relatively flat rock strewn field is located at the end of the fjord and is one of the three most productive areas in the complex. Significant exploration in the 1960s revealed large deposits of beryllium, and finds of Tugtupite and other rare minerals. Some of the nicest features of this area are several beautiful areas to camp, driftwood to build a fire, a couple of rapidly flowing streams, and a never-ending supply of fluorescent minerals. The fluorescent collector could not go wrong to spend several nights here.

Several major fluorescent finds have been made in this area. In the summer of 2001 a large boulder of gem quality green Sodalite was found simply laying in the rock field. Upon splitting open a few pieces, a deep purple coloration appeared and slowly faded in the sunlight. Upon exposure to ultraviolet light, this deep purple color returns and the process can be repeated indefinitely.

There are reports from material written in the 1960s of a trail of large white boulders running from the base of the cliffs to the water's edge; the result of a vein of Albite/Tugtupite from which the surrounding syenites had eroded away. These boulders have since disappeared, but each winter the water and ice seem to "dig up" additional specimens of white material which, when put under UV, rate among the prettiest minerals of the complex. Collecting in these frost heave spots is easy and fun. It is simply a matter of finding a circle of rocks (frost heaves), throwing your tarp over the top of them and climbing under with a UV light. The resulting finds could be the highlight of a trip.

Getting Your Finds Home

After a week scouring the mountains it is a amazing how many rocks one can accumulate. A nightly ritual is the "culling hour"—no matter how tired you seem to be, the desire to examine the day's finds with fellow adventurers is overwhelming. Take this opportunity to discard the three kilo rock that you thought was so neat at the top of Kvanefjeld but now looks pitiful against the finds from Tasaq. Trading with your collecting partners can be rewarding also. They may have found material you didn't find, and vice-versa. In any case, it is important to pick and choose the best specimens, as there is a limit to how much you can carry home with you.

International flights limit your luggage to a total of twenty kilos per person. While they are somewhat flexible with this, grossly overweight baggage will be charged accordingly. Additionally, Greenland has recently adopted some strict laws regarding the export of minerals. Tourists are allowed only a select sampling to be carried in their luggage without an export license (MinerShop, in conjunction with Jewelstones of Greenland provides an export license for those who attend their Geo-Adventure tours).

Specimens should be wrapped in bubble wrap and carefully packed in your checked luggage. Hand carried specimens should be limited to only the most delicate (and lightest). Security at various airports has been known to cast a skeptical eye on rocks as they could be suspected of being weapons.

Greenland is a land of spectacular beauty and majestic landscapes. It is not for the timid but is probably one of the last unspoiled collecting areas where an average collector can expect to find specimens often only seen in museums. Perhaps the biggest challenge will be identifying the finds that have been made and will be made by future visitors.

Greenland Minerals
RFL—Reported to be fluorescent in similar locales (MSH, Langban)

Mineral	SW	LW
Albite	dark red	
Analcime	green	
Arfvedsonite	green	
Barylite	violet, red	
Bertrandite	RFL green	
Beryllite	red	
Calcite	red	
Catapleiite	green	
Cerussite	RFL yellow	
Chabazite	RFL green	
Chkalovite	green	
Cookeite	RFL yellow	
Diopside	RFL blue/white	
Elpidite	green	
Evenkite	RFL yellow/orange	
Fluorapophyllite	RFL various	
Fluorite	blue	blue
Genthelvite	RFL green	
Gibbsite	RFL bluish white	
Gmelinite	RFL yellow	
Halloysite	RFL yellow/white	
Hydrocerussite		RFL white
Lepidolite	RFL yellow/white	
Leucosphenite	RFL yellow/white	
Lorenzenite	RFL yellow	
Lovdarite	RFL green	
Microcline	blue/white, red	
Montmorillonite	RFL white	
Natrolite	RFL white, green, pink	
Nenadkevichite	RFL green	
Nepheline	RFL dark red	
Pectolite	RFL pink	orange
Plagioclase	dark red	
Polylithionite	yellow/white	
Prehnite	RFL bluish	
Quartz	blue	
Rosenbuschite	RFL yellow	
Sodalite	orange	bright orange
Sorensenite	yellow/white	
Steenstrupine	green	
Tetranatrolite	RFL green, white, pink	
Tugtupite	red	salmon, orange
Ussingite	orange green	
Villiaumite	red, orange	
Vinogradovite	RFL green	
Zircon	yellow	

Chapter Three

Classic Fluorescent Minerals That Fit into Every Collection

The most easily recognized stones from the Franklin Zinc Mine and the nearby Sterling Hill Zinc Mine are sometimes referred to as Christmas Calcites or Crazy Calcites. Stones from these areas are Calcite (glows red-orange SW) and Willemite (glows green SW). Black pieces are often non-fluorescent (noted as "NF") Franklinite while the reddish bits are NF Zincite or sometimes Andradite Garnet (usually tan in daylight). The Calcites and Willemites from these mines glow with a color and intensity that is generally not found anywhere else.

ALBITE: Albite, chemical formula $NaAlSi_3O_8$, is a sodium Feldspar (silicate). Feldspars are common minerals, but when they appear in pegmatites, they can fluoresce. Albite usually glows weak velvety red under SW UV. Under daylight it appears as dull gray crystals. It is related to Microcline.

ARAGONITE: Aragonite is a calcium carbonate. It can be found in many shapes—sharp thin crystals, bubbly surface coatings, etc. In daylight it is usually white and it glows white or blue-white under SW and generally has a good phosphorescence. It will react to dilute hydrochloric acid.

BARITE: Barite, chemical formula $BaSO_4$, is a sulfate. It is found worldwide, but most of it does not fluoresce. Franklin area Barites glows white or yellow-white under SW UV and is usually found associated with green Willemite and Calcite. Under SW, it looks like white glowing grains of rice in a red-orange rock. Some Mead County, South Dakota Barite glows blue-white (SW). There are orange glowing Barites from Ohio, Tennessee, and Arizona.

BENITOITE: Benitoite, a gorgeous blue gemstone with an unmistakable blue fluorescence, is named after San Benito County, California where it was discovered in 1907. When it was first discovered by prospectors who thought that they had found sapphires. Dr. George Louderback of the University of California studied it and found it to be a new mineral. In his studies of Benitoite, he found other minerals closely associated with Benitoite, one of which was named Joaquinite (NF). Another that appeared with Benitoite was Neptunite (NF), a dark red long, slender crystal (resembling Aegerine), that had also been found in Greenland and Russia. Although Benitoite has been found in a few other Southwest mines, the quality of that found in San Benito County was often of gem quality. The best quality is cut into gem stones that resemble Sapphire or Tanzanite.

Fluorescent collectors can buy a few pounds of Benitoite/Neptunite ore from the mine. When it arrives it is covered by white Natrolite (NF) on a light blue matrix. You soak the ore in a diluted solution of hydrochloric acid (sold in hardware stores as Muriatic Acid). Over a period of days, the Natrolite dissolves and exposes the minerals attached to the blue matrix. The collector then washes off the stone, coats the exposed areas of Benitoite or Neptunite sticking out of the Natrolite with wax to protect the supporting Natrolite from further attack by the acid. It then goes back into the acid bath. When the collector is satisfied with the results, the stone is boiled in water and the wax floats to the surface. Acetone on the end of a cotton swab sometimes helps to remove stubborn wax. You never know what you are getting under the Natrolite, hence the best exposed Benitoite and Neptunite is expensive.

BUSTAMITE: Bustamite, chemical formula $CaMn(SiO_2)_3$, is a silicate. It can be found in the Franklin, New Jersey area as a cream to pink mineral under daylight, which looks like a fibrous Rhodonite. It was once called "Manganese Wollastonite." Generally, it does not glow under UV light. Some Franklin Bustamite (usually associated with Clinohedrite or Hardystonite) glows red under LW UV. A smaller percentage glows cherry red under both SW and LW. This is the stuff that fluorescent collectors want and it is expensive. Red glowing Bustamite can also found from Sweden.

CALCITE: Calcite is a common carbonate with a chemical formula of $CaCO_3$ that can glow several different colors under SW and LW UV light or more commonly, not glow at all. There are fluorescent Calcites from all over the world that one can collect and the prices of these are usually reasonable. In the Franklin, New Jersey area, Calcite usually glows bright red-orange and is extremely plentiful. Manganese is the activator and Lead is a co-activator. Generally the closer to the ore body it is found, the brighter it glows. A single rock may have both fluorescent and NF varieties of Calcite in it.

In the Southwestern US and some places in Canada, Calcite can be found with Fluorite for a great combination of colors. Red-orange fluorescing Calcite is usually found in areas with base metals—Zinc, Copper, etc. Calcite can be found that fluoresces other colors and you may find some Calcites that show two distinct colors. Many Calcites will fluoresce under both SW and LW UV. Among the most beautiful and interesting Calcites are those from Terlingua, Texas and Terlingua-type Calcites from Mexico. These fluoresce blue under SW UV and pink under LW UV and they have a strong phosphorescence. Calcite can also fluoresce cream, yellow, gray, blue, or if uranium is present, green.

Calcite reacts with hydrochloric acid. If a weak solution of Muriatic acid is dropped on Calcite, the area will usually bubble and fizz. This is a good test to tell it apart from other minerals.

CLINOHEDRITE: Clinohedrite, chemical formula $H_2CaZnSiO_5$, is a silicate. It is a Franklin, New Jersey fluorescent and beautiful and rare when it covers more than 50% of a stone. Clinohedrite is usually found as a surface coating on Hardystonite or Bustamite, but can be found as a vein or as crystals. If you crack the stone along the vein, you can get two pieces with an amazing surface coating of Clinohedrite. It glows pumpkin orange under SW UV and weaker under LW. It is usually found associated with Hardystonite, Bustamite, Willemite, and NF Andradite. Assemblages with Clinohedrite combined with other fluorescent minerals can be incredibly beautiful. Collectors call it "Clino."

DIOPSIDE: Diopside, chemical formula $CaMg_3Si_2O_6$, is a pyroxene silicate. It can be found in the Franklin, New Jersey area (generally Sterling Hill and surrounding quarries). It was originally called "white Schefferite" and usually appears in NF Franklin Marble (Limestone) as sky blue-white glowing grains (SW). It is often associated with Norbergite. It is really a beautiful color and can also be found in mines in New York and Canada.

ESPERITE: Esperite, chemical formula $PbCa_3Zn_4(SiO_4)_4$, is an orthosilicate of calcium, lead, and zinc and is another classic, rare Franklin, New Jersey fluorescent. It glows a brilliant lemon yellow and can be found with Hardystonite, Willemite, Calcite, and Clinohedrite. It was relegated to the mine dump from the picking table because it contained lead and could contaminate the purity of the Zinc ore. Esperite was originally called Calcium Larsenite. Esperite, when found in large patches on a rock, is usually the result of its replacing Hardystonite. Esperite is only found at Franklin (from the Parker Shaft) although a tiny quantity has been reportedly found at the El Dragon Mine in Bolivia. Rocks containing a combination of Esperite with Willemite, Hardystonite, Clinohedrite, Calcite, and other fluorescent minerals are among the most actively sought by collectors.

FLUOBORITE: Fluoborite, chemical formula $6MgO \cdot B_2O_3 \cdot F_2H_2O$, is a borate and can be found in the Franklin, New Jersey area. It usually appears in NF Calcite or Limestone as yellow-white glowing rice-like grains (SW). Usually it is found in the quarries other than Franklin Mine, although some is found at Sterling Hill. It can also be found in mines in California, Canada, and Sweden.

FLUORAPATITE: Fluorapatite (sometimes called "Svabite" or "Apatite"), chemical formula $Ca(FOH)(CAZnMn)_4(ASO_4PO_4)_3$ (or Johnbaumite, chemical formula $Ca_5(ASO_4)_3OH$) is an Apatite phosphate and can also be found at Franklin, New Jersey. Apatites are found in many places in the world, but the New Jersey Apatites are usually light blue-green or gray-white in daylight. In Franklin they are more often massive, that is, they show no crystal structure. In Sterling Hill, they are often found as crystals. Most Apatites do not fluoresce, but the fluorescing Apatites glow orange, pink-orange, burnt orange, yellow, and occasionally blue under SW UV and generally not at all under LW. The exceptional examples are bright in color or cover large portions of the stone. The New Jersey pieces are usually found with NF Andradite and Willemite. New Jersey Fluorapatite is sometimes called "Svabite," which it generally is not, but most collectors call it Apatite or Fluorapatite unless they can scientifically identify it as true Svabite or as Johnbaumite. It can also be found in Pakistan and New Mexico.

FLUORITE: Fluorite, chemical formula CaF_2, is found throughout the world. It is the source of the word "fluorescent" and generally is mined for the fluorine and fluorides that can be extracted from the ore. Fluorite comes in an assortment of colors and formations (bubbly veins, crystals, veins, etc.). The fluorescent activators are usually rare earths such as Europium, Yttrium, Samarium, and some organic impurities. Fluorite is usually a later-forming mineral that moves into an existing vein, vug, or gas pocket. Some of the pieces most highly prized by fluorescent collectors comes from the hundreds of mines in Weardale, Durham County in England. The finest pieces have beautifully green or blue tinted clear crystals that fluoresce (change color) in sunlight. These usually have a bright purple glow under LW and a slightly less bright glow under SW. There are also amber colored Fluorite crystals from Cave in Rock, Hardin County, Illinois that glow creamy white (LW) while Clay Center, Ohio is known for its white glowing Fluorite (LW and SW). There are some incredibly beautiful Fluorites available from China that are mixed in with Muscovite and other minerals. They mostly glow purple or purple-blue under LW. Almost every part of the world can boast of some version of Fluorite. There are enough varieties that some collectors specialize in collecting just Fluorites.

HARDYSTONITE: Hardystonite, chemical formula $Ca_2ZnSi_2O_7$, is a calcium Zinc silicate and is a classic Franklin, New Jersey fluorescent. It is named for Hardyston Township in which the Franklin Mine is located. Hardystonite originally came out of the 900 foot level of the Parker Shaft. It is found no where else in the world. It was often relegated to the mine dump. Although Hardystonite is considered "rare," it is probably the most common of the rare Franklin fluorescents. Collectors usually want three, four, or more colors (Calcite, Willemite, Clinohedrite, Esperite, etc.) combined with Hardystonite. Hardystonite glows purple-blue under SW UV light and often glows a lesser blue under LW UV.

Under daylight, the most desirable Hardystonite is a very white colored mineral. Flesh colored is also very nice. It can also be found as a light brown or very dark colored mineral. There are other minerals that are closely associated with Hardystonite. These are Andradite, a NF tan color mineral (that is the source of Garnet), Clinohedrite (which is usually found as a surface coating that is sometimes micro-crystalline in nature), Willemite, and occasionally Esperite. Hardystonite is subject to alteration and replacement by Esperite and Clinohedrite, hence they can be found together.

HYALOPHANE: Hyalophane, chemical formula $K_2BaAlSi_3O_8$, is a barium feldspar. Feldspars are common minerals, but when they appear in pegmatites, they can fluoresce. Hyalophane is found in the Franklin, New Jersey area and glows weak velvety red-purple under SW UV. Under daylight it appears as sharp glassy-white crystals resembling Calcite. The glow is usually weak, so a good light, and time to allow your eyes to adjust to the dark is usually necessary to view it.

HYDROZINCITE: Hydrozincite, chemical formula $ZnCO_3 \cdot Zn(H_2O)$, is a silicate that is an alteration product of Sphalerite. It is found in the Franklin, New Jersey area as well as in many other areas where there are Zinc mines. Hydrozincite, under daylight, is usually a chalky white surface coating caused by water flowing through Zinc bearing rock. This causes oxidation on the host rock which glows bright blue-white under SW UV. In Nevada and Mexico, Hydrozincite can be found that glows an orange color under LW in addition to its blue-white glow under SW. It can have a long phosphorescence.

MANGANAXINITE: Often called "Axinite," Manganaxinite, chemical formula $Ca_2MnAl_2(BO_3OH)(SiO_3)_4$, is an acid borosilicate of calcium, aluminum, and manganese, with possibly a touch of iron and Zinc. It is another hard-to-find Franklin, New Jersey fluorescent. Axinites from Franklin are usually tan or whitish tan in daylight and often do not glow at all under UV light. Franklin Manganaxinite, at its fluorescent finest, glows cherry red under SW UV and weakly if at all under LW. It is usually found with NF Andradite and Willemite.

MARGAROSANITE: Margarosanite, chemical formula $PbCa_2(SiO_3)_3$, is a silicate. It is a rare Franklin, New Jersey fluorescent that only came out of the Parker Shaft. It was sent to the mine dump from the picking table because it contained lead. It has a hardness of 2.5 to 3 so it would not make a very good lapidary material. Margarosanite is usually white or blue-white in daylight and glows light violet blue or light pink under SW UV

and red-pink or tan under MW UV. Under a 10x to 20x magnifier, you may be able to see silvery bladed crystals. It is usually found with NF Andradite, Calcite, and Willemite and sometimes Clinohedrite.

Margarosanite is one of the most actively sought fluorescent minerals by collectors. The demand vastly outstrips the supply. At this time it seems to run about $1,000 per pound. In addition to New Jersey, Margarosanite can also be found from Sweden. Swedish Margarosanite is usually found as a platy surface coating. It does not demand the prices paid for the New Jersey material.

MICROCLINE: Microcline, chemical formula $KAlSi_3O_8$, is a potassium Feldspar (silicate). Feldspars are common minerals. Some wonderful Microcline is found in the Franklin, New Jersey area and may glow light blue-gray, light pink-red, or dark purple-red under SW UV. Under daylight it can appear as a blue-green Amazonite or more typical blue-gray Microcline. Microcline is fairly common, but often very attractive. While sometimes available from mineral dealers, it is usually easy to find on your visit to the Franklin Mine dump. It is related to Albite. Interestingly, iron, usually a quencher of fluorescence, is actually the activator of fluorescence in Feldspars.

NORBERGITE: Norbergite is a relatively easy to obtain mineral from Sterling Hill Mine in Ogdensburg, New Jersey and from some of the nearby quarry dumps and road cuts through the Franklin marble. Its chemical formula is $Mg_3(SiO_4)(FOH)_2$ and it is a humite silicate. It has a pleasing golden yellow color under daylight and can appear as rice-like grains to larger crystals up to half an inch or larger. Under SW light is glows a golden yellow color. It can appear in bands in the usually NF Franklin marble (limestone). It is often associated with Diopside and can be confused with the rarer Chondrodite that fluoresces a similar color. The best examples are rich in the mineral and often contain other fluorescent minerals.

PREHNITE: Prehnite, chemical formula $Ca_2Al_2Si_3O_{10}(OH)_2$, is an acid orthosilicate of calcium and aluminum and can be found at Franklin, New Jersey. It sometimes appears with orange or purple glowing crystals of Pectolite. Prehnite glows peach or pink (SW). Under a 10x magnifying glass, look for the glistening white crystals. A very unusual Prehnite has recently been discovered on an old mine dump in Franklin. It glows golden tan under SW and does not exhibit a crystal appearance under magnification. Prehnite can also be found in mines in California and Canada. Prehnite from Asbestos, Quebec Canada can fluoresce blue (LW).

SCAPOLITE: Scapolite (var. Marialite or Meionite), chemical formula Na (or Ca)$_4$(SiAl)$_{12}$O$_{24}$Cl, is found in many places and in many shades of color. The fluorescence is best described as mild rather than bright. It is best when associated with other fluorescent minerals giving the stone a multi-colored look under UV. Examples from California can be yellow-white (SW) and white-yellow, orange, or pink (LW). Franklin, New Jersey examples can be blue or orange (SW), peach pink or sky blue (LW). Sterling Hill, New Jersey examples can be dull yellow (SW and LW) or crimson red (SW). Connecticut examples can be yellow or pink (LW). Nevada examples can be pink (LW and SW). Quebec (MSH) examples can be yellow-white (SW) or red (LW). New York examples can be pink or dark red (SW) and Pennsylvania examples can be weak white (LW). Wernerite is a Scapolite and it glows brightly yellow under LW UV.

SCHEELITE: Scheelite, chemical formula $CaWO_3$, is mined as the source of Tungsten metal. It can fluoresce a brilliant blue-white to a duller yellow SW. The purer the Scheelite is, the whiter the glow. Just before America entered World War II, it anticipated that its source of Tungsten from China would be cut off by German submarines. Miners started looking for Scheelite in the Southwestern US. They quickly learned that Scheelite was highly fluorescent under SW UV. Miners bought up all of the portable mineral lights that were available (at that time, made by Ultra Violet Products of California) and began their search. Many searched abandoned silver and gold mines and found that the dumps from these mines contained tons of Scheelite. The United States had a new source of Tungsten. The government put out a small chart that contained examples of Scheelite of different purities with a hole in the card next to the sample. The miner could hold the card up to his sample, hit it with the SW UV light, and compare the sample to the different examples on the card to determine the purity of the mineral.

Some of the finest Scheelite comes from Sichuan China and appears as beautiful large tan crystals growing on Muscovite, a mica. Scheelite can also be found in Connecticut, throughout the Southwest United States, Canada, Sweden, Italy, and other countries.

SODALITE: Sodalite, chemical formula $Na_8Al_6Si_6O_{24}Cl_2$ (this formula varies depending upon the type of Sodalite), an aluminosilicate, is found in quite a few places and is easily identified by its bright orange color under LW UV. The brightest and most varied (many colors under SW) Sodalites come from Greenland and are also highly tenebrescent: that is they can change to a (daylight) grape or raspberry color after exposure to SW UV. Sodalite can also be found in Canada, Afghanistan, Russia, and Norway. An attractive daylight blue Sodalite comes from Bancroft, Ontario, Canada. It can be cut into cabochons and used as jewelry. It is also mildly tenebrescent. Sodalite stones that change color are generally called Hackmanite. Hackmanite that forms as a clear crystal (usually from MSH, Canada) can be cut and polished into gemstones. The best cut pieces sell for about $500 a carat.

SPHALERITE: Sphalerite, chemical formula ZnS, is a Sulphide and is found in many places. It is a major ore of Zinc, but does have the disadvantage of containing sulfur, which increases the cost of smelting the ore.

Under daylight it can be many colors and often appears in its crystalline form. Not all Sphalerites fluoresce, but many do and when they do, the colors can be creamy white to pink, orange or even blue. Some Franklin Sphalerite that have pinkish daylight color glows orange, blue, and pink under LW and SW. LW will consistently give a better response. Blue glowing Sphalerite is sometimes called "Cleiophane" which is actually Sphalerite that is free of iron. Manganese is the activator. Collecting New Jersey Sphalerites gives the collector a good reason to have both a SW and LW UV light. Under SW some Sphalerite (the Sterling Hill Mine variety is a good example) glows weakly and shows up dark. If you were searching in the field with your SW light, you might have thrown the rock away. Under LW light, the Sphalerite jumps out as a glowing orange vein. Sphalerite is often "triboluminescent"—that is, it produces light when scratched. Sphalerite is a beautiful and varied mineral that usually looks good in daylight. Balmat, New York produced some very nice Sphalerites including one that glows green and pink under LW.

TUGTUPITE: Tugtupite, chemical formula $Na_4AlBeSi_4O_{12}Cl$, is found in Greenland. It glows red-orange under LW, but really shines a brilliant cherry red under SW. Some rocks containing Tugtupite also exhibit a white glow around the edges of the cherry red which is also believed to be white Tugtupite. Some Tugtupite bleaches out in sunlight and regains its red color when again exposed to SW. The best examples come from Kvanefjeld, Ilimaussaq, Greenland. Tugtupite is also available from the Tasaq slope of Ilimaussaq, Greenland, but it is a more porous, softer stone that, although it glows beautifully under SW UV, it does not make a very good gem stone for lapidary work. Some tugtupite from the Tasaq Slopes glows white under MW UV. Small crystals of Tugtupite have been found at MSH.

WERNERITE (SCAPOLITE): Wernerite (a name given to Scapolite var. Marialite or Meionite), chemical formula Na (or Ca) $_4(SiAl)_{12}O_{24}Cl$, is found in Grenville, Quebec and Bancroft, Ontario, Canada. It glows a bright orange-yellow (LW) and is less bright under SW. It can also be found in mines in New York and New Jersey.

WILLEMITE: Willemite is a Zinc silicate ore with a chemical formula of Zn_2SiO_4. It glows green under SW UV light and often glows green under LW. Willemite occasionally has a strong green phosphorescence. Manganese and Lead are the activators. Willemite is found in several parts of the world and when it is fluorescent, it generally glows green. It is one of the main fluorescents at Franklin and Sterling Hill and can be found in great abundance there. Willemite's daylight colors can be white, yellow, gray, green, red, brown, and black. Brown Willemite is often called "Troostite."

Since green glowing Willemite is very common in the Franklin, New Jersey area (the ground at the mine dumps glows green and red under SW UV at night), collectors look for unusual varieties or unusual configurations, such as interesting veins of Willemite in Calcite or Calcite in Willemite. Collectors should try to find examples of gemmy Willemite which has small distinct crystals or rare crystalline Willemite which is usually transparent green, red, or amber and when big enough, can be cut into faceted gemstones. Some lapidary enthusiasts occasionally offer cut gem stones from transparent topaz-yellow crystals of Willemite. Also rare are radiating Willemites where the crystals of Willemite grow out from a central point (these are usually highly phosphorescent) and straw Willemite which looks like pieces of straw in Calcite or other host rock. A bit less rare are large hexagonal crystals of brown or black Willemite sticking out of Calcite. The harder to find daylight colors of Willemite are blue, yellow, red, and bright green. Daylight green Willemite is generally found at Franklin and not at Sterling Hill.

Beta Willemite, a micro-crystalline yellow to yellow-orange fluorescing Willemite with a strong phosphorescence, is a great, rare addition to your fluorescent collection. Small amounts have been found at the Sterling Hill Mine or neighboring Andover Mine and even less has been found at the Franklin Mine.

The Southwestern part of the United States produces some yellow-white glowing (SW) Willemite as well as the standard green Willemite. The Willemite green glow is distinctly different from a Uranium green glow. By studying the two, you can pretty quickly determine which one is Willemite. You can assemble a collection of just Willemites from around the world or just every variety from the Franklin area.

WOLLASTONITE: Wollastonite, chemical formula $CaSiO_3$, is found in the Franklin, New Jersey area as well as in other areas. In daylight it usually exhibits a glazed china-looking surface. Franklin area Wollastonite glows orange, yellow-orange, or yellow under SW UV. It will phosphoresce the same color. In the Franklin area it is usually found associated with Calcite and looks like yellow or orange glowing grains of rice, blades, or fans in a red-orange rock. It has a Manganese activator and the higher the concentration of Manganese, the more orange the color. In the Franklin area, there are Wollastonites called "1st Find," "2nd Find," "3rd Find," etc. These indicate the place in the mine where the fluorescing mineral was first found, etc. 1st Find usually has large patches of Wollastonite and usually contains Willemite and sometimes Margarosanite. 2nd Find usually has large patches of Wollastonite and contains Hardystonite. 3rd Find Wollastonite contains white glowing Barite. There are other varieties such as "fibrous," etc. Wollastonite can also be found in New York, California, Canada, China, and Mexico. Wollastonite contains Calcium, Silicon and Oxygen. It is a metamorphic mineral, meaning it changed from its original composition, due to the earth's pressure and heat, to form this mineral.

Radioactive Mineral Collecting

If you have a hankering for radioactive minerals that fluoresce, you might look for Autunite, Torbernite, Carnotite, Uraninite, Monazite, Pitchblende, and other uranium ore minerals for your collection. When dealing with radioactive minerals, there are a few additional rules that must be obeyed.

1) Store them in an airtight container. They produce radioactive gas (radon) and dust that can get into the air and onto your skin or clothing. The dust can also be inhaled. If you accumulate numerous specimens, they should be kept in lead containers.

2) Keep your specimens away from places occupied by people (such as kitchens, bedrooms, etc.) and away from children.

3) Make sure that they are labeled as "Radioactive." Clean up flakes and broken pieces that might work their way into clothes, food, lungs, etc. Your LW UV light will help you find the particles.

There is no reason why a group of radioactive fluorescents can not be an interesting addition to your fluorescent collection.

Chapter Four

A Photographic Display of Fluorescent Minerals

In this section, the first photo is the stone in daylight. The second is usually SW UV or LW UV. Additional photos may show a close up, MW UV, Tenbrescence, or Phosphorescence.

Note: Fluorescent minerals exhibit very pure colors when they fluoresce. I have included a color chart that covers the most basic of the fluorescent colors. Since colors vary from stone to stone and from person to person seeing the colors, the actual colors of the stones may be more or less saturated, lighter or darker, brighter or duller, or the hue may vary from what you see here on paper. I have tried to accurately capture the colors that were present, but the printing process cannot show color the way that the eye actually sees it. The photos should give you a good representative feel for what you will see with your own rocks. Most of the photographs were taken using a new UV Systems' SuperBright™ brand UV light. If you have an older (pre-1995) UV light, the colors you see with the same stones may not be as bright and may have a slightly bluer look. There are now quite a few very good mineral lights on the market. As you build your collection of fluorescent minerals, you will probably want to invest in the latest UV light available.

white	yellow	yellow-green	green-yellow	green	blue-green	green-blue
blue	purple-blue	purple	violet	pink	peach	reddish peach
orange	pumpkin orange	burnt orange	orange-red	red	velvet red	brown
creamy white	creamy yellow	gold	lawn green	tourquoise	slate grey	tan

Franklin Mine, Sterling Hill Mine, and Vicinity, New Jersey

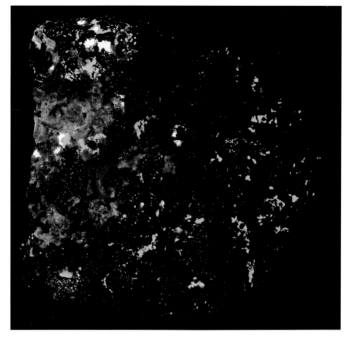

AMAZONITE: A piece of dark brown Augite with Amazonite, a variety of Microcline (a potassium Feldspar) from the Old Mill Site, Franklin, New Jersey. Amazonite is blue-green in daylight and fluoresces a mild blue-gray under SW UV. 10 oz. 2.5" x 2" x 2". Value $12-14.

Same under SW UV.

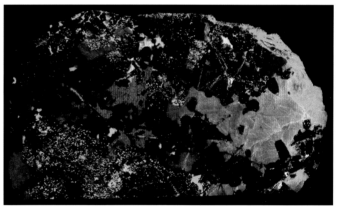

AMAZONITE: An unusual four color polished slice of a rock containing Amazonite, a variety of Microcline, along with a daylight reddish Apatite, Willemite, Calcite, and NF Augite from the Old Mill Site, Franklin. This Amazonite is blue-green in daylight and fluoresces gray-blue under SW. The Apatite glows a burnt orange, the Calcite red-orange, and the Willemite glows green. 2.5 oz. 3.25" x 2" x .25". Value $45-55.

Same under SW UV.

AMAZONITE: A group of four polished cabochons containing Amazonite from the Old Mill Site, Franklin, New Jersey. This Amazonite is blue-green in daylight and fluoresces a range of colors – gray-blue to gray-blue with peach-pink veins under SW. Each about 1" wide by 1.5" tall. Value $45-55 each.

Same under SW UV.

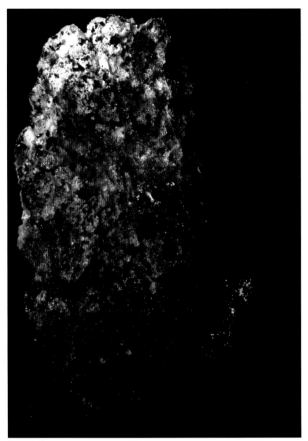

AMAZONITE and MEIONITE: Amazonite is a form of Microcline (Feldspar family) that has a porcelain-like texture and blue-green color in daylight. It fluoresces a mild blue-gray. The Meionite, (a variety of Scapolite) located under the Amazonite is an unusual find. It fluoresces mild orange (SW), a very offbeat color. From the Old Mill Site, Franklin, New Jersey. 11.5 oz. 4" x 3" x 1.75". Value $55-65.

Same under SW UV.

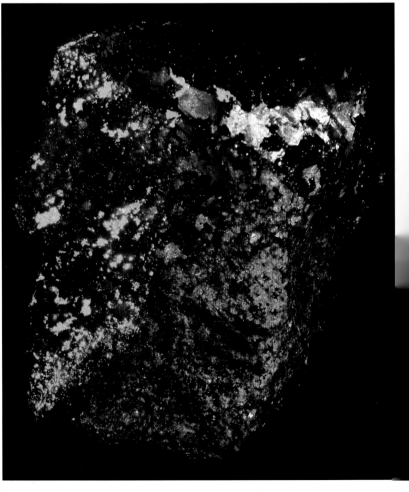

AMAZONITE and MICROCLINE: A rock containing daylight blue-green Amazonite, Microcline, Willemite, and Calcite from the Old Mill Site, Franklin, New Jersey. Microcline is often an under-appreciated mineral. It fluoresces nicely and looks great under daylight. This piece is pretty exceptional in that it glows a few unusual colors under SW. The Amazonite glows mild blue-gray, the Microcline Feldspar glows light violet, the Willemite glows green, and the Calcite red-orange (SW). 1 lb. 6 oz. 3.25" x 3" x 2.125". Value $20-25.

Same under SW UV.

ANDRADITE: Andradite is usually found as a tan mineral without crystalline shape. It is sometimes a good indicator of rarer Franklin minerals. This piece has Andradite Garnet crystal shapes and is from the Old Mill Site, Franklin, New Jersey. Andradite is a NF (tan-brown color in daylight) garnet. 1 lb. 8 oz. 4" x 3" x 2". Value $12-15.

Same under SW UV.

ARAGONITE: Small needle-like (acicular) Aragonite crystals on matrix from Sterling Mine, Ogdensburg. Aragonite glows greenish white (SW and LW). 6.5 oz. 3.5" x 2.5" x 1". Value $10-15.

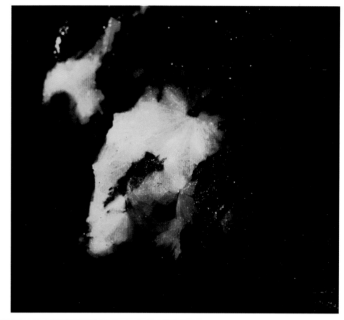

Same under SW UV.

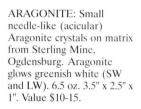

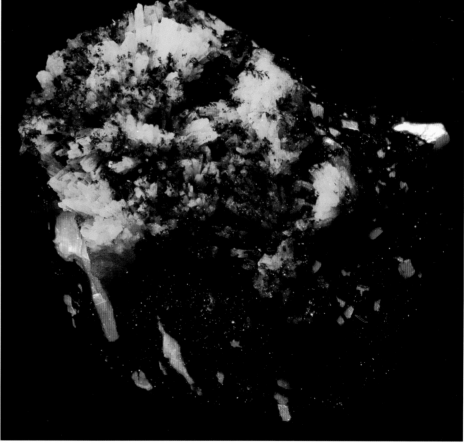

ARAGONITE: A dark stone with off-white crystals of Aragonite. The stone also contains NF Galena (lead crystal) and Calcite. This is from the Sterling Hill Mine, Ogdensburg. Aragonite glows greenish white (SW and LW). Calcite fluoresces orange-red. 6.5 oz. 2.25" x 1.75" wide. Value $15-20.

Same under SW UV.

AZURITE with MALACHITE: A recent find of Sterling Hill material with substantial evidence of copper was found in the west wall of the sand pit (a part of the Passaic pit). Copper containing Sterling Hill material, up to the time of this find was considered very rare. The Azurite is daylight blue and the Malachite is daylight green. Both are hydrous copper carbonates that form when copper sulfides weather. The Franklin limestone acts as the source of carbon dioxide which joins the copper ions together to form these two minerals. Under SW UV, the Calcite in the stone glows typical red-orange. 6 oz. 2" x 2" x 1". Value $18-22.

BARITE with WILLEMITE: A rare combination from Franklin – Barite, Grape Willemite, and Calcite. Barite is rarely found with Willemite. It is almost always attached to Calcite. The Barite glows white (SW), the Willemite glows green (SW), and the Calcite glows red-orange (SW). 11.75 oz. 3" x 2.5" x 1.75". Value $250-300.

Same under SW UV.

BARITE: A rare Franklin mineral, Barite on Calcite, from the Franklin Mine. Barite from the Franklin Mine is usually found as a dirty white color rather than this bright white which is a more Sterling Hill Mine color. This is a museum quality large display piece. Barite glows white (SW). 3 lb. 13 oz. 6" x 4.25" x 2.25". Value $450-500.

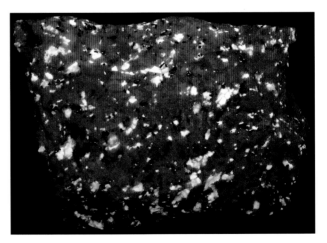

Same under SW UV.

BARITE: A very nice stone from Franklin, New Jersey containing a massive chunk of Barite. Barite glows white (SW). Barite is usually found as smaller grains spread throughout a matrix of Calcite. This is an exceptionally large area of Barite. 9 oz. 2.75" x 2.25" x 1.5". Value $120-135.

Same under SW UV.

BARITE: Barite on Calcite from the Franklin Mine. Franklin Barite often can be differentiated from Sterling Barite in that the Franklin material is usually found in a Rose Calcite (under daylight) while the Sterling Barite is found in a whiter Calcite. Barite glows white (SW). 1 lb. 1 oz. 5" x 3.5" x 2.25". Value $70-85.

Same under SW UV.

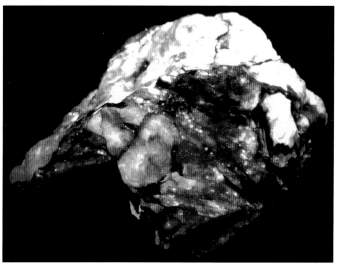

BARYLITE: An incredibly rare fluorescent mineral from the Franklin Mine. Barylite glows violet-blue (SW). 5 oz. 3" x 2.75" x 1". *From the George Elling collection.*

Same under SW UV.

BETA WILLEMITE: A rare mild yellow fluorescing Willemite made up of many tiny sparkling crystals (druzes) with Calcite from Sterling Hill Mine, Ogdensburg. This mild yellow to intense yellow glowing (SW) Willemite is called Beta Willemite. 16 oz. 4.5" x 5.5" x 1.5" thick. Value $200-235.

Close up showing the crystalline nature of the Beta Willemite.

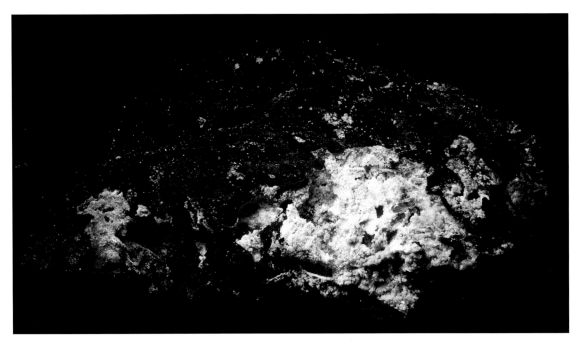

Same under SW UV.

BETA WILLEMITE: Beta Willemite and Willemite from the Sterling Hill Mine. This Beta Willemite glows yellow-orange (SW) and the Willemite glows green. 8.75 oz. and 3.75" x 2.25" x 1.75". Value $100-120.

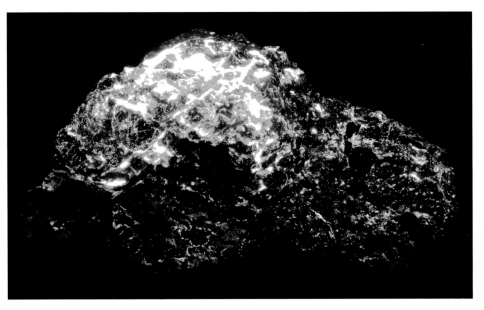

Same under SW UV.

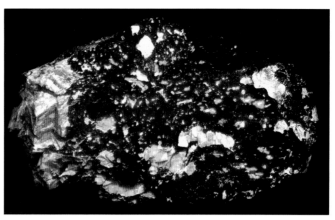

BUSTAMITE, CALCITE and WILLEMITE: An interesting Franklin combination rock containing Willemite, Calcite, NF Bustamite, and NF Biotite Mica from the Old Mill Site, Franklin, New Jersey. The Willemite glows green, and the Calcite glows red-orange (SW). 3 lb. 3 oz. 5.5" x 3" x 2.75". Value $14-18.

Same under SW UV.

BUSTAMITE: Bustamite looks like a fibrous light pink to red-pink Rhodonite in daylight. Most Bustamite does not fluoresce. This piece is a rare SW and LW fluorescent Bustamite with Clinohedrite from the Franklin Mine. Bustamite, when it fluoresces usually glows red under long wave UV. This rarer type glows red long wave and is equally bright under short wave. The Clinohedrite glows pumpkin orange (SW). 3.5 oz. 2.75" x 1.5" x 1". Value $150-175.

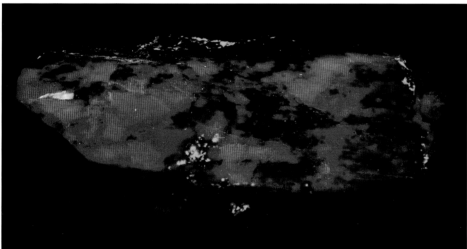

Same under LW UV.

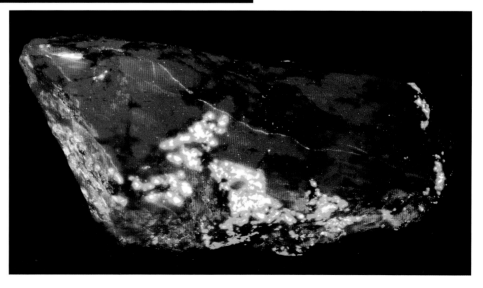

Same under SW UV.

BUSTAMITE: Another example of a rare SW fluorescent Bustamite. This piece glows red long wave and is equally bright under short wave. 2.5 oz. 3.25" x 1 x .75". Value $125-135.

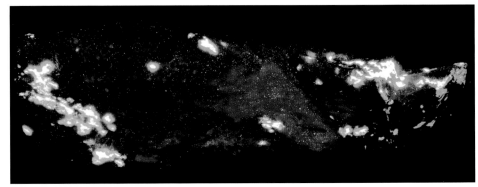

Same under LW UV.

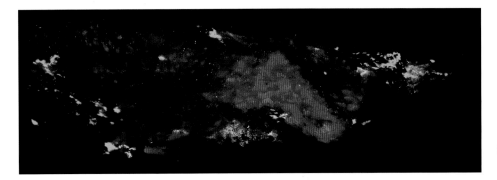

Same under SW UV.

BUSTAMITE: Bustamite, with Hancockite and Prehnite from the Franklin Mine. This Bustamite glows red (SW), Prehnite glows peach (SW), Hancockite is NF (daylight) light brown. 11 oz. 4" x 2.75" x 1.5". Value $60-75.

Same under SW UV.

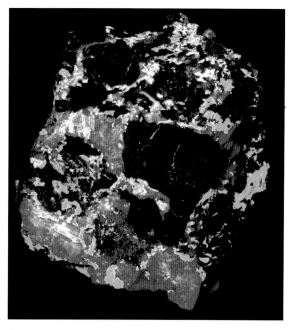

Same under SW UV.

CALCITE and WILLEMITE: Calcite, Franklinite, and Willemite, Franklin. A particularly nice Franklin stone. When it comes to red and green glowing stones, the more advanced collector looks for something different–veins, unusual patterns, etc. This stone just has a bright pleasing pattern. Calcite glows red-orange (SW) and Willemite glows green (SW). 4 lbs. 6" x 4" x 3.5". Value $40-55.

Same under LW UV.

CALCITE: An unusual tiny piece of Calcite from the Buckwheat dump of the Franklin Mine, Franklin. The Calcite glows the typical red-orange (SW) but it glows a purple-blue under LW in a style similar to Terlingua Calcite. .75" x .5". Value $5-6.

Same under SW UV.

CALCITE and WILLEMITE: Calcite, Franklinite, and Willemite from the Sterling Hill Mine. Another nice stone. With red and green glowing stones, one should look for something different–veins, unusual patterns, etc. This stone has great veins. Calcite glows red-orange (SW) and Willemite glows green (SW). 15.5 oz. 7 x 3.5". Value $25-30.

Same under SW UV.

CALCITE: Calcite balls and chips in brown NF Augite with NF Andradite from the Old Mill Site, Franklin. This is an oddity that is not found very often. It can be fashioned into very nice jewelry. The Calcite glows a rich red-orange (SW). 2 lb. 4 oz. 4" x 3.75" x 2". Value $20-25.

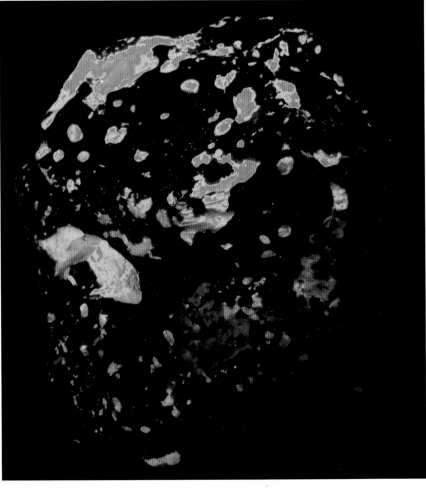

Same under SW UV.

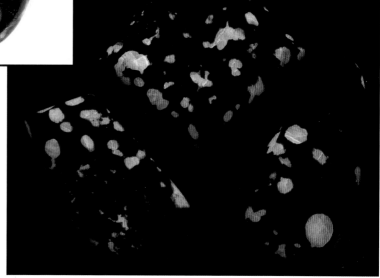

CALCITE IN AUGITE: An unusual form of Calcite from the Franklin Mine, Franklin cut into cabochons. The Calcite, which appears as white "pearls" is nested in brown Augite (NF) with tan Andradite (NF). The Calcite glows a strong red-orange. 1 to 1.5" across.

Same under SW UV.

SALMON CALCITE: Calcite from the Franklin Mine occasionally turns a beautiful salmon color. Salmon Calcite rarely occurs at the Sterling Mine. This is from the Old Mill Site, Franklin and is an exceptionally bright red-orange under SW. The closer to the ore body the Calcite is, the brighter it glows. 3.5 lb. 6" x 5" x 3". Value $35-45.

Same under SW UV.

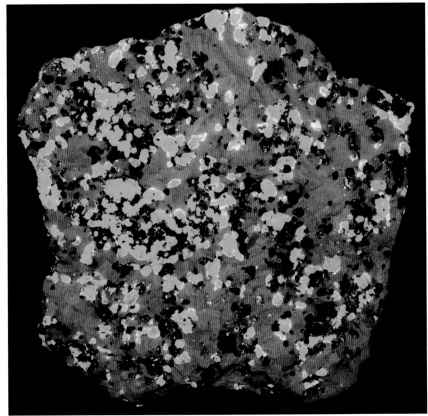

CALCITE and WILLEMITE: A great example of gemmy Willemite and Calcite. This is the classic Sterling "Christmas Calcite" that is so easily identified as coming from this mine. It is called "gemmy" since the Willemite and Franklinite are nice individual crystals. The Calcite fluoresces orange-red (SW) with loads of Willemite and also has crystals of Franklinite and some Zincite. From Sterling Hill Mine, Ogdensburg. 1 lb. 11 oz. 4.5" x 4.5" x 1". Value $20-25.

Same under SW UV.

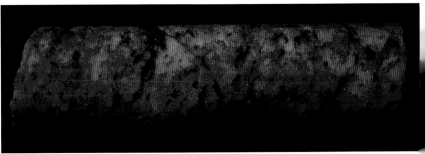

CALCITE CORE SAMPLE: Cores were taken in the mine to allow the miners to follow the vein of Zinc bearing rock. Most core samples from the mine do not fluoresce. Calcite glows orange-red (SW). From Sterling Hill Mine, Ogdensburg. 6 oz. 4" x 1". Value $12-15.

Same under SW UV.

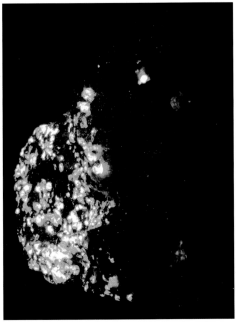

CALCITE: A group of nail head and regular NF Calcite crystals on a matrix of Willemite crystals. Nail head Calcite is an unusual shaped blade of Calcite that looks like the head of a nail. These came from a fault line on the north wall of the Passaic Pit at the Sterling Hill Mine that contained vugs (open areas in the rock) containing Calcite crystals. The Willemite glows green (SW). 5.5 oz. 2.5" x 2.25" x 1.5". Value $20-30.

Same under SW UV.

CALCITE and MANGANESE: Two small but interesting pieces of rock containing nail head and regular NF Calcite crystals on a matrix of Willemite crystals. The smaller piece has a perfect, rare, pyramid shaped crystal growing on the Manganese ball with nail head Calcite in front of it. These came from a fault line on the north wall of the Passaic Pit at the Sterling Hill Mine that contained vugs (open areas in the rock) containing Calcite crystals. The Willemite glows green (SW).

CHLORITE: Greenish plates of Chlorite, a NF Mica material in Calcite from the Old Mill Site, Franklin. The Calcite glows red-orange (SW). 1 lb. 4" x 3" x 1.25". Value $10-12.

Same under SW UV.

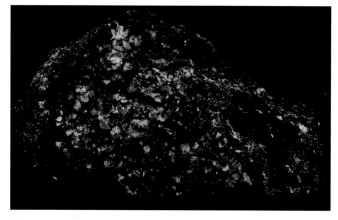

Same under SW UV.

CHLOROPHANE and SPHALERITE: Chlorophane, a brown fluorite, with Sphalerite and Willemite from the Old Mill Site, Franklin (it can also be found at Sterling Hill). Chlorophane glows a beautiful teal blue-green under SW and LW and has a phosphorescent afterglow. Some Chlorophane becomes luminescent when heated (thermoluminescence). Some is so sensitive that it will glow from the heat of one's hand. Chlorophane must be kept out of direct sunlight or it will lose its fluorescence over time. Some collectors keep theirs wrapped in aluminum foil. The Sphalerite glows orange and blue. 9 oz. 3.5" x 2.25" x 1.5". Value $30-40.

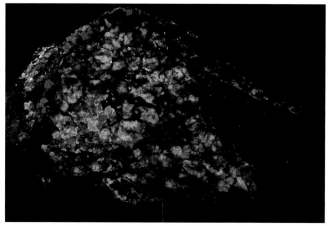

Same under LW UV.

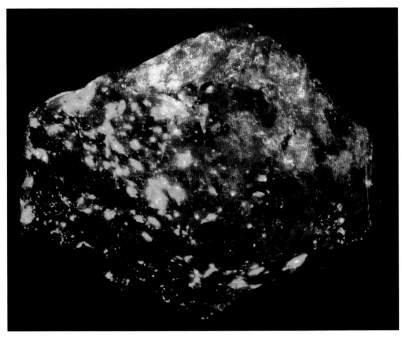

CLINOHEDRITE: Clinohedrite, Hardystonite, Willemite and touches of Calcite, Franklin. This is an exceptionally nice looking rock under SW UV. It looks like it is on a pink Bustamite under daylight. Under the SW light, the Clinohedrite, which is usually a surface coating, seems to permeate the stone. Clinohedrite glows pumpkin orange (SW), Hardystonite glows purple-blue (SW). 8 oz. 2.75" x 2" x 2". Value $100-125. *Originally from the Nick Zipco collection.*

Same under SW UV.

CLINOHEDRITE with BUSTAMITE: Franklin Parker Shaft Clinohedrite on gemmy NF Bustamite with Hardystonite. The Clinohedrite has seeped into the Bustamite. Clinohedrite glows a bright pumpkin orange. The Hardystonite glows purple-blue and the Willemite glows green all under SW. 7.5 oz. 3.5" x 1.5" x 1.25". Value $55-65.

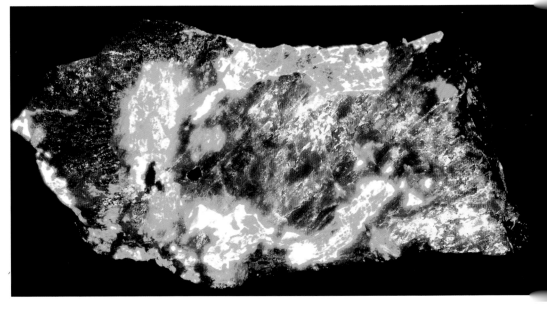

Same under SW UV.

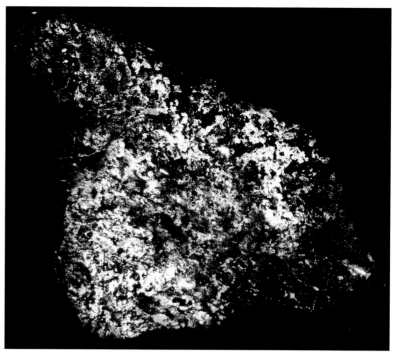

CLINOHEDRITE: Clinohedrite with Hardystonite, Willemite, and Franklinite from the Parker Shaft, Franklin. This stone has exceptional coverage of Clinohedrite. Clinohedrite glows a Halloween orange (SW), Willemite glows green (SW), and Hardystonite glows purple-blue (SW). 1 lb. 8 oz. 4" x 4" x 1.25". Value $85-95.

Same under SW UV.

CLINOHEDRITE: Platy Clinohedrite, Hardystonite, Willemite, Franklin. Often the Clinohedrite is a thin layer of mineral. This has lovely thicker plates of Clinohedrite which glows orange (SW), Hardystonite glows purple-blue (SW). 6.5 oz. 3.5" x 2.25" x .75". Value $55-65. Originally from the Nick Zipco collection.

Same under SW UV.

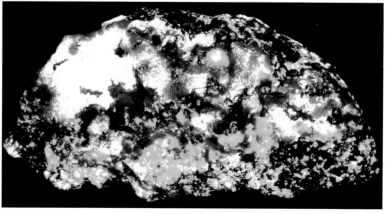

CLINOHEDRITE: Clinohedrite crystals, Willemite, a touch of Calcite, and Franklinite from the Parker Shaft, Franklin. This stone has incredible coverage of crystalline Clinohedrite. Clinohedrite glows orange (SW), Willemite glows green (SW), and Calcite glows red-orange (SW). 1 lb. 7 oz. 5.25" x 3" x 2.25". *From the George Elling collection.*

Same under SW UV.

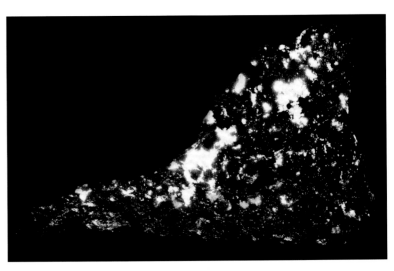

CLINOHEDRITE and MARGAROSANITE: Clinohedrite with small blebs of Margarosanite and NF Andradite from the Parker Shaft, Franklin. A small piece, but very pretty. Margarosanite glows sky blue (SW) and Clinohedrite glows orange (SW). .5 oz. 1.75" wide. Value $40-45.

Same under SW UV.

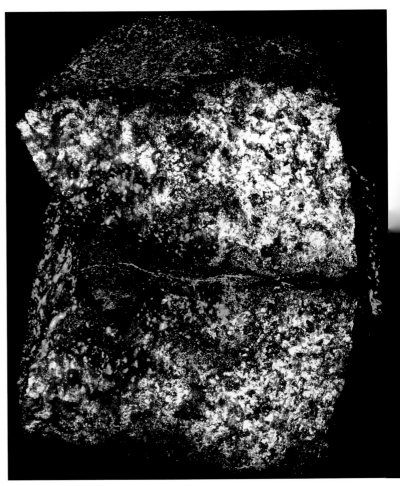

CLINOHEDRITE: Franklin Clinohedrite on Hardystonite. Clinohedrite glows a bright pumpkin orange under SW. This stone looked like a solid piece of Hardystonite. After careful examination under a SW light, a tiny orange vein was detected. The stone was place in a precision rock cracker and pressure was applied. The rock cracked along the vein and exposed two beautiful faces of Clinohedrite. The rock went from a two color stone (there was some Willemite) to two three color stones.

Same under SW UV.

48

CUSPIDINE: A very rare Franklin Mine mineral. A small quantity was found in 1997 by Dru Wilbur among stones from a demolished building foundation in Franklin, New Jersey. It was first visually identified as Johnbaumite, but an X-ray powder diffraction analysis by Excalibur Mineral Co. confirmed that it was the rare fluorescent mineral Cuspidine. This is from that find. This Cuspidine glows peach-orange under SW and rose-pink under MW. 4 oz. 2" x 1.625" x 1.125". Value $225-250.

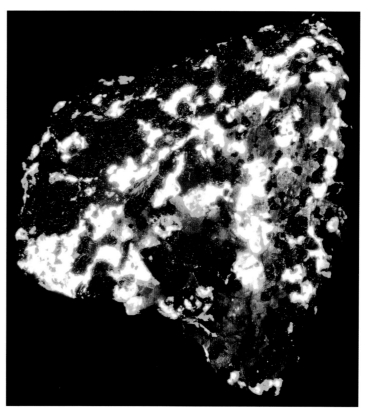

Same under SW UV.

DIOPSIDE: Diopside from Sterling Hill Mine. This example has a particularly nice larger fibrous crystal of Diopside on the left side. Diopside glows light blue (SW). 7 oz. 3.5" x 2". Value $20-25.

Same under MW UV

Same under SW UV.

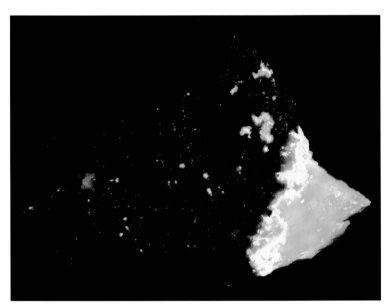

ESPERITE: A fish shaped piece of stone containing green Willemite crystals at the nose, then a band of Esperite, then more Willemite and some spots of Calcite in the body. Esperite glows lemon yellow (SW), Willemite glows green (SW), and Calcite glows red-orange (SW). From the Parker Shaft of the Franklin Mine. 5 oz. 2.5" x 2" x .25". Value $50-55 (mostly for its unusual shape).

Same under SW UV.

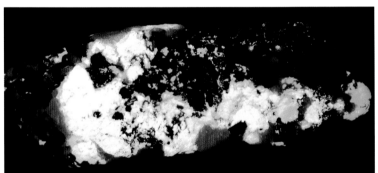

ESPERITE: Esperite, Calcite, Franklinite, and Willemite, Franklin. A nice three color stone. Esperite glows yellow (SW). 6 oz. 3.75" x 1.25". Value $60-65.

Same under SW UV.

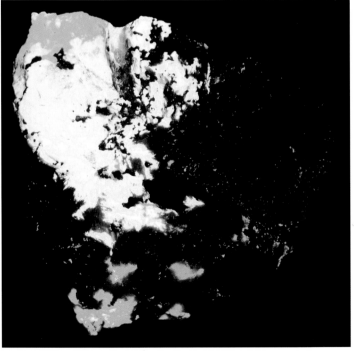

ESPERITE: Esperite with Hardystonite, and Willemite from the Parker Shaft, Franklin. This is a great three color stone with a nice band of yellow Esperite. Esperite glows a bright yellow (SW), Willemite glows green (SW), and Hardystonite glows purple-blue (SW). 11 oz. 3" x 2.25" x 2". Value $85-100.

Same under SW UV.

ESPERITE: A very large stone that is almost half solid Esperite. In most cases, you find Esperite within Willemite. In this stone, the Willemite is just an eye in the Esperite. 4 lb. 3 oz. 5.5" x 4.5" x 3.25". Value $600-700. *From the Gar Van Tassel collection.*

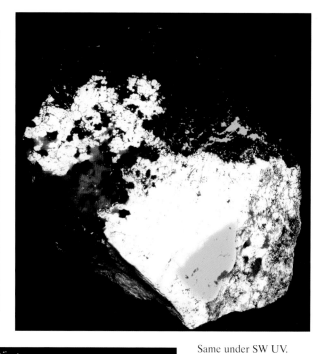

Same under SW UV.

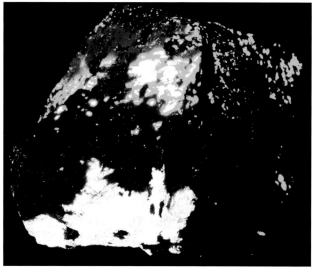

ESPERITE and HARDYSTONITE: A great four-color stone containing Esperite, Hardystonite, Clinohedrite, Willemite, and Franklinite. From the Parker shaft, Franklin. Esperite glows lemon yellow, Hardystonite glows purple-blue, Clinohedrite glows pumpkin orange, and Willemite glows green. 3 lb. 5" across. Value $200-250.

Same under SW UV.

FLUOBORITE: Fluoborite in Franklin marble (Limestone) from the Bodner Quarry, Rudeville, New Jersey. Fluoborite glows yellow-white (SW). 7 oz. 4" x 1.75" x 1.25". Value $30-35.

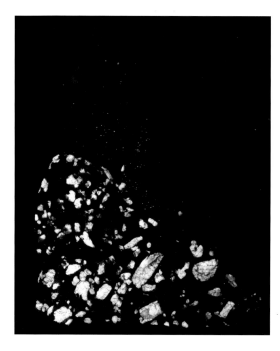

Same under SW UV.

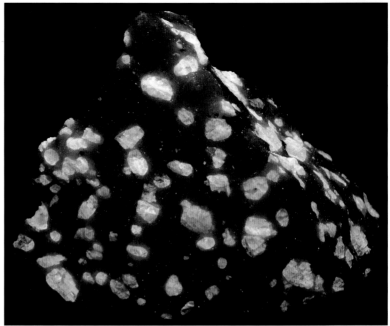

FLUOBORITE: Fluoborite in Franklin marble from the Bodner Quarry, Rudeville. This is a particularly rich example. Fluoborite glows yellow-white (SW). 2 oz. 2.25". Value $15-18.

Same under SW UV.

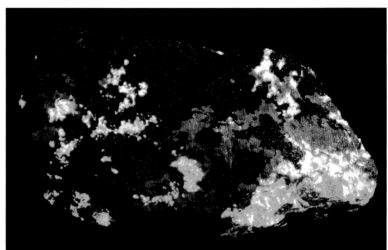

FLUORAPATITE: Massive Fluorapatite and Willemite with tan Andradite garnet (NF) from Franklin. Fluorapatite glows orange to burnt orange (SW). Fluorapatite, while hard to find, is not considered rare. The best examples have a lot of the mineral in the stone (great coverage) and under SW UV, it glows bright orange. Standard examples glow a burnt orange and only have a few blebs of the material on the stone. 1 lb. 7 oz. 5" across. Value $85-110.

Same under SW UV.

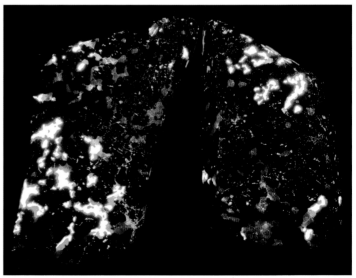

FLUORAPATITE: A pair of free form cabochons cut and polished from a stone containing Fluorapatite with Willemite, NF Zinc Schefferite and NF Andradite from Franklin. The Fluorapatite, glows orange (SW). 2.75" to 3" tall. Value $40-50 ea.

Same under SW UV.

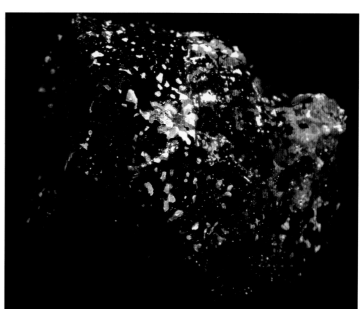

Same under SW UV.

FLUORAPATITE and SPHALERITE: An unusual combination of Fluorapatite (on the right side of the stone) and Sphalerite from the Passaic Pit at the Sterling Hill Mine. This came from the same trench in which the Genthelvite was found. The Fluorapatite glows golden orange (SW). The Sphalerite glows blue and pink. 6 oz. 2.5" x 2" x 1.5". Value $20-25.

Same under LW UV.

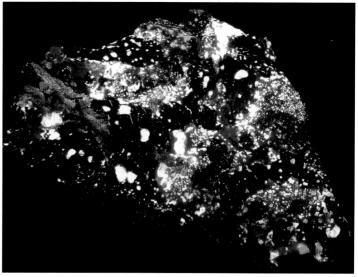

FLUORAPATITE: Fluorapatite (on the center and left side of the stone) from the Sterling Hill Mine. The Sterling Hill Fluorapatite is more often found in the crystalline form rather than the massive form found from the Franklin mine. This came from the same trench in the Passaic Pit where the Genthelvite was found. The Fluorapatite glows golden orange (SW). 6 oz. 2.5" x 2" x 1.5". Value $25-30.

Same under SW UV.

FLUORAPATITE: Crystals of Fluorapatite in Calcite and Willemite from the Passaic Pit, Sterling Hill Mine. Fluorapatite glows orange (SW), Calcite glows red-orange, Willemite glows green under SW. 3.5 oz. 2.5" x 1.75" x 1". Value $25-30.

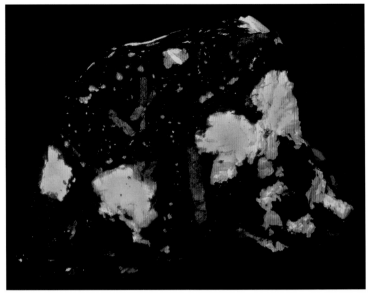

Same under SW UV.

FLUORITE: A white limestone containing crystals of Franklin Fluorite. This Fluorite is not very fluorescent. It appears as purple Amethyst-looking fluorite crystals sparsely disseminated in limestone. The fluorite barely glows under SW and not at all under LW, but there is a light Hydrozincite glow around the crystal. Hydrozincite glows blue white (SW). 6 oz. 2.5" x 1 x 1". Value $30-35.

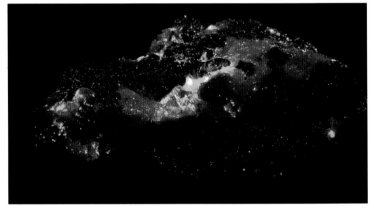

Same under SW UV.

FRANKLIN PARKER SHAFT COMBO: Tan Manganaxinite, altered Hendricksite, Clinohedrite, Prehnite, Smithsonite, Margarosanite, and Willemite from Parker Shaft, Franklin. This is a great example of the amazing groupings that come out of the Parker Shaft. Manganaxinite glows red, Prehnite glows pink-peach, Smithsonite glows white, Margarosanite glows blue-white, Clinohedrite glows pumpkin orange (SW), Willemite glows green (SW), and altered Hendricksite is a NF Zinc Mica. 16 oz. 3.75" across. Value $175-200.

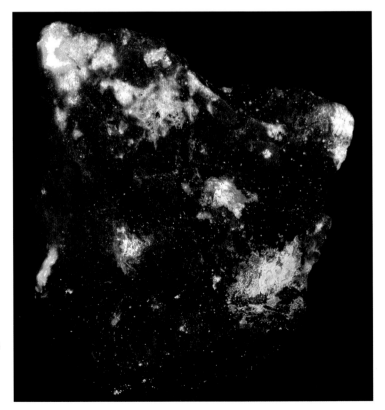

Same under SW UV.

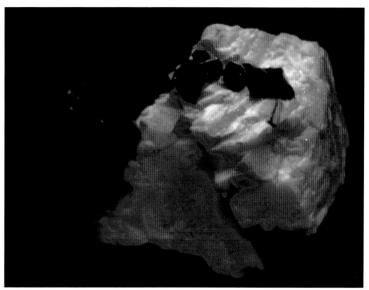

FRANKLINITE: A stone with a large Franklinite crystal (1" across) and some smaller crystals on a piece of Calcite from Franklin, New Jersey. The Calcite glows red-orange (SW). 4.5 oz. 2.25" x 1.25" x 1.25". Value $40-50.

FRIEDELITE: Friedelite crystals with Willemite and touches of blue glowing Sphalerite from Sterling Hill. Friedelite is a tough to find mineral and can have two completely different appearances. Here it is as a tan NF crystalline coating on Calcite and Franklinite. This is a particularly fine example. 2 lb. 4" x 4" x 2". Value $45-55.

FRANKLINITE: A nice large partially weathered octahedron crystal of Franklinite with Calcite from the Noble Pit at the Sterling Hill Mine, Ogdensburg. This area is in the top of the Noble Pit where Franklinite can be dug out. It is said that the area was picked over for Franklinite crystals for many years in the mid to late 1800s as the heavy mineral worked well as bird shot. The largest side of the crystal is 2.5". The Calcite glows red-orange (SW). 1 lb. 12 oz. 4.5" x 3.25" x 2". Value $80-100.

FRANKLINITE: Larger, weather worn crystals of NF Franklinite from Sterling Hill Mine, New Jersey. There is an area in the Noble Pit where these clumps of Franklinite can be dug out. It is said that the area was picked over for Franklinite crystals for many years in the mid to late 1800s as the heavy mineral worked well as bird shot. 10 oz. 4" x 2.75". Value $9-13.

FRIEDELITE: A very gemmy red liver colored Friedelite from Sterling Hill. The Friedelite is NF. This can be cut into cabochons. 3.5 oz. 2" x 2" x .75". Value $40-45.

GAHNITE: Dark green crystals of Gahnite (a NF Zinc Spinel) in Calcite, from Sterling Hill Mine. Calcite glows red (SW). 1 lb. 2.5 oz. 3.5" x 3". Value $35-40.

Same under SW UV.

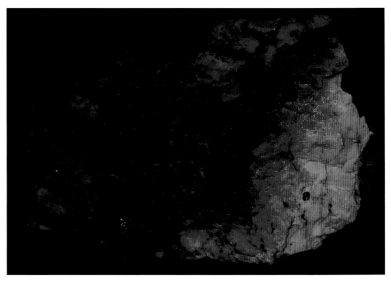

GALENA and CALCITE: Calcite, and non-fluorescing Galena (lead crystals). Calcite glows orange-red (SW). From Sterling Hill Mine, Ogdensburg. 7 oz. 3.75" x 2.25". Value $30-35.

Same under SW UV.

GENTHELVITE: This is a very rare Sterling Hill Mine mineral. Genthelvite was discovered at Sterling in late 2002 in one area of the Passaic Pit. It got its name as it is a Helvite named after Dr. Gent. Most finds are a few tiny spots on the very hard-to-break host rock (amphibole). The pointer shows a small 2mm patch on a larger stone. Genthelvite glows (a Willemite) green under LW and barely glows green under SW. It has also been found in Mont Saint-Hilaire Canada, Langesundfjord Norway, and Motzfeldt Center Greenland. There is a Wisconsin version that glows weak blue-white under SW. 13.5 oz. 2.5" x 2.5" x 2". Value $45-55.

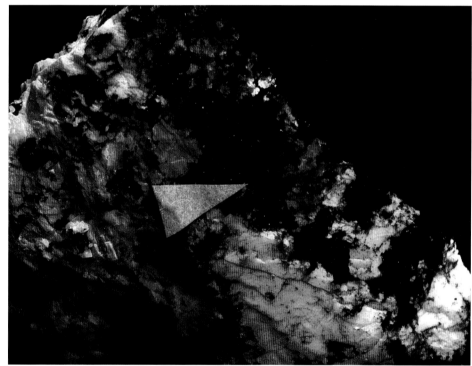

Same under SW UV showing the minimal response of the Genthelvite and the better response of the Calcite.

Same under LW UV.

GENTHELVITE: Another example of this rare Sterling Hill Mine mineral. This piece has a substantial area of Genthelvite which has a greenish hue in daylight. It glows green under LW and barely glows green under SW. Genthelvite can also be found in Mont Saint-Hilaire. That variety glows stronger under SW UV. 13.5 oz. 6" x 3.5" x 1". Value $300-350.

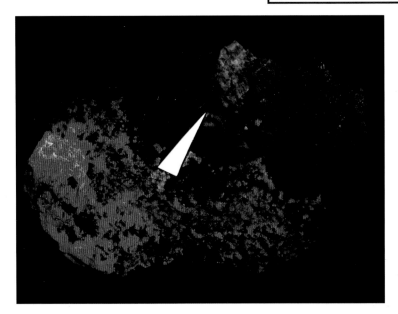

Same under SW UV.

Same under LW UV.

GENTHELVITE: Another example of this rare mineral, Genthelvite. .5 oz. 1.75" x 1 x .4". Value $25-30.

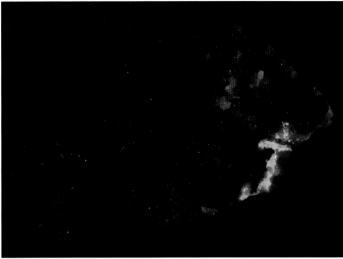

Same under LW UV.

HARDYSTONITE: Massive gray Hardystonite enclosing large anhedral masses of deep red Zincite, minor granular Franklinite and Willemite, Franklin. Hardystonite glows purple-blue (SW). Zincite is NF red. Hardystonite can be found as a very dark material to a very light material. It is a hard to find material, but not considered to be rare. The best examples show four, five, or more fluorescent minerals on the same rock. 1 lb. 13 oz. 4" x 3.25". Value $65-75. *Originally from the E. Packard "Sunny" Cook collection.*

HARDYSTONITE: Calcite with Franklinite, Willemite and Hardystonite from the Old Mill Site, Franklin. Hardystonite glows purple-blue (SW), Calcite glows red-orange, and Willemite glows green (SW). 2 lb. 4.5" x 3" x 2". Value $35-40.

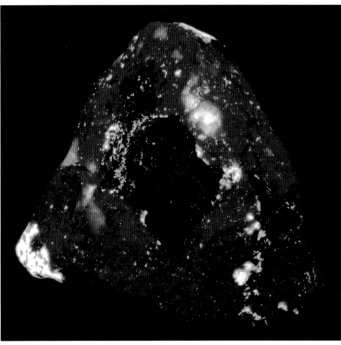

Same under SW UV.

Same under SW UV.

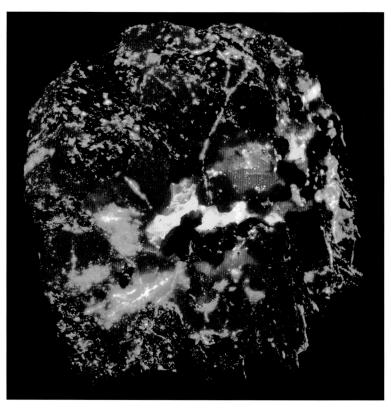

HARDYSTONITE: A very light colored Hardystonite with Andradite, Calcite, and Willemite, Franklin. Hardystonite glows purple-blue (SW). A nice 3 color stone. 9 oz. 2.5" x 2.25". Value $40-45.

Same under SW UV.

HARDYSTONITE: A very dark Hardystonite with Willemite veins crisscrossing, (NF) Franklinite, and Calcite from the Parker Shaft, Franklin. Hardystonite glows purple-blue (SW) and Calcite glows red (SW), and Willemite glows green (SW). 15 oz. 4.25" across. Value $35-40.

Same under SW UV.

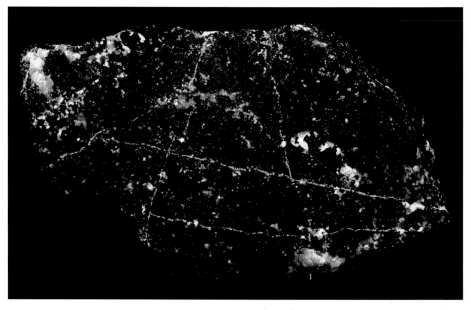

 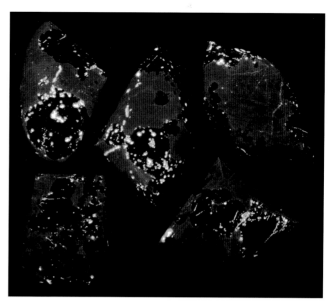

HARDYSTONITE: A group of cabochons made of Hardystonite and Andradite from the Parker Shaft of the Franklin Mine, Franklin. The Hardystonite glows purple-blue (SW) 1 to 2" across.

Same under SW UV.

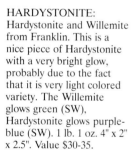  

HARDYSTONITE: Hardystonite and Willemite from Franklin. This is a nice piece of Hardystonite with a very bright glow, probably due to the fact that it is very light colored variety. The Willemite glows green (SW), Hardystonite glows purple-blue (SW). 1 lb. 1 oz. 4" x 2" x 2.5". Value $30-35.

Same under SW UV.

HARDYSTONITE and CLINOHEDRITE: Hardystonite with Clinohedrite and Willemite from Franklin. The Clinohedrite glows pumpkin orange, Willemite glows green (SW), Hardystonite glows purple-blue (SW). Clinohedrite is often found with Hardystonite. 1 lb. 11 oz. 3.75" wide. Value $55-65.

Same under SW UV.

HARDYSTONITE and CLINOHEDRITE: Rebecca holds a large chunk of Hardystonite with a beautiful Clinohedrite coated face. There is also a nice smattering of Willemite. From the Franklin Mine. The Clinohedrite glows pumpkin orange, Willemite glows green (SW), Hardystonite glows purple-blue (SW). This is an exceptionally beautiful rock. 5 lbs. 8" x 4.5" x 3". Value $250-300.

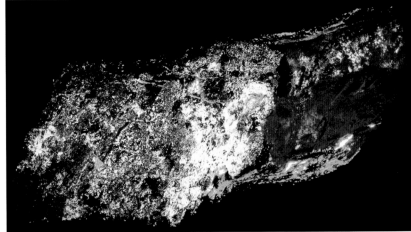

Same under SW UV.

HARDYSTONITE and CLINOHEDRITE: An unusual stone from the Franklin Mine. Mostly Andradite that contains Hardystonite and Clinohedrite that seems to have formed in the stone in solution. On other parts of the stone, there are a few blobs of Hardystonite, but inside the stone, there are no easily discernible areas of Hardystonite in daylight. When the SW UV light is turned on, there are thin veins and areas of Clinohedrite (pumpkin orange) and lots of bright purple-blue glowing specks of Hardystonite along with Willemite. 4 oz. and 3" x 1" x 1". Value $12-16.

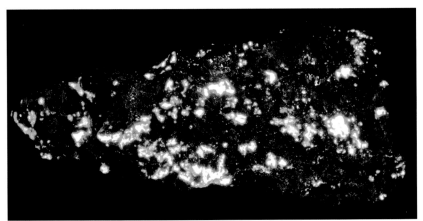

Same under SW UV.

HARDYSTONITE and CLINOHEDRITE: An exceptionally beautiful example of Hardystonite with Clinohedrite and Willemite from Franklin. The Clinohedrite glows pumpkin orange, Willemite glows green (SW), Hardystonite glows purple-blue (SW). 1 lb. 9 oz. 4.25" x 3" x 2". Value $60-75. *From the Gar Van Tassel collection.*

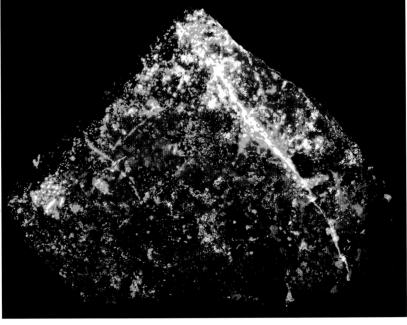

Same under SW UV.

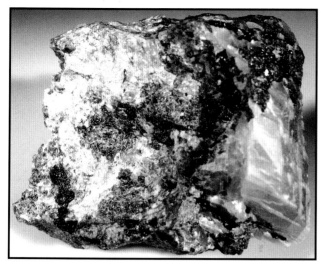

HARDYSTONITE with FLUORAPATITE: An unusual five color combination of Hardystonite with Fluorapatite, Calcite, Willemite, and Clinohedrite from Franklin. The Fluorapatite glows a burnt orange, Hardystonite glows blue-purple, Clinohedrite glows orange, Willemite glows green, and the Calcite glows red-orange. 3.5 oz. 2.75" x 1.75" x 1.25". Value $40-50.

Same under SW UV.

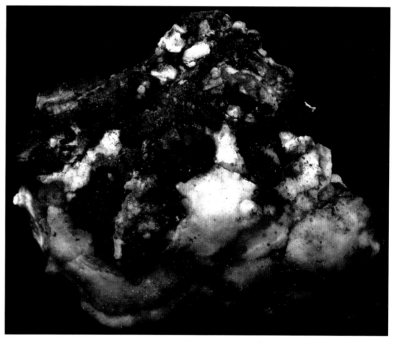

HEMIMORPHITE: A bubbly crust of white Hemimorphite from Sterling Mine, Ogdensburg, New Jersey. Hemimorphite is sometimes called "Maggot Ore." Hemimorphite glows white (SW). 4 oz. 3.25" x 3.25" x 1". Value $55-60.

HENDRICKSITE: Hendricksite is a somewhat rare NF Zinc Mica, Andradite is a NF (golden color) garnet. This is from the Old Mill Site, Franklin. 1 lb. 3.25" x 3" x 1.75". Value $20-25.

Same under SW UV.

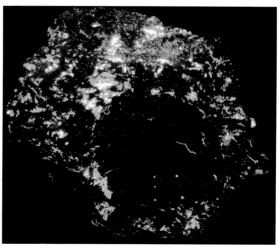

Same under SW UV.

63

HYALOPHANE, A light colored stone containing Hyalophane from Franklin. Usually it is found in conjunction with other minerals, but this stone is mostly Hyalophane. Hyalophane is a barium Feldspar, a close relative to Microcline and Amazonite (both potassium Feldspars) and Albite (sodium Feldspar), and glows a weak to moderate velvety purple-red under SW. Hyalophane looks like Calcite in daylight, but it does not react like Calcite (which bubbles and fizzes) if you drop dilute hydrochloric acid on it. 4 oz. 3" x 1.75" x 1". Value $8-10.

Same under SW UV.

HYALOPHANE and FLUORAPATITE: Blue-gray areas of Fluorapatite, light gray Hyalophane, Willemite, NF brown Zinc Schefferite, and Andradite from the Old Mill Site, Franklin. Fluorapatite glows soft orange (SW), Hyalophane glows velvety red (SW). 1 lb. 3.5 oz. and 4" x 2.75" x 2". Value $55-65.

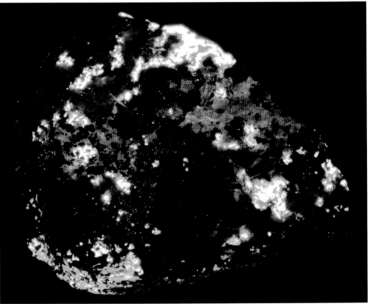

Same under SW UV.

HYDROZINCITE: Hydrozincite from the Trotter dump, Franklin. Hydrozincite glows blue-white (SW). 3 lb., 8 oz. 5.25" across. Value $20-30.

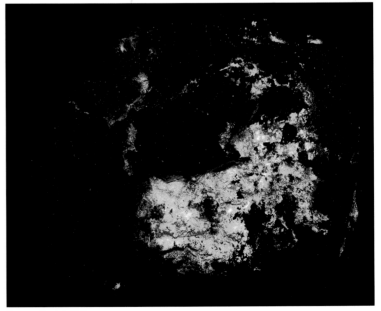

Same under SW UV.

HYDROZINCITE: Hydrozincite on Calcite from the Buckwheat dump of the Franklin Mine, Franklin. The Hydrozincite is a coating on the Calcite and it glows bright blue-white (SW). The Calcite glows red-orange (SW). 3 oz. 3" x 1.75" x 1.25". Value $20-25.

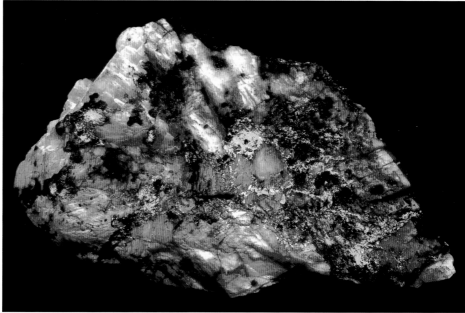

Same under SW UV.

JOHNBAUMITE: Johnbaumite with NF Franklinite, and Hendricksite, a NF daylight brown Zinc Mica from the Parker Shaft, Franklin. Johnbaumite, a very rare Apatite, glows orange (SW). 16 oz. 3.25" across. Value $300-350.

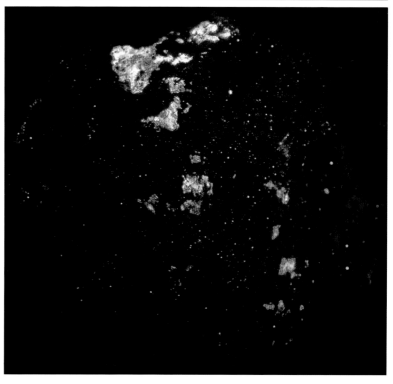

Same under SW UV.

LOELLINGITE: Although Loellingite (pronounced "Lo Ling Ite") is not fluorescent, this is a tough to find Franklin area mineral that compliments a fluorescent collection. Metallic Loellingite with Franklinite from Sterling Hill Mine, Ogdensburg. There is also some Willemite in the stone. 15 oz. 3.5" x 2.5". Value $40-65.

Same under SW UV.

MAGNESIORIEBECKITE: Grayish Magnesioriebeckite on Sphalerite with Lenilenapeite and Calcite. A nice stone from the Old Mill Site, Franklin. It is mostly Calcite that glows a orange-red (SW) and it has some gray lumps of Sphalerite that is coated with Magnesioriebeckite that glows a gray-white (SW). There is a nice glassy surfaced mineral that is Lenilenapeite. 1" to 1.5" across on a 1 lb. stone. Value $60-65.

Same under SW UV.

Same under LW UV.

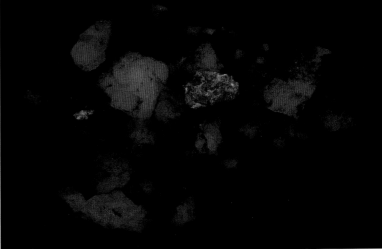

MANGANAXINITE: Tan Manganaxinite with Xonotlite from Franklin. This is a good example of an Axinite that glows red, but only faintly. Most Axinites do not glow at all, while some glow brightly. The value of the stone is dependent upon the strength of the glow. Xonotlite glows blue-purple (SW) and Manganaxinite glows red. 4.5 oz. 3.25" across. Value $55-60.

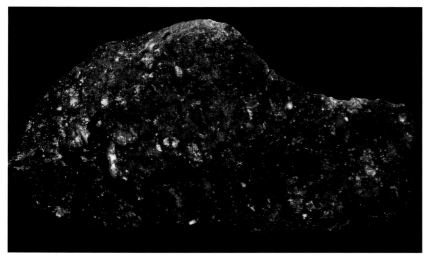

Same under SW UV.

MANGANAXINITE: Manganaxinite, Willemite, and Andradite from Franklin. This great example of Manganaxinite glows a strong cherry red (SW). 5 oz. 3" x 2.25" x 1.125". Value $85-95.

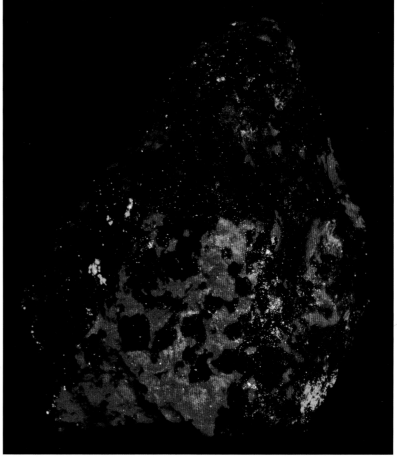

Same under SW UV.

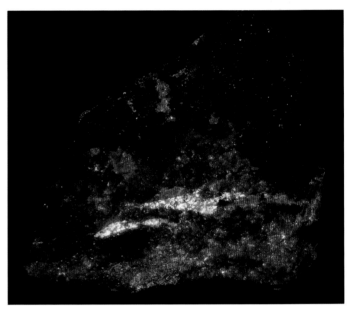

MANGANAXINITE: Tan Manganaxinite, Clinohedrite and Andradite from Franklin. Manganaxinite glows cherry red (SW), Clinohedrite glows orange. 10.5 oz. 3" x 2.75" x 2. Value $125-140.

Same under SW UV.

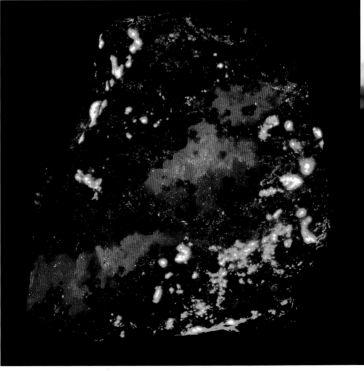

MANGANAXINITE: A tan stone from the Parker Shaft of the Franklin Mine containing fluorescent Manganaxinite, Xonotlite, Willemite, blebs of Fluorapatite, and a small patch of Clinohedrite. The Axinite glows a bright red, Xonotlite glows purple, Willemite glows green, Fluorapatite glows orange, and Clinohedrite glows pumpkin orange, all under SW. 1 lb. 6 oz. 3.5" x 3.5" x 2.5. Value $225-250.

Same under SW UV.

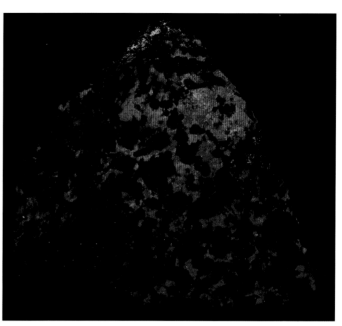

MANGANAXINITE and HENDRICKSITE: Manganaxinite with Hendricksite (a NF Zinc Mica), and tan NF Andradite from the Parker Shaft of the Franklin Mine. Manganaxinite glows cherry red (SW). 11 oz. 3.5" x 3" x 1.25". Value $135-150.

Same under SW UV.

MARGAROSANITE: Rare Margarosanite with Willemite, a touch of Calcite and (NF) Hancockite from the Parker Shaft of the Franklin Mine. Margarosanite glows sky blue or pink (SW) and red-pink or tan under MW UV, Calcite glows red (SW), and Willemite glows green (SW). Hancockite is NF (daylight) light brown. Margarosanite is one of the most actively sought fluorescents from Franklin. 10 oz. 3" wide. Value $350-400.

Same under SW UV.

MARGAROSANITE: A superb example of this rare mineral with lots of coverage of Margarosanite with Willemite and Hyalophane from the Parker Shaft, Franklin. Margarosanite glows a sky-blue (SW) and red-pink or tan under MW UV, Willemite glows green (SW), and Hyalophane glows a weak red (SW). 4.25 oz. 3" x 1.5" x .75". Value $250-300.

Same under SW UV.

MARGAROSANITE: Margarosanite (a wide vein) and Willemite, from the Franklin Mine. This Margarosanite glows pink and sky blue (SW) and red-pink or tan under MW UV. 4.75 oz. 2.75" x 2.25" x 1.75". Value $350-400.

Same under SW UV.

MARGAROSANITE and PECTOLITE: A rock with areas of Margarosanite that glows sky blue (SW) and areas of Pectolite that glows pink-peach (SW). From the Parker Shaft, Franklin. 1.75 oz. 2.25" x 1.125". Value $75-85.

Same under SW UV.

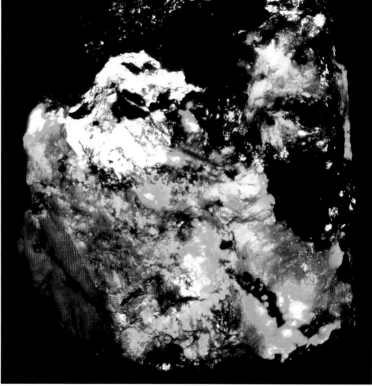

MARGAROSANITE and WOLLASTONITE: Margarosanite, Wollastonite, Willemite, and Calcite, from the Parker Shaft, Franklin. An incredible assemblage of rare Parker Shaft minerals. The Margarosanite glows a sky blue with touches of pink. Wollastonite glows yellow-orange (SW), Willemite glows green (SW), and Calcite glows red-orange (SW). 1 lb. 9 oz. 4.5" x 2.75" x 2". *From the George Elling collection.*

Same under SW UV.

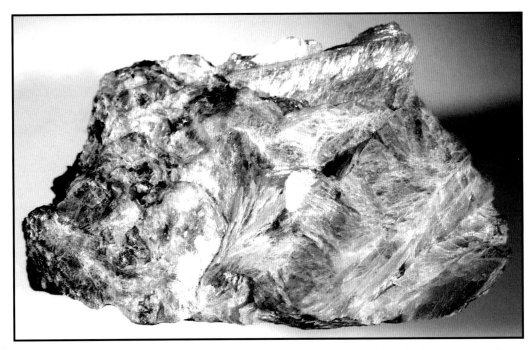

MARGAROSANITE: Beautiful glistening blades of Margarosanite from the Franklin Mine. Margarosanite glows a sky blue (SW) and a red-pink under MW. 2.5 oz. 2.25" x 1.5" x 1". *From the George Elling collection.*

Same under SW UV.

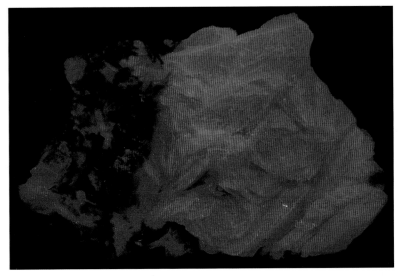

Same under MW UV

MARGAROSANITE with WOLLASTONITE and ROEBLINGITE: A stunningly beautiful combination of rare minerals – Margarosanite with Roeblingite and Wollastonite – from the Parker Shaft of the Franklin Mine. Margarosanite glows a sky blue color (SW). The Roeblingite glows red (SW) and the Wollastonite glows yellow-orange (SW). 8.5 oz. 3.75" x 2.25" x 1.5". *From the George Elling collection.*

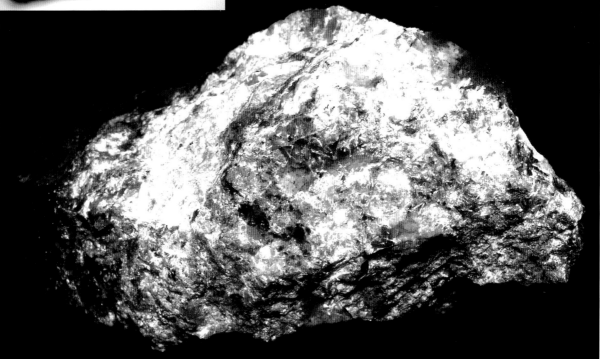

Same under SW UV.

MARGAROSANITE and MINEHILLITE: A large stone of rare minerals – Margarosanite with Calcite and Minehillite – from the Parker Shaft of the Franklin Mine. Margarosanite glows a sky blue color (SW). The Calcite glows red-orange (SW) and the Minehillite glows violet-sky blue (SW). 2 lb. 4 oz. 4.25" x 4" x 2.25". *From the George Elling collection.*

Same under SW UV.

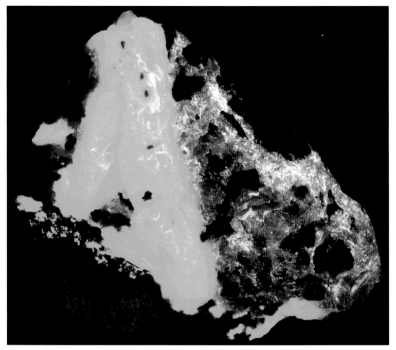

MARGAROSANITE and WILLEMITE: A combination of Margarosanite with Calcite and Willemite crystals from the Parker Shaft of the Franklin Mine. Margarosanite glows a sky blue with touches of pink (SW). The Calcite glows red-orange (SW) and the Willemite glows green (SW). 1 lb. 2 oz. 3.75" x 3" x 2.25". *From the George Elling collection*.

Same under SW UV.

MARGAROSANITE with HARDYSTONITE and ROEBLINGITE: Among the rarest six color combinations, this stone has Margarosanite with Hardystonite, Roeblingite, Clinohedrite, Calcite, and Willemite from the Parker Shaft of the Franklin Mine. Margarosanite glows a sky blue, Roeblingite glows red, Clinohedrite glows orange, Calcite glows red-orange and the Willemite glows green (all SW). 2 lb. 3 oz. 4.25" x 4" x 2". *From the George Elling collection.*

Same under SW UV.

Same under SW UV.

MICROCLINE: Microcline from Franklin. This Microcline glows gray-white (SW). The dark mineral in the rock is graphite and the glowing red material is Calcite. From the Trotter dump, Franklin, New Jersey. 1 lb. 9 oz. 5" across. Value $15-20.

MICROCLINE: An unusual bright green Microcline from Franklin. This Microcline glows gray-white (SW). From the Old Mill Site, Franklin, New Jersey. 7 oz. 3" x 2" x 2". Value $12-16.

Same under SW UV.

Same under SW UV.

MINEHILLITE: An incredibly rare fluorescent mineral from the Franklin Mine. Minehillite is often confused with Margarosanite, however Minehillite glows violet-sky blue (SW) and a similar color under MW and Margarosanite tends to glow a redder color under MW. There is also red-orange glowing Calcite. 9.5 oz. 3" x 2.75" x 2.25". *From the George Elling collection.*

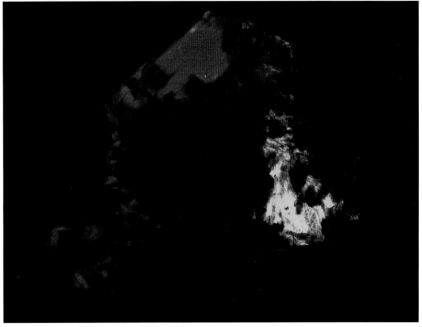

Same under MW UV

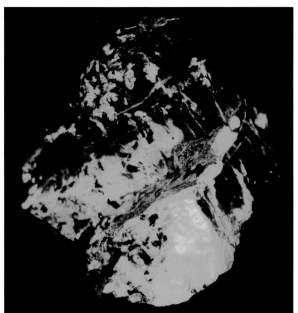

Same under SW UV.

MONOHYDROCALCITE: Willemite with Franklinite and a touch of Sphalerite from the Sterling Hill Mine, Ogdensburg. There is a patch of Monohydrocalcite on the front end of the stone. The Willemite, under SW, makes the Monohydrocalcite invisible until the stone is examined under LW. Willemite glows green (SW), Monohydrocalcite glows bright green (SW and LW) and the Sphalerite glows orange (LW). 5 oz. and 3.5" x 2". Value $100-110.

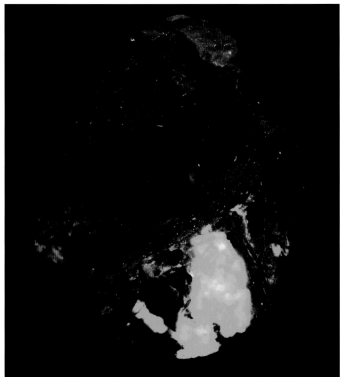

Same under LW UV. showing the Monohydrocalcite.

NORBERGITE: Norbergite crystal in limestone from the Limecrest Quarry, Sparta, New Jersey. Norbergite glows yellow (SW). 2 oz. 3" wide. Value $20-25.

Same under SW UV.

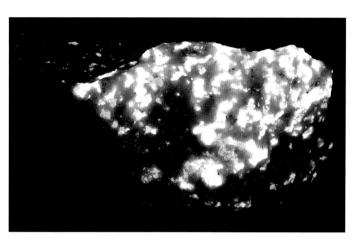

NORBERGITE and DIOPSIDE: Norbergite and Diopside in Limestone from Sterling Hill Mine, New Jersey. Norbergite glows yellow (SW) and Diopside glows light blue-white (SW). This combination is also known to come from the Atlas Quarry, Hamburg, New Jersey. 9.5 oz. 4" x 2.25". Value $15-20.

Same under SW UV.

PECTO-PREHNITE: A white crystalline rock that has Prehnite and Pectolite from the Parker Shaft of the Franklin Mine. The Prehnite glows a peach color and the Pectolite glows a purple color (similar to the glow of Xonotlite) (SW). 6 oz. 2" x 1.75" x 1.75". Value $140-150.

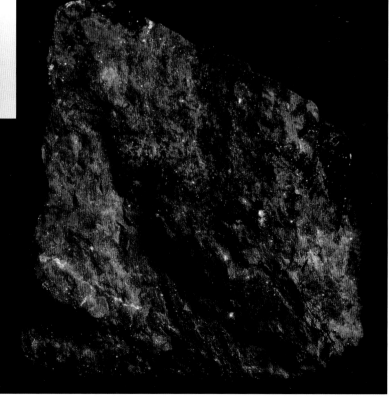

Same under SW UV.

PARGASITE with PHLOGOPITE: Daylight blue Pargasite with Phlogopite Mica from the Bodner Quarry, Rudeville, Sussex County, NJ. The Pargasite glows light blue (SW) and the Phlogopite glows creamy yellow (SW). 1 lb. 1 oz. 3.5" x 3" x 2". Value $30-35.

Same under SW UV.

PARGASITE with CHONDRODITE and PHLOGOPITE: Daylight blue Pargasite with Chondrodite, and Phlogopite Mica from the Bodner Quarry, Rudeville, Sussex County, NJ. The Pargasite glows greenish blue (SW), the Chondrodite glows yellow-orange (SW), and the Phlogopite glows creamy yellow (SW). 2 lb. 3 oz. 5" x 3.5" x 2.5". Value $50-55.

Same under SW UV.

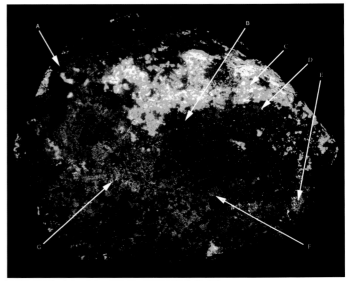

PARKER SHAFT 7 COLOR COMBINATION: A super rare seven color Parker Shaft combination from Franklin–Barite, Hardystonite, Willemite, Calcite, Clinohedrite, Fluorapatite, and Hydrozincite. It is so unusual to find a large stone with seven different fluorescent colors on one face that this piece can be the centerpiece of any collection. 4 lb. 4 oz. 5" x 4.25" x 3". Value $1,250-1,400. *From the Gar Van Tassel collection.*

Under SW UV the Barite (A) glows white; the Hardystonite (B) glows purple-blue; the Willemite (C) glows green; the Calcite (D) glows red-orange; the Clinohedrite (E) glows pumpkin orange; the Fluorapatite (F) glows burnt orange; and the Hydrozincite (G) glows blue-white.

POWELLITE: A double pinhead sized section of the rare (at Sterling Hill) mineral, Powellite, on a dark stone from the Passaic Pit at the Sterling Hill Mine. The area containing the Powellite is circled and enlarged and shown under SW UV. This came from the trench in which the Genthelvite was found. The Powellite glows light yellow (SW and a touch brighter under LW). 3 oz. 2" x 1.25" x 1". Value $20-25.

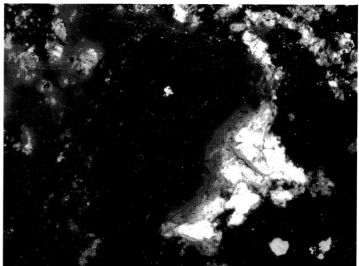

Same under SW UV.

POWELLITE and GENTHELVITE: Two rare minerals for Sterling Hill– A pinhead sized portion of Powellite and a larger area of Genthelvite from the Passaic Pit at the Sterling Hill Mine. The area containing the Powellite and Genthelvite is noted and enlarged and shown under SW and LW UV. The Powellite glows light yellow (SW and a touch brighter under LW). The Genthelvite glows green under LW and very weak green under SW. The area shown is about 2.5" on a larger rock weighing about 10 oz. Value $50-65.

Same under LW UV.

PREHNITE with XONOTLITE: Prehnite with Xonotlite from the Parker Shaft of the Franklin Mine. Prehnite glows peach colored (SW) and Xonotlite glows purple (SW). 9 oz. 3.75" x 2" x 1.75". Value $250-300. *Formerly from the Claude Poli collection.*

Same under SW UV.

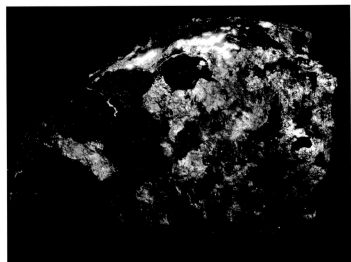

PREHNITE: Prehnite with Clinohedrite, Willemite, and tan NF Andradite from the Franklin Mine. Prehnite glows pink-peach (SW), Clinohedrite glows orange, and Willemite glows green (SW). 14 oz. 4" x 2.5" x 2". Value $135-150.

Same under SW UV.

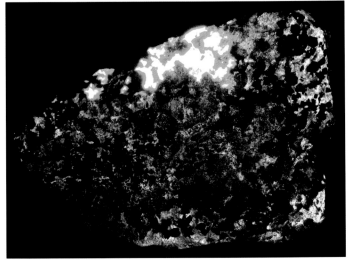

PREHNITE and MANGANAXINITE: Prehnite (upper right side and left side) with Andradite, Willemite (at the top), Manganaxinite (in the middle), and a touch of Calcite. This is a great assemblage from the Parker Shaft of the Franklin Mine. Prehnite glows peach (SW), Manganaxinite glows red (SW). 1 lb. 5 oz. 4" x 2.5" x 2". Value $95-110.

Same under SW UV.

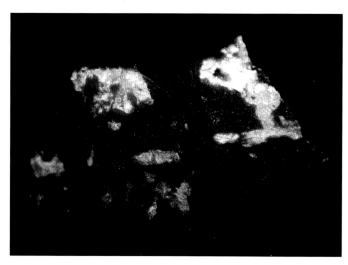

PREHNITE: A new and very rare Prehnite with Caryopolite from the Franklin Mine. This Prehnite glows mustard (SW) rather than the usual pink-peach color. 2 oz. 1.5" x 1.25" x 1". Value $100-125 (due to its small size).

Same under SW UV.

RHODONITE: Red Rhodonite crystals with Franklinite, Calcite, and Willemite from the Old Mill Site in Franklin. Willemite glows green (SW). Calcite glows red-orange (SW). Rhodonite is NF. 1 lb. 3" x 3". Value $20-25.

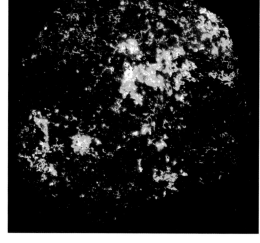

Same under SW UV.

Left:
RHODONITE: Larger individual Rhodonite crystals on Calcite with touches of Willemite from Franklin Mine. Rhodonite is pinkish red to red in daylight and NF. This Calcite is very yellow-orange (SW). 8 oz. 2.5" x 2.5". Value $40-50.

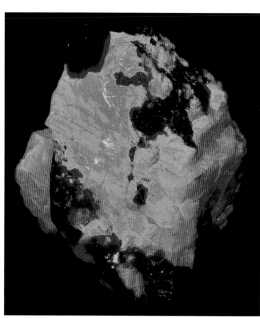

Same under SW UV.

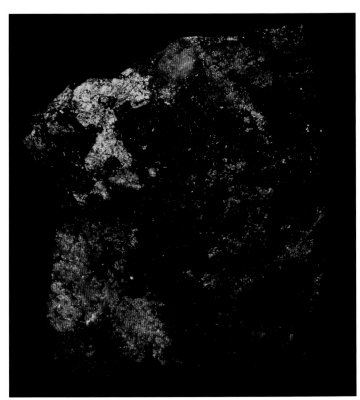

ROEBLINGITE: A super rare Franklin mineral, Roeblingite, with Xonotlite and Prehnite (on the other side of the stone), from the Franklin Mine. Roeblingite is a white mineral that glows red (SW), Xonotlite glows blue, and the Prehnite glows peach (SW). This is a superb Parker Shaft assemblage. Roeblingite was named in honor of Washington A. Roebling, an engineer and Franklin mineral collector. 8.5 oz. 2.5" x 2" x 1.25. Value $900-1,000.

Same under SW UV.c

ROEBLINGITE and XONOTLITE: An incredibly rare combination of Roeblingite with Xonotlite, crystals of Willemite, and Clinohedrite from the Parker Shaft of the Franklin Mine. Roeblingite glows red (SW). Xonotlite glows purple (SW), Clinohedrite glows orange, and the Willemite crystals glow green. 5 oz. 3" x 2.75" x 1.5". *From the George Elling collection.*

Same under SW UV.

ROEBLINGITE and AMETHYSTINE CLINOHEDRITE: A rare combination of Roeblingite with Amethystine Clinohedrite, Xonotlite, and Willemite from the Parker Shaft of the Franklin Mine. The Clinohedrite resembles daylight purple Amethyst. The Roeblingite glows red (SW). The Xonotlite glows purple (SW), Clinohedrite glows orange, and the Willemite glows green. 9.5 oz. 3" x 2.75" x 1.5". *From the George Elling collection.*

ROEBLINGITE with NASONITE: A rare Franklin mineral, Roeblingite with Nasonite, Xonotlite, Willemite, from the Parker Shaft of the Franklin Mine. Roeblingite glows red (SW), Nasonite glows pale yellow, Clinohedrite glows orange, Xonotlite glows purple, and Willemite glows green. 3.25 oz. 2.25" x 1.75" x .5". Value $350-400.

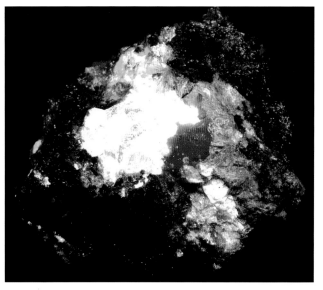

Same under SW UV.

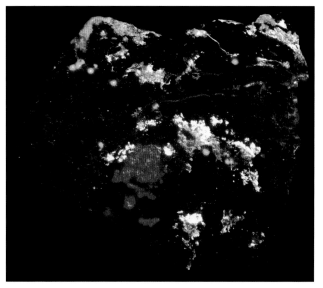

Same under SW UV.

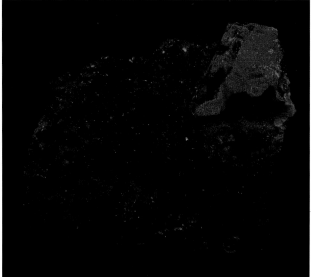

Same under LW UV.

RUBY: A red Ruby crystal from the Limecrest Quarry, Sparta, Sussex County, New Jersey. Ruby glows red under LW. 2.5 oz. 2.75" x 1.75" x .875". Value $12-15.

SCAPOLITE: Massive light greenish gray Scapolite with Calcite from the hump entering the Noble Pit at the Sterling Hill Mine, Ogdensburg. The Scapolite glows medium crimson red (SW), Calcite glows a bright red-orange. 12.5 oz. 4.25" x 2.75" x 1.5". Value $20-25.

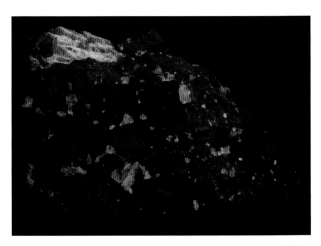

Same under SW UV. Scapolite next to Calcite looks almost a pink-red. If you isolate the chunk of Scapolite and hold it under SW UV, it shows as medium crimson red.

SCAPOLITE: Massive light gray-green Scapolite and Calcite from the hump entering the Noble Pit at the Sterling Hill Mine, Ogdensburg, NJ. The Scapolite glows medium crimson red (SW), Calcite glows a bright red-orange. 2 lb. 13 oz. 7 x 4.75" x 2". Value $35-45.

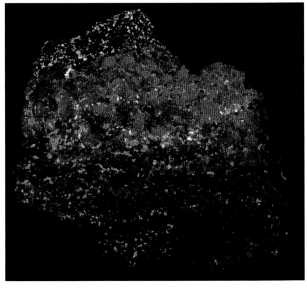

Same under SW UV.

Same under SW UV.

Left:
SCHEELITE: A dark stone containing Scheelite from Franklin. Scheelite from Franklin is usually found as sparse platy areas on the host rock. It glows light yellow under SW. 14 oz. 4.5" x 3.5" x 1.5". Value (this rock has very sparse coverage) $35-40.

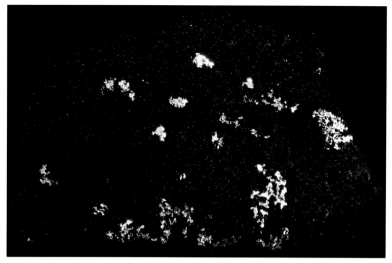

SCHEELITE: A dark stone containing Scheelite from Franklin. Scheelite from Franklin is usually found as sparse platy areas on the host rock. It glows light yellow under SW. 3.75 oz. 3" x 2" x .75". Value (much better coverage, but a smaller rock) $30-35.

Same under SW UV.

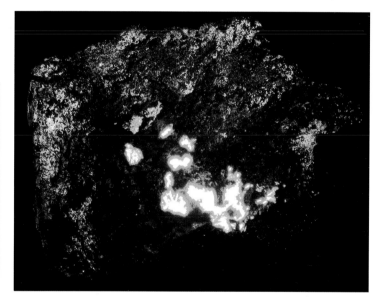

Same under SW UV.

SPHALERITE with WILLEMITE: Sphalerite with Radiating Willemite and Hydrozincite from the last remaining ore wall at the Trotter Dump in Franklin. Collected at the site of the discovery of the first radiating Willemite. Sphalerite glows orange (LW), Willemite glows green LW and brighter green SW, and Hydrozincite glows blue white SW and lesser white LW. 5 oz. 3.25" x 2.5" x .75". Value $45-50.

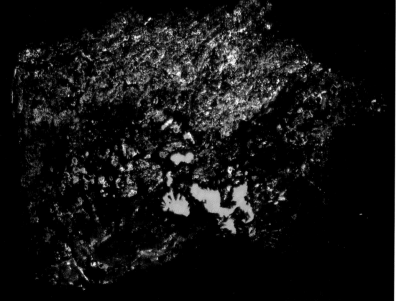

Same under LW UV.

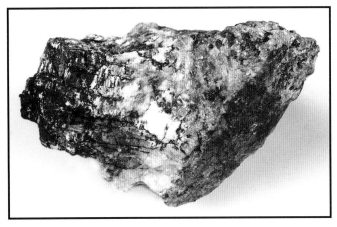

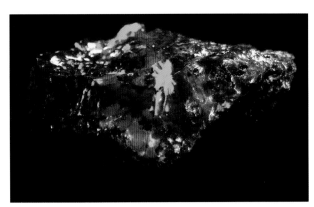

SPHALERITE with WILLEMITE: Sphalerite with Radiating Willemite and Hydrozincite from the last remaining ore wall at the Trotter Dump. Sphalerite glows orange (LW), Willemite glows green LW and brighter green SW, and Hydrozincite glows blue white SW and lesser white LW. 2.5 oz. 2.25" x 1.5" x 1.25". Value $35-40.

Same under LW UV.

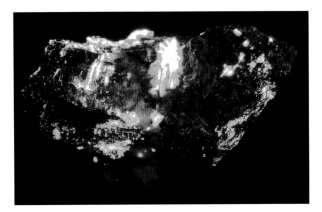

Same under SW UV.

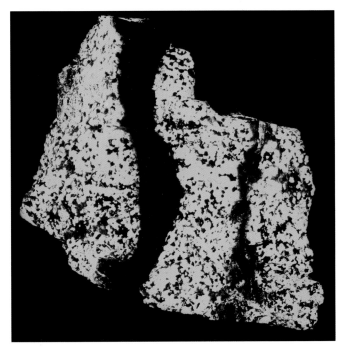

Same under SW UV.

Same under LW UV.

SPHALERITE: Willemite with Sphalerite and Franklinite from the Sterling Mine, Ogdensburg. This piece has great veins of Sphalerite. This is a good example of why you need a long wave light as well as a short wave light. If you checked this piece only under SW, you might have considered it just a piece of Willemite. The long wave light brings out the orange glowing Sphalerite. Willemite glows green (SW), and Franklinite is NF. 2 lb. 12 oz. 4.75" x 3.5" x 2". Value $80-90.

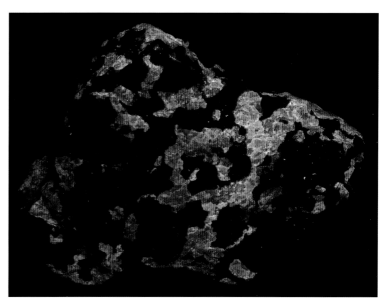

SPHALERITE: Sphalerite crystals with Willemite (this Willemite is NF under LW), and NF Andradite from the Old Mill Site, Franklin. This Sphalerite glows orange (LW and SW). 2 lb. 4.5" x 2.5" x 2.5". Value $65-70.

Same under LW UV.

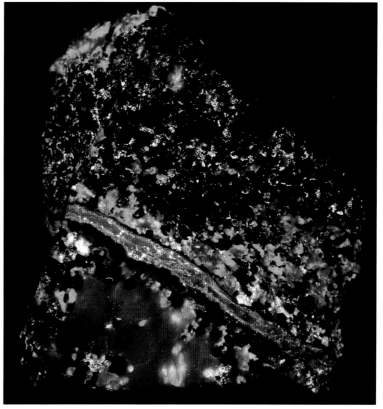

SPHALERITE-CLEIOPHANE with ZINCITE: A super attractive stone containing a vein and patches of Sphalerite-Cleiophane (blue glowing Sphalerite) along with fluorescing Zincite from the 500 foot level of the Sterling Hill Mine, Ogdensburg, New Jersey. The Sphalerite glows orange (best under LW). The Zincite, found sparsely disseminated in the top half of the stone, glows creamy yellow (LW). The Cleiophane glows blue (LW). 4.5 oz. 2.5" x 2" x .875". Value $40-45.

Same under LW UV.

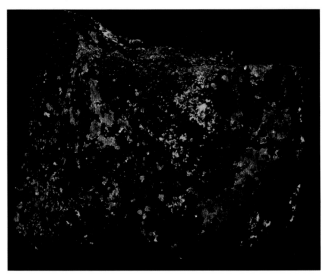

Same under SW UV.

SPHALERITE: An unusual stone that has Sphalerite with Willemite, magnetic Franklinite, and Loellingite. Sphalerite glows blue and orange (SW and LW), Willemite glows green (SW), NF Franklinite and NF Loellingite. From the Sterling Hill Mine, Ogdensburg. 1 lb. 11 oz. 3.5" across. Value $50-55.

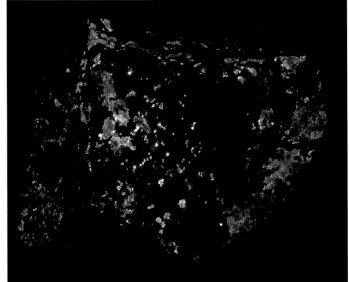

Same under LW UV.

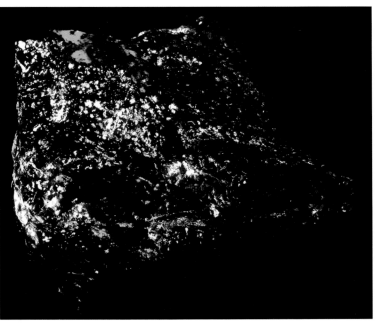

SPHALERITE: A very beautiful rock containing Sphalerite with Willemite from the Franklin Mine. Cleiophane was an early name given to iron-free Sphalerite. Today, collectors generally use the term "Cleiophane" to indicate Franklin or Sterling Sphalerite that glows blue or pink. This Sphalerite glows violet-blue and orange-pink (LW), Willemite glows a mild green under the LW UV. 15.25 oz. 3.25" x 2.75" x 2". Value $45-55.

Same under LW UV.

SPHALERITE: Sphalerite crystals with Willemite from the Old Mill Site, Franklin, New Jersey. Sphalerite glows pink-orange-blue (SW and LW). 11 oz. 3.5" x 2.25" x 2". Value $65-70.

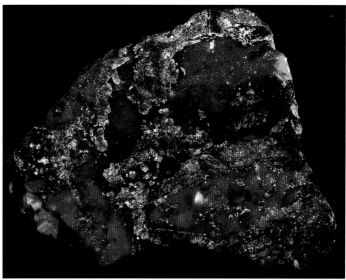

same under SW UV

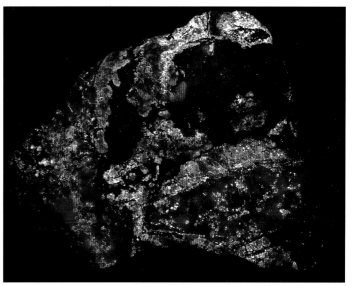

Same under LW UV.

SPHALERITE: Sphalerite grains in a white Limestone containing Pyrite from Sterling Hill. It glows orange SW and brighter pumpkin orange LW. 12.5 oz. 3.25" x 2.75" x 1". Value $15-20.

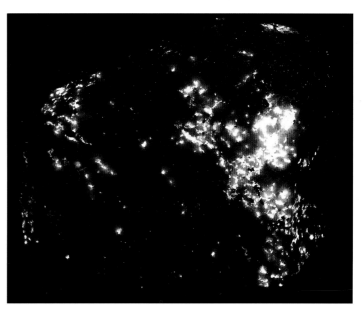

Same under LW UV.

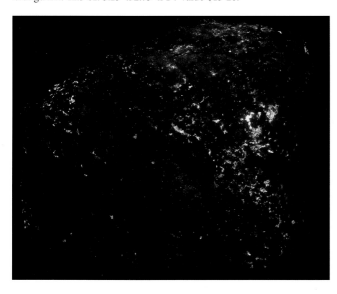

Same under SW UV.

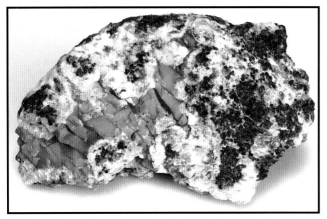

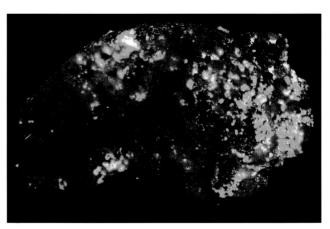

SUSSEXITE: Willemite, Calcite, Franklinite, Albite, and non-fluorescing Sussexite from Franklin. Albite glows Purple (SW), Calcite glows red-orange (SW), Sussexite, named after the county in which it is found, is a NF pink-flesh colored material. 5 oz. 3.5" x 2". Value $25-35.

Same under SW UV.

TURNEAURITE: A rare mineral (and especially rare in the Franklin Mine), Turneaurite, with a beautiful Turneaurite crystal on top, with Calcite and NF Andradite from the Franklin Mine. Turneaurite glows bright yellow-orange (SW). Calcite glows red-orange (SW). 1.25 oz. 1.5" x 1.25" x .5". Value $300-350.

Same under SW UV.

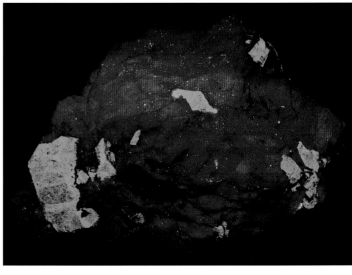

WILLEMITE and CALCITE: Large unusual dark gray Willemite crystals in Calcite with a bit of Sphalerite which glows pink-blue-orange (SW and LW) from the Sterling Hill Mine. The dark Willemite is magnetic. Willemite glows green (SW). 1 lb. 5.5 oz. 6" x 4.5" x 2". Value $75-100.

Same under SW UV.

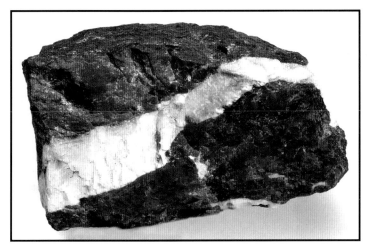

WILLEMITE and CALCITE: Brown Willemite (originally called Troostite) with a wide Calcite vein from Sterling Hill Mine. Calcite glows red (SW), Willemite glows green (SW). 12 oz. 3.75" x 2.5" x 2". Value $85-100.

Same under SW UV.

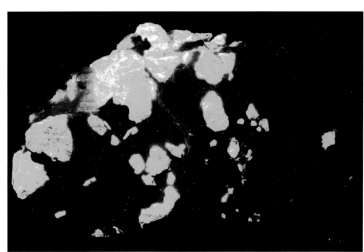

WILLEMITE: Brown Willemite (Troostite) in Calcite, and Franklinite from Sterling Hill Mine, Ogdensburg. This has the look of chunky chocolate chip cookie dough. Willemite glows green (SW). 8 oz. 3.5" x 2.25". Value $20-25.

Same under SW UV.

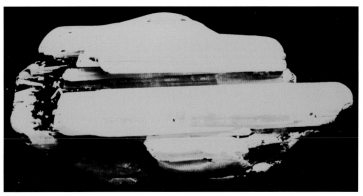

WILLEMITE: Beautiful, long crystals of Willemite from the Franklin Mine. This is called Trotter Willemite. Willemite glows green (SW). 3 oz. 2.5" x 1.5" x 1.125". *From the George Elling collection.*

Same under SW UV.

WILLEMITE: Gemmy light Green Willemite from the Franklin Mine. Willemite glows green (SW). This Willemite will actually get brighter green if left in direct sunlight. 12.5 oz. 3" x 2.5" x 2". Value $60-75.

Same under SW UV.

WILLEMITE: Gemmy green and grape Willemite from the Old Mill Site in Franklin. Willemite glows bright green (SW). 2 lbs. 3.5" x 3". Value $45-60.

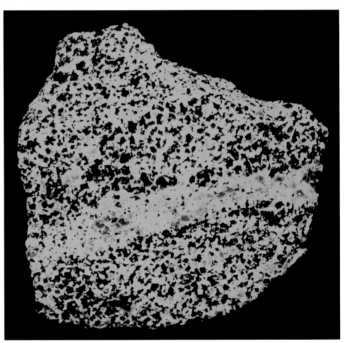

Same under SW UV.

WILLEMITE: Yellow Willemite crystals with Calcite from the Franklin Mine. In sunlight, this Willemite is an unusual light yellow color. The top of the stone sparkles with small Willemite crystals. Willemite glows bright green (SW). 8 oz. 3.25" x 2.25". Value $55-65.

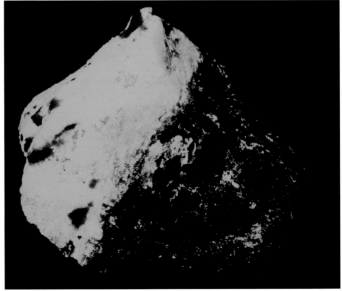

Same under SW UV.

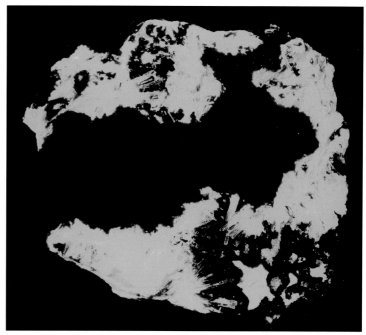

Same under SW UV.

WILLEMITE: Bright white radiating, highly phosphorescent Willemite with Dolomite and Serpentine from the Franklin Mine. Up close, you can see the radiating crystals.. Willemite glows bright green (SW). 3 oz. 2.25" x 2". Value $90-100. *Originally from the E. Packard "Sunny" Cook collection*

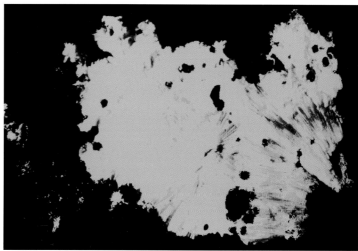

WILLEMITE: Bright white radiating, highly phosphorescent Willemite from the Franklin Mine. Up close, you can see the radiating crystals. Willemite glows bright green (SW). 1 lb. 4.25" x 2.75" x 1". *From the George Elling collection.*

Same under SW UV.

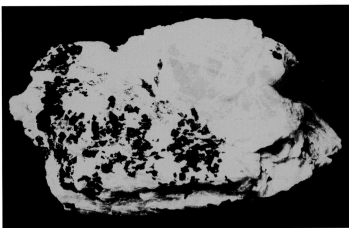

WILLEMITE: Bright yellowish green translucent Willemite mass with Franklinite from the Franklin Mine. Willemite glows bright green (SW). 5.5 oz. 3" x 2". Value $35-45. *From the E. Packard "Sunny" Cook collection.*

Same under SW UV.

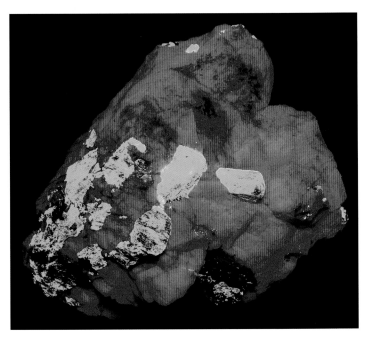

WILLEMITE: Brown Willemite nuggets in Calcite from Sterling Hill Mine. Calcite glows red (SW), Willemite glows green (SW). 2 lb. 6 oz. 6" tall. Value $55-65.

Same under SW UV.

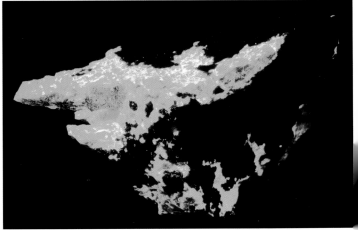

WILLEMITE: Gem red Willemite crystal 7/8th inches long on NF Andradite with touches of Fluorapatite, from the Old Mill Site, Franklin. The Willemite glows a very bright green (SW) and the Fluorapatite glows orange (SW). 3 oz. 2.5" x 1.5" x 1 .25". Value $45-50.

Same under SW UV.

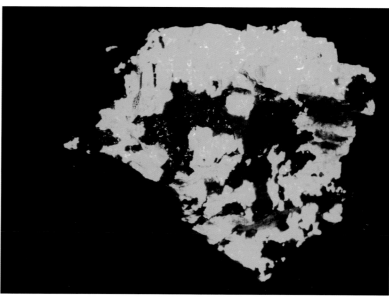

WILLEMITE: Gem red Willemite crystals on NF Andradite with touches of Fluorapatite from the Old Mill Site, Franklin. The Willemite glows a very bright green (SW) and the Fluorapatite glows orange (SW). 1 lb. 1 oz. 3.75" x 2" x 2". Value $50-60.

Same under SW UV.

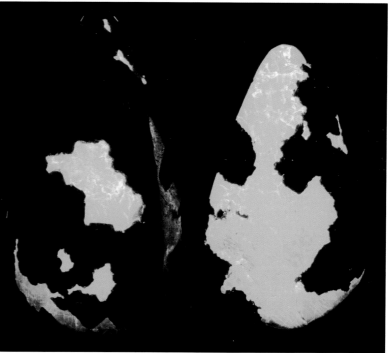

WILLEMITE: Rare gem red Willemite crystals on NF Andradite with touches of Fluorapatite, from the Old Mill Site, Franklin. A piece containing this mineral was knocked off a larger stone and then sawed with a slab saw. The slabs were rough cut into a shape that took advantage of the red Willemite and then fine shaped on a Diamond Pacific 6 wheel grinder/polisher. This material was very hard to work with since the crystals of Willemite often broke off or apart during cutting or even when polishing. Willemite glows a very bright green (SW) and the Fluorapatite glows orange (SW). Each is about 1.5" tall. Value $45-55ea.

Same under SW UV.

WILLEMITE: A group of cabochons made of Willemite and Calcite from the Franklin Mine, Franklin. The Willemite glows green (SW). 1 to 1.5" across.

Same under SW UV.

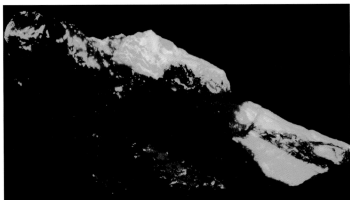

Same under SW UV.

WILLEMITE: A rock with areas of light green Willemite with lots of small fibrous crystals on the top area. It glows a bright green under SW and a slightly duller green under LW. From Sterling Hill Mine, Ogdensburg. 14 oz. 7" across. Value $35-40.

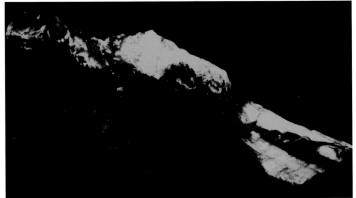

Same under LW UV.

Same under SW UV.

Same under LW UV.

WILLEMITE SLICKENSIDE: A piece of Slickenside with Willemite and what appears to be Sphalerite or Bustamite. "Slickenside" is a piece of rock from a fault line that shows a face that has been scraped smooth when the two sides of the fault rubbed against each other. Under SW light, the rock looks mostly like Willemite. Under LW light, some of the other minerals make an appearance. From Sterling Mine, Ogdensburg. Sphalerite glows Orange LW, Bustamite glows red LW. Willemite glows green SW and to a lesser extent LW, Calcite glows red-orange SW, and Franklinite is NF. 12.5 oz. 3.5" x 2.25" x 1.75". Value $45-55(more if Bustamite).

WILLEMITE and CALCITE (Mylonitized): Willemite and Calcite that flow together (mylonitized) with Franklinite from Sterling Hill Mine. The Willemite glows green, the Calcite red-orange (SW). 14 oz. 3.75" x 2.5" x 1.25". Value $50-60.

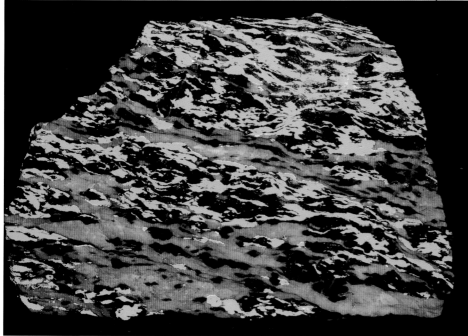

Same under SW UV.

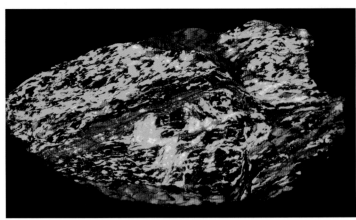

WILLEMITE and CALCITE (Mylonitized): Willemite and Calcite that flow together with Franklinite from Sterling Hill Mine. The Willemite glows green, the Calcite red-orange (SW). 1 lb. 15 oz. 6" x 2.75" x 1.75". Value $60-70.

Same under SW UV.

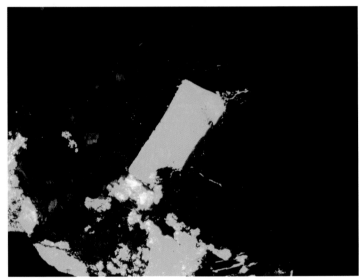

WILLEMITE: An unusual gray Willemite rectangular crystal embedded in mica on Andradite. There is also a bit of Fluorapatite. From the Old Mill Site in Franklin. The crystal glows bright green (SW) and the Fluorapatite glows burnt orange. 9.5 oz. 2.75" x 2.75" x 1.5". Value $30-35.

Same under SW UV.

WILLEMITE: A large stone of gem green Willemite from Franklin Mine. The Willemite glows green (SW). 1 lb. 2 oz. 4" x 2.75" x 1.75". Value $40-50.

Same under SW UV.

WOLLASTONITE, 1st Find: A great example of 1st Find Wollastonite from the Parker Shaft of the Franklin Mine. The Wollastonite glows yellow-orange (SW) and the Willemite glows green. 7 oz. 3.25" x 2.5" x 1.5". *From the George Elling collection.*

Same under SW UV.

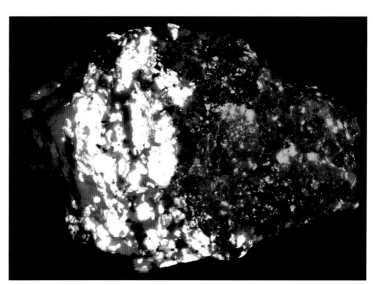

WOLLASTONITE, 2nd Find: A great example of 2nd Find Wollastonite from the Parker Shaft of the Franklin Mine. The Wollastonite glows yellow-orange (SW), Hardystonite glows purple-blue, and the Willemite glows green. 1 lb. 9 oz. 4.75" x 2.75" x 2.5". *From the George Elling collection.*

Same under SW UV.

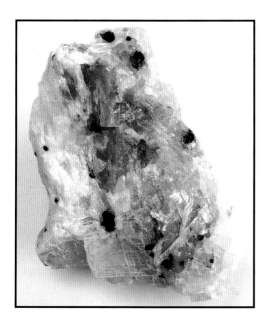

WOLLASTONITE, 3rd Find: Wollastonite with Barite from the Franklin Mine. 3rd Find is characterized by the inclusion of Barite in the stone. Wollastonite glows orange-yellow (SW), Barite glows white (SW). .5 oz. 1.5" x 1 x .25". Value $20-25.

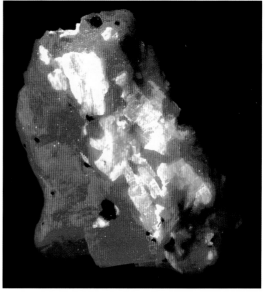

Same under SW UV.

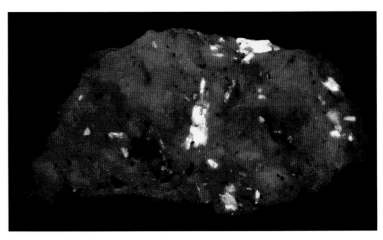

WOLLASTONITE, 3rd Find: 3rd Find Wollastonite with Barite on Calcite from the Franklin Mine. Wollastonite glows orange-yellow (SW), Barite glows white. 13.5 oz. 6.25" x 3" x 1". Value $75-85.

Same under SW UV.

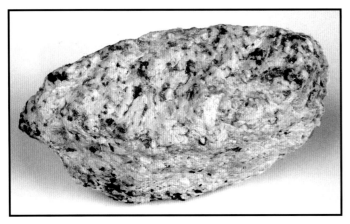

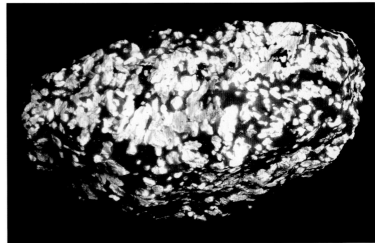

WOLLASTONITE: Wollastonite from the 340 foot level of the Sterling Hill Mine, Ogdensburg. Wollastonite glows bright yellow-orange (SW) 8 oz. 3.5" x 2". Value $15-20.

Same under SW UV.

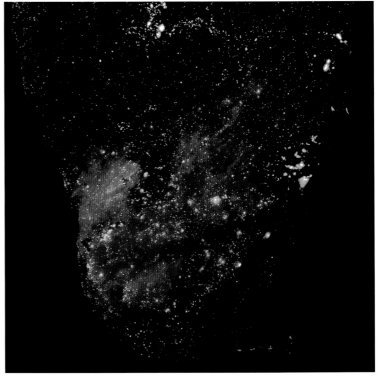

WOLLASTONITE: Radiating white Wollastonite as a vein in Andradite from the Old Mill Site, Franklin. This unusual Wollastonite glows violet (SW). 2.25 oz. 2" x 1.75". Value $20-25.

Same under SW UV.

XONOTLITE: Xonotlite with Hyalophane, a touch of Clinohedrite and tan NF Andradite from the Parker Shaft of the Franklin Mine. Xonotlite glows blue-purple (SW), Hyalophane, a barium bearing feldspar, glows purple-red (SW), and Clinohedrite glows pumpkin orange (SW). 5 oz. 3" x 1.75" x 1.5". Value $85-95.

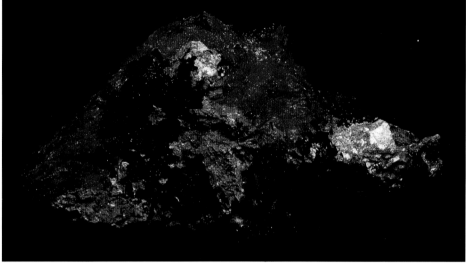

Same under SW UV.

XONOTLITE: Another example of a stone containing Xonotlite, Prehnite, Calcite, and Willemite from the Parker Shaft of the Franklin Mine. Xonotlite glows purple, Prehnite glows peach, Willemite glows green, Calcite glows red-orange. 2 oz. 2.5" x 2" x 1.5". Value $70-80.

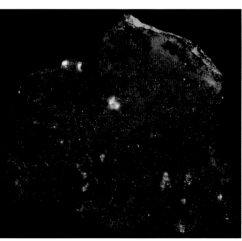

Same under SW UV. showing the Prehnite side

Same under SW UV. showing the Xonotlite side

101

 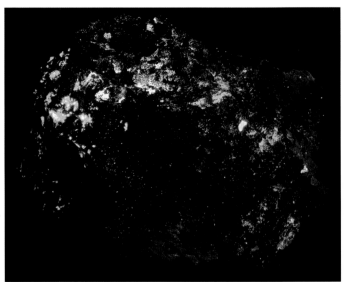

XONOTLITE and CLINOHEDRITE: A stone containing Andradite, Hendricksite, Willemite, Xonotlite, and Clinohedrite from the Old Mill Site, Franklin. Xonotlite (daylight – white) glows bright blue-purple, Clinohedrite glows pumpkin orange, Willemite glows green, Hendricksite is a NF Zinc Mica, and Andradite is NF. 11 oz. 3.5" x 2.5" x 1.5". Value $55-65.

Same under SW UV.

 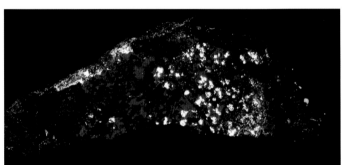

XONOTLITE and CLINOHEDRITE: Franklin Xonotlite and Clinohedrite. Xonotlite glows electric purple and Clinohedrite glows a bright pumpkin orange under SW. This stone is an interesting Parker Shaft combination– Andradite, Willemite, Franklinite, Schefferite, and Hendricksite. After careful examination under a SW light, a tiny orange vein was detected. The stone was placed in a precision rock cracker and pressure was applied. The rock cracked along the vein and exposed two beautiful faces of Clinohedrite and Xonotlite. The Xonotlite was in the vein.

Same under SW UV.

 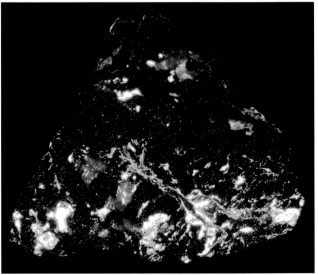

ZINCITE: Red Calcozincite, Zincite, Calcite, Willemite, and possibly Guerinite, from Sterling Hill Mine. Guerinite, a rare arsenate, glows white (SW and LW). 2 oz. 2" x 1.5". Value $6-9.

Same under SW UV.

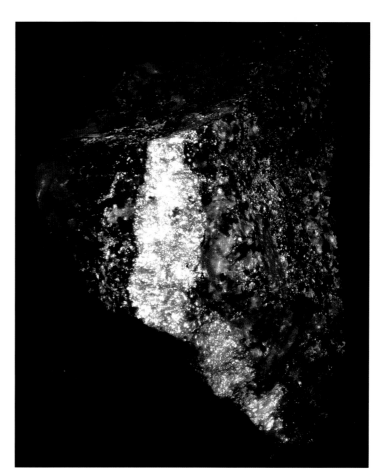

ZINCITE (Fluorescing): Willemite and NF Calcite with a vein of Fluorescing Zincite with Franklinite and red Zincite from the Sterling Mine, Ogdensburg. Fluorescing Zincite is rare. Most Zincite does not fluoresce. When it does, it glows a mild yellow-white (LW and slightly less bright SW). Willemite glows green (SW), and Franklinite and red Zincite are NF. 1 lb. 8 oz. 4.25" x 3" x 2.5". Value $200-225.

Same under LW UV.

ZINCITE and WILLEMITE: Red NF Zincite, black NF Franklinite, and (fluorescent green) Willemite ore from the Buckwheat Mine, Franklin. This was the desirable ore that the miners sought. These are heavy pieces of rock. 3 lb. 4" x 5" x 2.5". Value $30-40.

Same under SW UV.

103

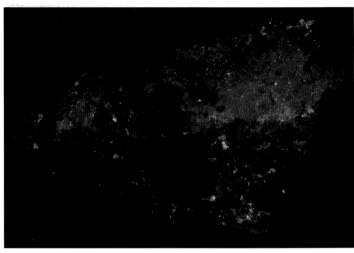

Same under SW UV.

ALBITE: A black and white, opaque stone containing Albite and Gahnite (NF green crystals) from East Pitcairn, New York. The few white spots may be Diopside. Albite fluoresces purple-red (SW) and blue-purple (LW). 1 lb. 3 oz. 5" x 3.5" x 2". Value $10-12.

Same under LW UV.

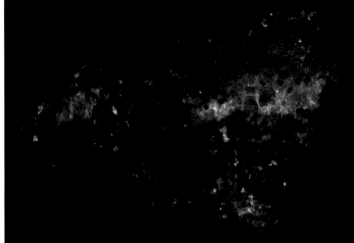

CHLOROPHANE and FLUQRAPATITE: Chlorophane and Fluorapatite from a former Scheelite mine in Trumbull, Connecticut. Chlorophane, a variety of Fluorite, glows a beautiful teal green-blue under SW and about the same color under LW and has a strong light green phosphorescence. Fluorapatite has a yellow glow under SW and a creamy white glow under LW. Chlorophane is sensitive to light and UV exposure. It should be kept in the dark (some people wrap it in aluminum foil) as it loses its ability to fluoresce after repeated exposure to steady light or UV. 2 oz. 2" x 1.75" x 1". Value $16-20

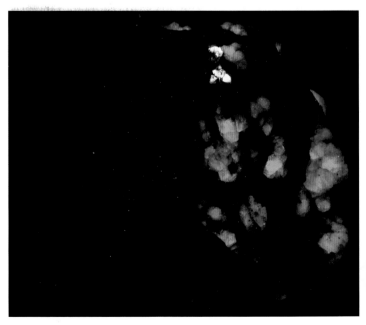

Same under SW UV.

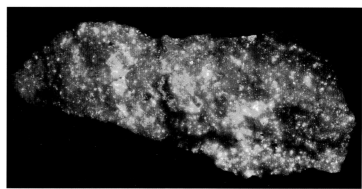

DIOPSIDE and PHLOGOPITE: Diopside and Phlogopite Mica from Pierrepont, New York. Diopside glows bright light blue (SW), Phlogopite glows yellow-orange (SW). 12.5 oz. 7" wide. Value $20-25.

Same under SW UV.

EUCRYPTITE: Eucryptite from Parker Mountain Mica Mine, Stafford, New Hampshire. This stone is fairly unattractive under daylight, but once the UV hits it, it glows a beautiful red color (SW). It is hard to find with additional fluorescent minerals mixed in (as a two or three color stone). 7.5 oz. 3.25" x 2". Value $35-45.

Same under SW UV.

FLUORITE: A plate of purple Fluorite crystals that glow creamy white (SW and LW). From the Minerva #1 mine, Cave-in-Rock, Hardin County, Illinois. The company, Elf Atochem NA, came in 1937 and discovered fluorspar north of Cave-In-Rock. Mining started in November 1939. Countless small shafts were sunk. Only three are in operation today. They include the Anna Belle Lee, the Denton, and the oldest, the Ozark-Mahoning #1 (formerly called the Minerva). 1 lb. 4" x 3". Value $40-45.

Same under LW UV.

FLUORITE: A plate of amber colored Fluorite crystals from Cave-in-Rock, Hardin County, Illinois. This Fluorite glows white (LW). 1 lb. 5.25" x 4" x 1.5. Value $40-45.

Same under LW UV.

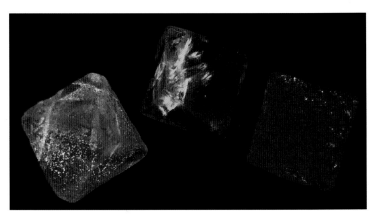

FLUORITE: Three Fluorite Octahedron crystals from Cave-in-Rock, Hardin County, Illinois. Fluorite glows purple (LW). About .75" wide. Value $4-6 each.

Same under LW UV.

FLUORITE: White Fluorite crystals from White Rock Quarry, Clay Center, Ohio. Clay Center is known for its cream-white glowing Fluorite (LW and SW). 4.5 oz. 3" x 2.5". Value $30-35.

Same under LW UV.

FLUORITE: Cubic crystals Fluorite from Clay Center, Ohio. The Fluorite glows creamy tan color (SW and LW). The white base under the Fluorite may be Aragonite or Fluorite. It glows white and has a strong phosphorescence (SW). 1 lb. 9 oz. 4" x 3" x 2.75". Value $40-45.

Same under SW UV.

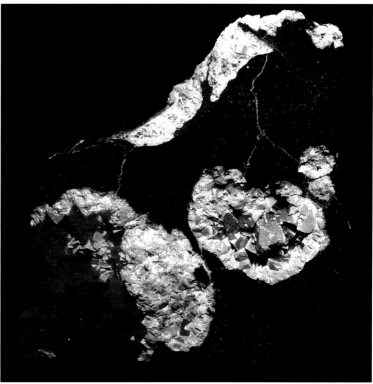

FLUORITE: Brown Fluorite crystals on a matrix of limestone. From Woodville, Ohio. The Fluorite crystals glow white (SW) and a bit more yellow (LW). 1 lb. 4.5" wide. Value $25-30.

Same under SW UV.

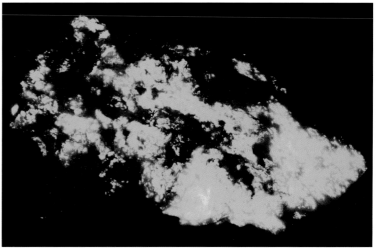

HYALITE: Hyalite Opal with some Biotite Mica from the gas pipe line, Gastonbury, Connecticut. The Hyalite glows green (SW and LW). 7 oz. 4.5" wide. Value $8-12.

Same under SW UV.

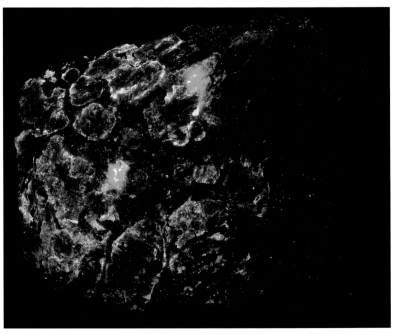

MANGANAPATITE: Manganapatite in Feldspar with Hyalite from the Bennet Quarry in Brickfield, Maine. Manganapatite glows yellow (SW), Hyalite glows green (SW). 7 oz. 3.5" x 2.25" wide. Value $12-14.

Same under SW UV.

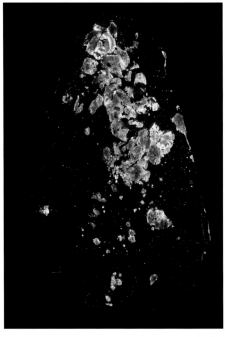

Far left:
MANGANAPATITE: Manganapatite in Feldspar from Bennet Quarry, Brickfield, Maine. Manganapatite glows yellow (SW). 10 oz. 3.5" x 2.25" x 2". Value $15-20.

Left:
Same under SW UV.

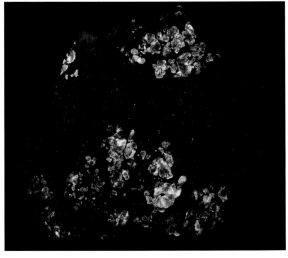

MANGANAPATITE: Manganapatite in feldspar from near Tamminen Quarry, Greenwood, Maine. Manganapatite glows yellow (SW). 8.5 oz. 3.75" wide. Value $27-33.

Same under SW UV.

MANGANAPATITE: Manganapatite from Strickland Quarry, Portland, CT. Manganapatite glows yellow (SW), Hyalite glows green (SW). 1.5 oz. 2" x 1.25" wide. Value $8-12.

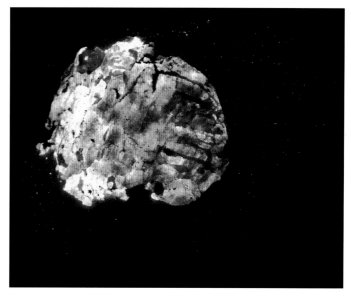

Same under SW UV.

MAGNASITE ($MgCo_3$): A white china-like coating on green Serpentine, from the Cedar Hill Quarry, Lancaster County, Pennsylvania. The glow is a bluish white under LW and slightly less bright under SW. It has a nice blue-white phosphorescence after exposure to SW. 4 oz. 2" x 2" x .5. Value $8-10.

MAGNASITE: A white china-like coating on Serpentine with bits of NF Tremolite from the Cedar Hill Quarry, Lancaster County, Pennsylvania. This is a much more interesting stone than the other more typical example of Magnasite. The glow is a bluish white under LW and slightly less bright under SW. It has a nice blue-white phosphorescence after exposure to SW. Magnasite from this area can be found that glows red (rarer than the white glowing variety). 8 oz. 2" x 2" x .5". Value $15-20.

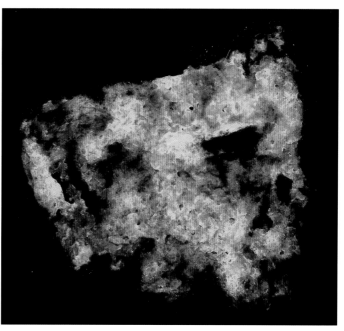

Same under SW UV.

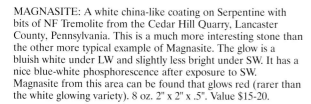

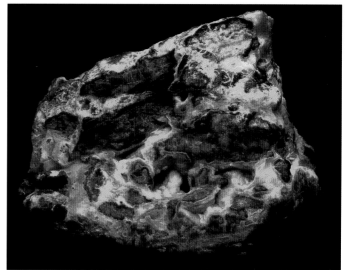

Same under SW UV.

PYROPHYLLITE: Pyrophyllite, a talc family mineral, comes from a mine west of Staley, North Carolina. Pyrophyllite glows yellowish white under LW. 14 oz. 4.5" x 3.5" x 1.5". Value $15-20.

Same under LW UV.

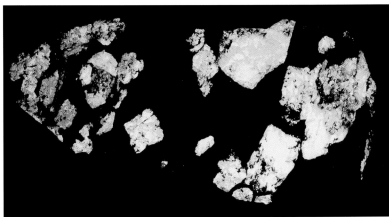

SCHEELITE: Scheelite from near Old Mine Park, Trumbull, Fairfield, Connecticut. Scheelite glows bright blue-white (SW). This is a classic location for great Scheelite. 4 lbs. 7.5" x 3.5". Value $95-125.

Same under SW UV.

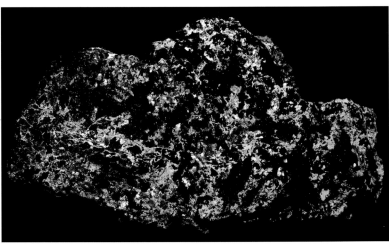

SPHALERITE: A stone containing rare two color Sphalerite from ZCA #2, Balmat, NY. This was part of a small find that was quickly sold out at the 2003 fall Franklin Mineral Show. This unusual Sphalerite glows a super distinct light green and a pink, under LW. Under SW it glows a greenish-yellow and pink. 11 oz. 4" x 2" x 1.25". Value $100-115.

Same under LW UV.

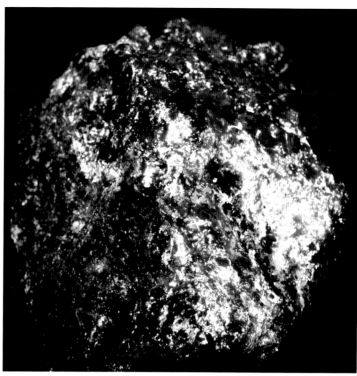

SPHALERITE: A stone containing rare three color Sphalerite from ZCA #4, Balmat, NY. This unusual Sphalerite glows blue, gold, and orange under LW. 9 oz. 3.5" x 3.25" x 1.5". Value $90-105. *From the Greg Lesinski collection.*

Same under LW UV.

SPHALERITE, DIOPSIDE, PHLOGOPITE: A stone containing Sphalerite, Diopside, and Phlogopite from West Pierrepont, New York. This piece is from a closed area that is no longer accessible. The Sphalerite glows orange (LW and SW), The Diopside is blue-white (SW), and the Phlogopite glows yellow-orange (SW). .75 oz. 2" x 1.5" x .4". Value (because of the small piece), $15-20.

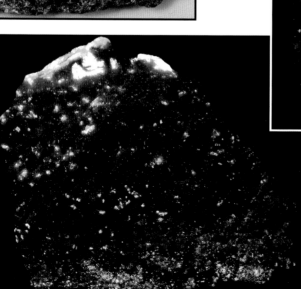

Same under LW UV.

Same under SW UV.

111

TALC and TREMOLITE: Talc and Tremolite, from Gouverneur Talc Company, Balmat, NY. Talc glows yellow-white (SW). Tremolite glows tangerine orange (better SW and less intense LW). 2 lb. 10 oz. 8 x 3.5" x 1.75". Value $30-35.

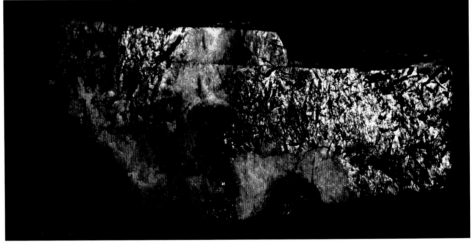

Same under SW UV.

TIRODITE and TREMOLITE: Tirodite and Tremolite, from Gouverneur Talc Company, Balmat, NY. Tirodite glows red (bright under LW and pinkish under SW). Tremolite glows tangerine orange (better SW and less intense LW). 7.5 oz. 2.75" x 2.25" x 1.5". Value $15-20.

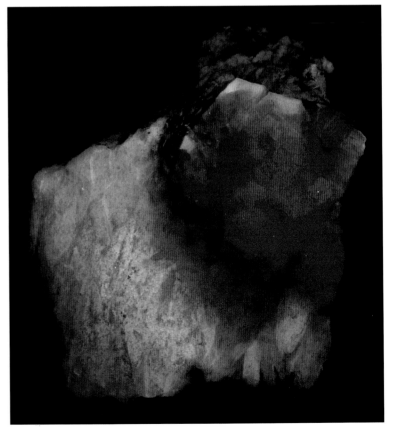

Same under LW UV.

TOURMALINE and DIOPSIDE: A light tan and rust colored opaque stone containing Tourmaline and Diopside from Richville, New York. The Tourmaline fluoresces orange-tan (SW) and the Diopside fluoresces pale blue (LW). 1 lb. 1 oz. 4" x 3" x 1.75". Value $10-13.

Same under SW UV.

ZIRCONIUM SLAG: A white, chalky opaque stone containing Zirconium Slag (Selenium/Fluorite). From Diamond Glass Works, Royersford, PA. It fluoresces a bright blue white (SW) and a slightly tanner white (LW). It has a strong phosphorescence. 4 oz. 3.75" across. Value $6-8.

Same under SW UV.

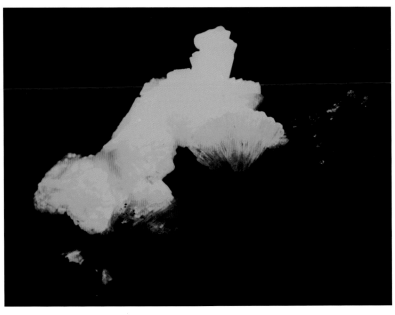

ADAMITE: Adamite crystal sprays on a brown matrix from Ojuela Mine, Mapimi, Durango, Mexico. This is the classic location for Adamite. It glows a bright green (SW). 1.5 oz. 2" x 1.75" x 1". Value $20-25.

Same under SW UV.

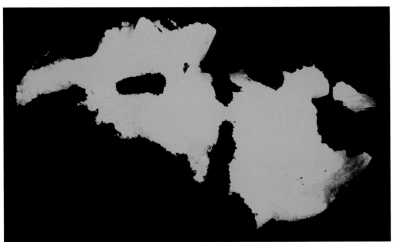

ADAMITE: Adamite crystal sprays on a brown matrix from Ojuela Mine, Mapimi, Durango, Mexico. It glows a bright green (LW and SW). 5 oz. 3" x 1.25" x 1.5". Value $30-35.

Same under LW UV.

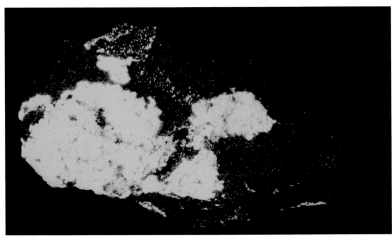

ANDERSONITE: Andersonite from the Atomic King Mine, above Kane Spring Wash, San Juan County, Utah. Andersonite is probably mildly radioactive. Andersonite glows bright blue green equally well under SW and LW UV. .5 oz. 1.75" x 1". Value $15-18.

Same under SW UV.

ARAGONITE: A white chunk of Aragonite from Texas. This Aragonite glows a bluish white (SW and LW). 6 oz. 2.25" wide. Value $8-10.

Same under SW UV.

Same under SW UV.

ARAGONITE: A white chunk of Aragonite from Texas. Aragonite glows a bluish white (SW and LW) and has a good phosphorescence. 2 oz. 1.75" x 1.5" x 1.25". Value $4-7.

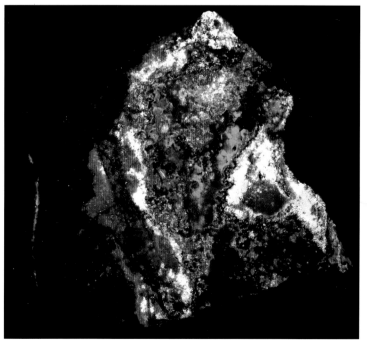

ARAGONITE, CALCITE, and HYALITE: A nice three color stone from the Lucky Jim Mine, Darwin District, Inyo County, California. The Aragonite glows white (SW) with great phosphorescence, the Calcite glows orange-red (SW) and the Hyalite glows green (SW). 4.5 oz. 3" x 2.5" x 1". Value $15-20.

Same under SW UV.

BARITE: A NF matrix with fluorescing Colemanite with Calcite crystals on top and with a golden Barite crystal growing in center. From Elk Mountain, Mead County, South Dakota. Barite glows blue-white (SW) and Colemanite glows peach (SW). 3 oz. 2.5" wide. Value $55-65.

Same under SW UV.

BARITE: Two Barite crystals from New Castle, Wyoming. Barite glows bright cream (SW), milder cream (LW). .5 oz. 1" wide. Value $5-8.

Same under SW UV.

BENITOITE: Benitoite on Natrolite from the Benitoite Gem Mine, San Benito County, California. Benitoite glows a striking bright blue (SW). Benitoite, a blue crystal, is only found in San Benito County and the best crystals are cut into gem stones. When the raw material comes out of the mine, the stone is covered in white Natrolite. It must be soaked in a weak Nitric acid for up to several days to slowly remove the Natrolite. If you want the Benitoite (and sometimes Neptunite) to stay attached to the stone, as the acid exposes the Benitoite, you must paint wax on the bottom of the exposed crystals to stop the acid from undercutting the Natrolite that holds it in place. This stone has especially nice crystals. 2 oz. 2" x 1.75" wide. Value $175-200.

Same under SW UV.

Same under SW UV.

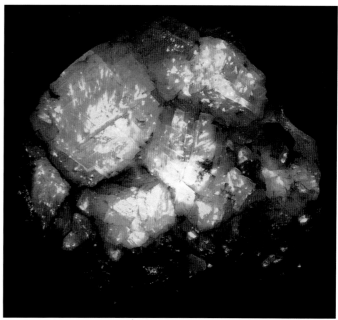

CALCITE: Calcite from Terlingua, Texas. It is difficult to find larger pieces of real Terlingua Calcite. It is almost identical to Boquillas Del Carmen, Coahuila, Mexico Calcite, but Terlingua fractures in curved lines while the other Terlingua-types fracture in straight lines. Terlingua Calcite glows light blue (SW), pink (LW) and has a high phosphorescence. 10.5 oz. 4" x 4" x 2". Value $60-70.

Same under LW UV.

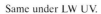

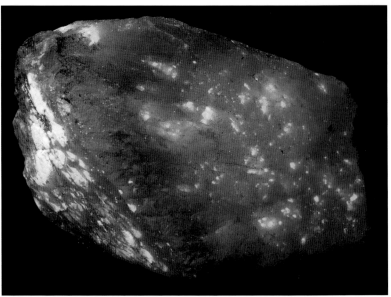

Same under SW UV.

CALCITE: A white, glassy pink opaque stone of Terlingua-type Calcite. From San Vincente Mine, Boquillas Del Carmen, Coahuila, Mexico. Fluoresces bright light blue (SW), pink (LW), and has a high phosphorescence. 7 oz. 3.5" across. Value $20-25.

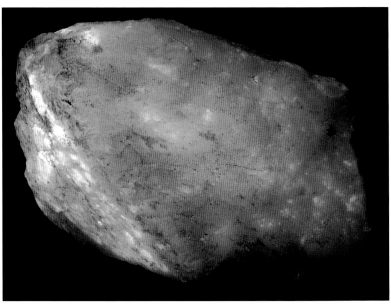

Same under LW UV.

CALCITE: A white, glassy pink opaque stone of Terlingua-type Calcite. From San Vincente Mine, Boquillas Del Carmen, Coahuila, Mexico. Fluoresces bright light blue (SW), pink (LW), and has great phosphorescence. 3.5 oz. 2" wide. Value $7-10.

Same under LW UV.

Same under SW UV.

CALCITE: Large Calcite crystals from the Gopher Valley Quarry, Yamhill, Oregon. This Calcite glows creamy white (SW and LW). 5.5 oz. 3.5" wide. Value $40-45.

Same under SW UV.

CALCITE: A transparent Calcite rhomb from near Muzquiz, Coahuila Mexico. It glows light blue (SW), pink to light orange-red (LW) and has a wonderful bright blue phosphorescence after exposure to SW UV. 1.5 oz. 2.5" x 1.5" wide. Value $12-15.

Same under LW UV.

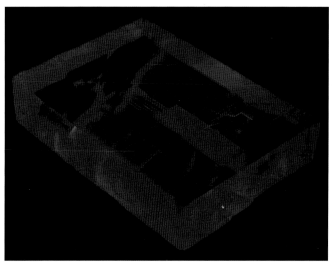

Same under SW UV.

Same showing phosphorescence five seconds after exposure to SW UV.

119

CALCITE: A rare prismatic red Calcite from the Santa Eulalia Mine, Chihuahua, Mexico. This red Calcite is from a very small find. Calcite glows crimson red-orange (SW). 7 oz. 4" x 2.625" x 1.5". Value $30-35.

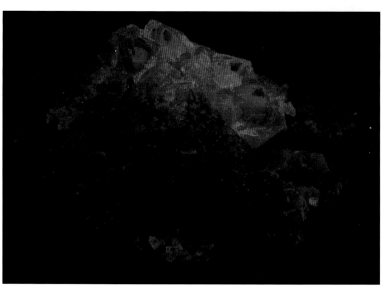

Same under SW UV.

CALCITE: Rounded crystals of Calcite from Chihuahua, Mexico. The Calcite glows blue-gray, but the tufts glow green, probably from a Uranium activator. 6 oz. 3" x 2" x 1.5". Value $10-15.

Same under SW UV.

CALCITE: Calcite from the Christmas Gift Mine, Darwin, California. This particular Calcite glows a bright orange (SW). 3 oz. and 3.5" x 2.25" x 1". Value $12-15.

Same under SW UV.

CALCITE: An interesting stone from Karnes·Uranium District, Wright-McGrady Mine, Texas. The druzy Calcite glows green (SW) and bluish-green (LW). There are veins of Caliche material (reacts with dilute hydrochloric acid) throughout the stone and they glow peach (SW). 7.5 oz. 4.5" x 1.5" x 1.25". Value $20-25.

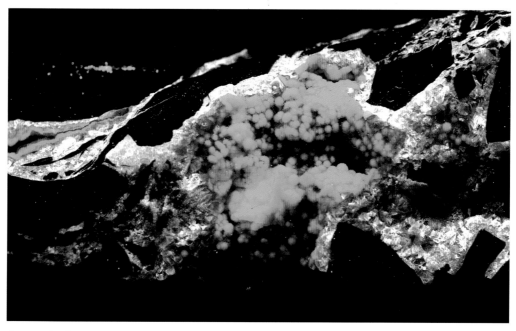

Same under SW UV.

CALCITE: Crystals of Calcite from Joplin, Missouri. The Calcite glows blue-gray. 4.5 oz. 2.5" x 2" x 1.5". Value $15-20.

Same under SW UV.

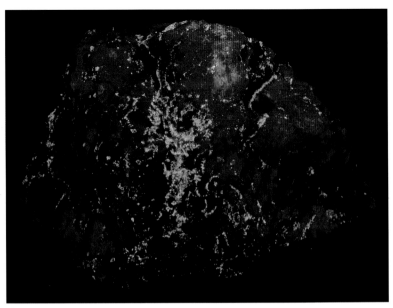

CALCITE, FLUORITE, and WILLEMITE: Calcite, Willemite, and Fluorite from the Hogan Claim, Yavapai County (near Wickenburg) Arizona. This is an exceptional stone from Arizona. The blue is almost Hardystonite-like and the Calcite is bright red-orange. If this piece were from Franklin, it would weigh more and there probably would be more Willemite and it would be brighter. The Calcite glows a bright red-orange, the Willemite glows blue-green and has a great phosphorescence, and the Fluorite glows blue (SW). Everything shows up best under SW UV. 9 oz. 3.75" x 3" x 2". Value $18-24.

Same under SW UV.

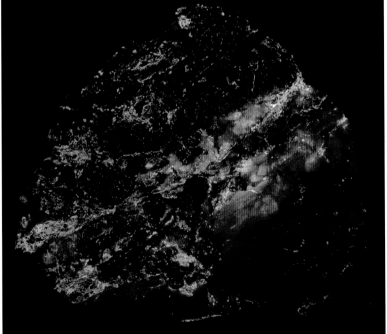

CALCITE and FLUORITE: Calcite with Fluorite crystals from Pure Potential Mine, La Paz County, Arizona. Fluorite fluoresces bright purple (SW and LW). Calcite is red under SW. There is a little bit of green glowing Willemite in the stone and a light blue glowing material that may be Scheelite. 13 oz. 4" wide. Value $20-25.

Same under SW UV.

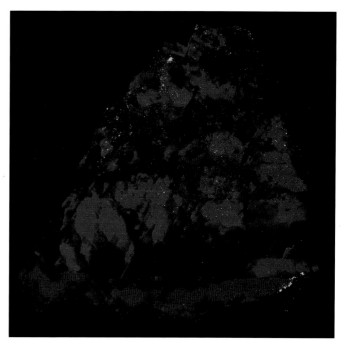

Same under SW UV.

CALCITE and FLUORITE: Calcite with bands of Fluorite crystals from Pure Potential Mine, La Paz County, Arizona. This is a particularly bright Arizona Fluorite. It is brighter under LW, but glows nicely under SW. Fluorite fluoresces bright purple (LW and SW). Calcite glows red under SW. 13 oz. 4" tall. Value $35-45.

Same under LW UV.

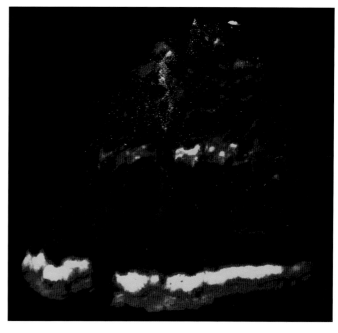

CALCITE and SCHEELITE: Calcite and Scheelite from the Princess Pat Mine, San Bernardino County, California. The Calcite glows red (SW) and the Scheelite glows blue-white (SW). 7 oz. 4" x 2.5" x 1". Value $20-25.

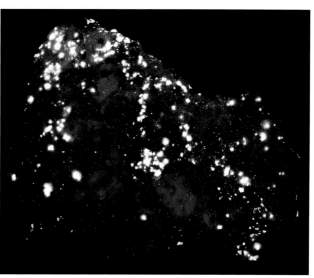

Same under SW UV.

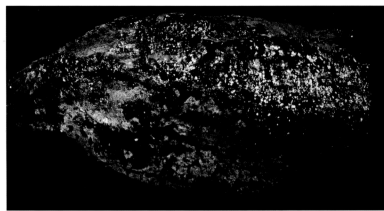

CALICHE with SCHEELITE and HYALITE: Caliche with Scheelite and Hyalite Opal from the Princess Pat Mine, San Bernardino County, California. The Scheelite glows blue-white (SW). The Caliche glows peachy-orange (SW) and the Hyalite glows green (SW). 3 lb. 9 oz. 8 x 3.5" x 3". Value $35-40.

Same under SW UV.

COLEMANITE on SULFUR: Colemanite on Calcite crystals from the US Borax Mine, Boron, California. Colemanite glows yellow-white and blue-white(SW), Calcite glows white (SW). 4 oz. 3" wide. Value $45-50.

Same under SW UV.

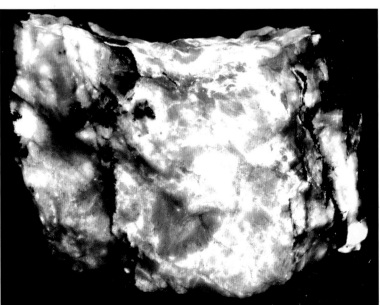

DATOLITE: Datolite from the Dry Creek Area, Heraldsburg, Sonoma County, California. This stone is beautiful under SW light. The Datolite glows yellow and creamy yellow (SW). Datolite is sometimes called the Esperite of the West. 14 oz. 3.5" x 3" x 2". Value $85-110.

Same under SW UV.

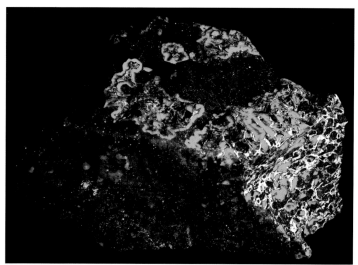

Same under SW UV.

DINOSAUR BONE: A fossilized piece of Dinosaur bone from Wyoming that has Calcite, Colemanite, and Chalcedony in it. The Colemanite glow Peach (LW and SW), the Calcite glows red (SW), and the Chalcedony glows green (SW). 7.5 oz. 3.25" x 2" x 1.25". Value $10-12.

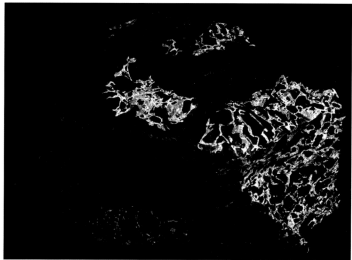

Same under LW UV showing the cell structure of the bone.

FLUORAPATITE: A stone of Fluorapatite with Quartz, Feldspar and Muscovite Mica from the Harding Pegmatite, Taos County, New Mexico. This Fluorapatite glows yellow (SW) and brighter yellow (MW). 5 oz. 2" x 2" x 1.75". Value $12-15.

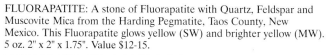

Same under SW UV.

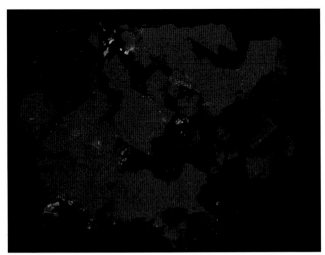

FLUORITE: A very nice group of Fluorite crystals from the Blanchard Mine, Bingham, New Mexico. This Fluorite fluoresces blue (LW). 1 lb. 4 oz. 4.5" wide. Value $25-30.

Same under LW UV.

FLUORITE: Blue Fluorite crystals on a matrix from Blanchard Claims, Bingham, New Mexico. The Fluorite glows purple (LW). 6.5 oz. 3" x 2" across. Value $10-14.

Same under LW UV.

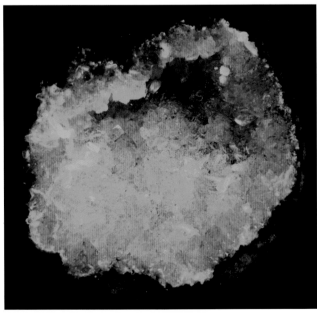

GEODE: Many geodes glow green. This rock is from the western United States. It also has a nice purple glowing ring around the outside edges of the geode. Uranium minerals or activators are suspected when the glow is this color green (SW). 5 oz. 2" x 2.25. Value $5-9.

Same under SW UV.

HALITE: Halite from Salton Sea near Niland, Imperial County, California. Halite from this area is salt with a mercury activator. Halite glows bright orange (SW). 1.5 oz. 3" x 1.5". Value $10-15.

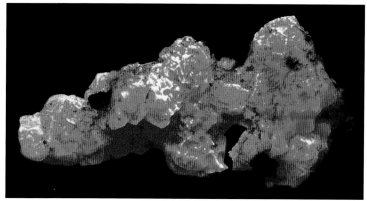

Same under SW UV.

Same under SW UV.

HYDROZINCITE: Hydrozincite from Goodsprings, Clark County, Nevada. It fluoresces bright blue-white (SW) and lesser blue-white under LW. 2 oz. 2" wide. Value $5-8.

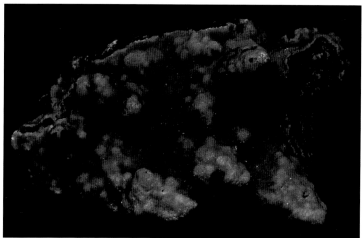

Same under LW UV.

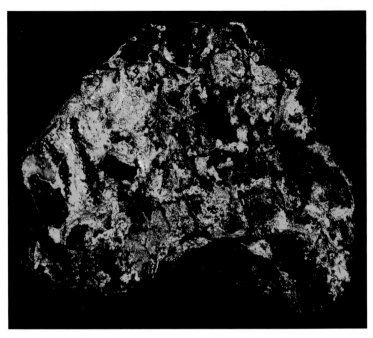

HYDROZINCITE: Hydrozincite from the Cerro Gordo Mine, Cerro Gordo District, Inyo County, California. The Hydrozincite glows blue (SW). 14 oz. 4" x 3.5" x 1.5". Value $12-15.

Same under SW UV.

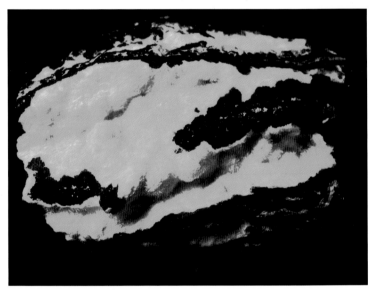

HYDROZINCITE: A stone containing Hydrozincite from Ojuela Mine, Mapimi, Durango, Mexico. The Hydrozincite glows bright bluish-white (SW) and cream (MW). 3.5 oz. 2.5" x 1.75" x 1.5". Value $7-9.

Same under SW UV.

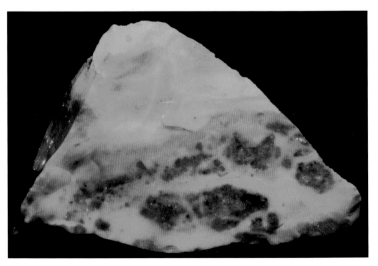

ICE CREAM OPAL: Common Opal (Hyalite) from Arizona. Opal glows green with touches of tan. 2" x 1.25". Value $4-6.

Same under SW UV.

OPAL: Common Opal with a slight opalescence on the top. The Opal glows bright light green under SW and less bright under LW. This piece came from Arizona. 12.5 oz. 3.5" x 2.5" x 2.5". Value $15-20.

Same under SW UV.

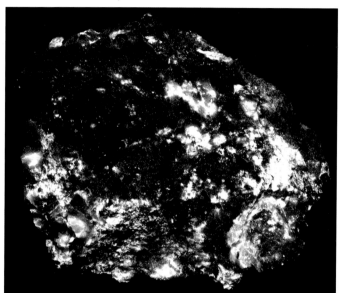

POWELLITE: Powellite from the Flying Saucer Claim, Maracopa County, Arizona. The Powellite glows yellow (SW). 8.5 oz. 3" x 3" x 1.5". Value $20-25.

Same under SW UV.

QUARTZ (var. Chalcedony): A Chalcedony rose from the Yankee Dog Field, Hildago County, New Mexico. This Chalcedony glows bright green (SW). It has a wonderful organic shape. 7 oz. 4" x 2.5" x 1.5". Value $20-30.

Same under SW UV.

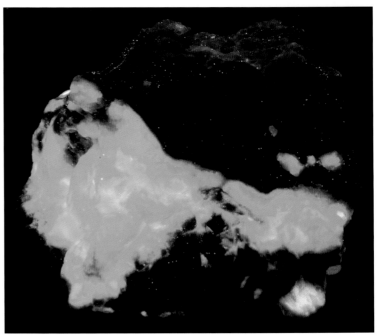

RHYOLITE, CHALCEDONY, and OPAL: Rhyolite, Chalcedony, and Opal from near Carefree, Arizona. The Rhyolite contains Feldspar, possibly Sanidine, that glows velvety red (SW); the Chalcedony and the Opal glow several shades of green (SW). 1 oz. 1.5" x 1". Value $5-6.

Same under SW UV.

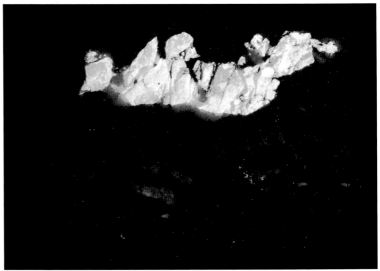

SCHEELITE: Scheelite patches in a Quartz vein with small Pyrite crystals in the quartz from New Ortiz Mine, Santa Fe, New Mexico. It glows bright blue white SW. There is also some red glowing Calcite in the stone and an unknown purple glowing material. 1 lb. 9 oz. 4.5" x 2.75" x 2". Value $20-25.

Same under SW UV.

SCHEELITE: Scheelite in a Quartz rock with Pyrite from New Ortiz Mine, Santa Fe, New Mexico. It glows bright blue white SW. 1 lb. 1 oz. 4.5" x 3.25" x 1.5". Value $30-35.

Same under SW UV.

130

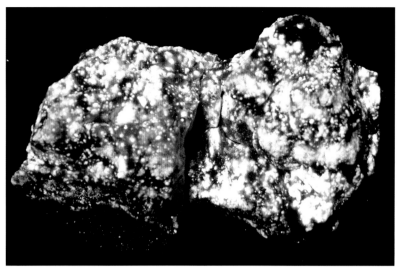

SCHEELITE: Scheelite from the Princess Pat Mine, San Bernardino County, California. The Scheelite glows blue-white and yellow (SW). 4 oz. 2.75" x 1.5" x 1". Value $12-15.

Same under SW UV.

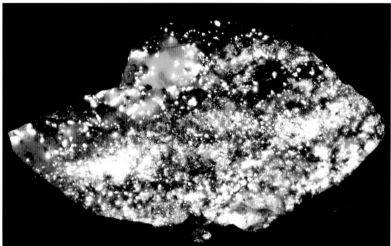

SCHEELITE: Scheelite from the Princess Pat Mine, San Bernardino County, California. The Scheelite glows blue-white and yellow (SW). 3.5 oz. 2.5" x 1.75" x 1". Value $8-10.

Same under SW UV.

SCHEELITE and HYALITE: Scheelite and Hyalite Opal from the Fernando Mine, Darwin District, Inyo County, California. The Scheelite glows blue-white (SW) and the Hyalite glows green (SW). 6 oz. 3" x 2" x 1.5". Value $20-24.

Same under SW UV.

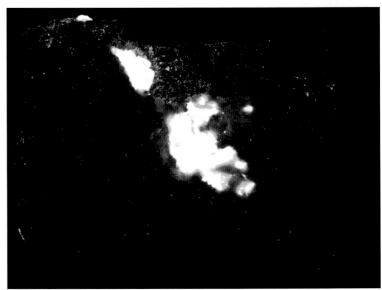

SCHEELITE and CALCITE: Scheelite and Calcite from the Cerro Gordo Mine, Cerro Gordo District, Inyo County, California. The Scheelite glows blue-white (SW) and the Hyalite glows green (SW). 14 oz. 4.25" x 2.75" x 1.25". Value $20-22.

Same under SW UV.

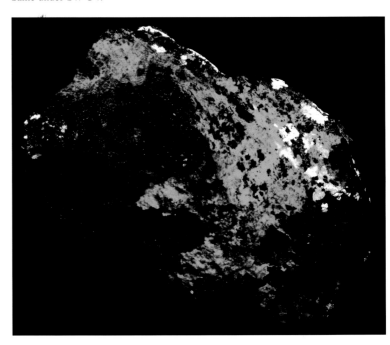

SCHEELITE and HYALITE: Scheelite and Hyalite Opal from the Fernando Mine, Darwin District, Inyo County, California. The Scheelite glows blue-white (SW) and the Hyalite glows green (SW). 13 oz. 4" x 2.5" x 2". Value $12-15.

Same under SW UV.

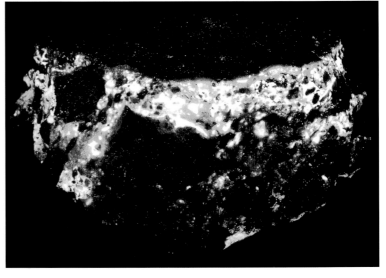

SCHEELITE: Scheelite from the Union Mine, San Bernardino County, California. The Scheelite glows blue (SW). 1 lb. 13 oz. 4.5" x 2.5" x 2". Value $25-30.

Same under SW UV.

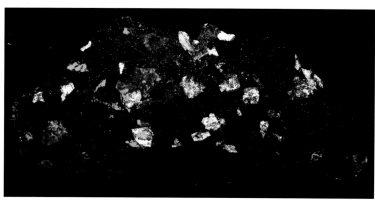

SCHEELITE and HYALITE: Scheelite and Hyalite Opal from the Fernando Mine, Darwin District, Inyo County, California. The Scheelite glows blue-white (SW) and the Hyalite glows green (SW). 1 lb. 8 oz. 6.5" x 3" x 2". Value $25-30.

Same under SW UV.

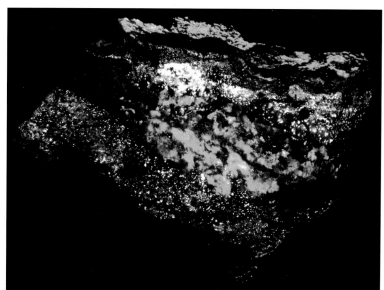

SCHEELITE with ARAGONITE and HYALITE: Scheelite with Aragonite and Hyalite Opal from the Princess Pat Mine, San Bernardino County, California. The Scheelite glows blue-white and yellow (SW). The Aragonite glows a blue-white and has a strong phosphorescence when the light is removed. The Hyalite glows green (SW). 2 lb. 4 oz. 6" x 4" x 3". Value $30-35.

Same under SW UV.

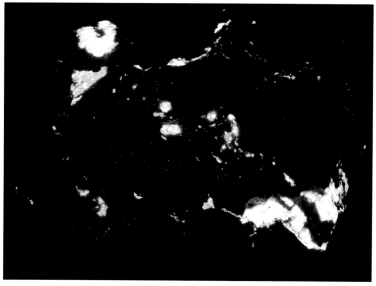

SCHEELITE: Scheelite from the Cerro Gordo Mine, Cerro Gordo District, Inyo County, California. The Scheelite glows blue-white (SW). 2 lb. 9 oz. 6" x 3.5" x 3". Value $25-30.

Same under SW UV.

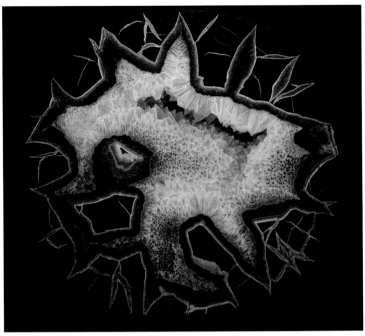

Same under SW UV.

SEPTARIAN NODULE: A Septarian Nodule slice from Southern Utah. It is a Cretaceous period mudball that cracked and Calcite entered the cracks and solidified. It has been sliced and one side is polished. It glows a soft blue white under LW and SW. 15 oz. 5.25" in diameter. Value $20-30.

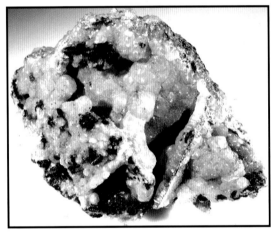

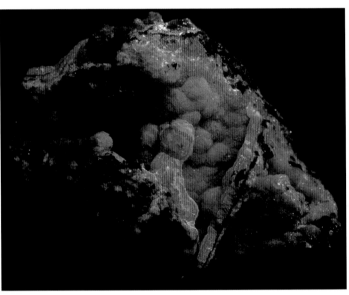

Same under SW UV.

SMITHSONITE: Bubbly Smithsonite from the Kelly Mine, Socorro, New Mexico. The Smithsonite glows blue-gray and where it is broken, it glows violet-pink (SW). 6.5 oz. 3" x 2.25" x 1.5". Value $30-35.

TREMOLITE: A dark flat stone with green radiating blades of Tremolite from Sunset South Mine, Harquahala Mountain, Maricopa County, Arizona. The Tremolite glows blue-white. 5.5 oz. 4.75" x 3" x .25". Value $15-20.

Same under SW UV.

134

TRONA: Trona crystals from Green River, Wyoming. Trona glows light gray-blue (SW and LW). Trona is a sodium sesquircarbonate that forms in non-marine evaporative deposits. It is subject to dehydration and/or hydration. It may form as crusts on the walls of caves and mines or in soils in arid regions. It gets its name from an Arabic word for native salt. Trona is the raw material for soda ash. Soda ash is used to make glass, paper, laundry detergents, etc. 2 lb. 4 oz. 4.5" x 4.5" x 2.5". Value $15-20.

Same under LW UV.

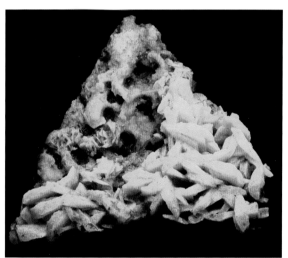

Same under SW UV.

TRONA: Trona crystals from Owens Lake, Inyo County, California. Trona glows light blue-green (SW and LW). 5 oz. 3" x 2.5" x 1.5". Value $12-15.

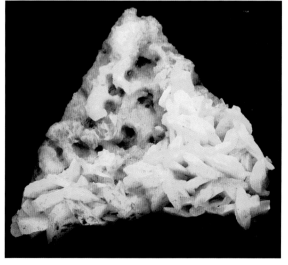

Same under LW UV.

135

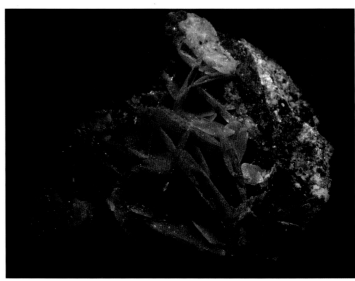

WULFENITE: Wulfenite from the Purple Passion Mine, Yavapai County, Arizona (near Wickenburg). This Wulfenite glows a weak tan (SW). 4 oz. 2.75" x 2.25" x 1.75". Value $30-35.

Same under SW UV.

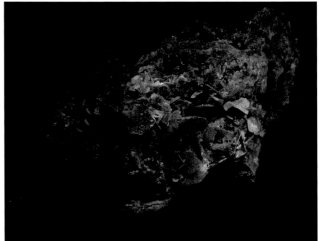

WULFENITE: Wulfenite from the Purple Passion Mine, Yavapai County, Arizona (near Wickenburg). This Wulfenite glows a weak tan (SW). 6 oz. 4.25" x 2.5" x 1.5". Value $30-40.

Same under SW UV.

Canada

AGRELLITE: Agrellite from Mt. Kipawa Complex, Sheffield Lake, Villedieu Township, Quebec. Agrellite fluoresces (SW and MW) lavender-pink. The piece also contains NF Eudialyte (red) and Aegerine (black), and a minor amount of thorium activated Calcite that fluoresces green (SW). The deep red color (SW) is Albite. 1 lb. 2 oz. 4.5" across. Value $22-28.

Same under SW UV.

AGRELLITE with PECTOLITE: Agrellite with a vein of Pectolite from Mt. Kipawa Complex, Sheffield Lake, Villedieu Township, Quebec. Agrellite fluoresces (SW and MW) lavender-pink. The Pectolite glows peach (MW). The piece also contains NF Eudialyte (red) and a minor amount of thorium activated Calcite that fluoresces green (SW). 12 oz. 4" x 3.5" x 1" across. *From the Greg Lesinski collection.*

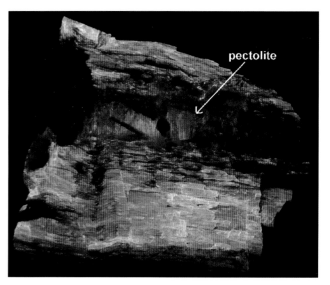

Same under MW UV.

Same under SW UV.

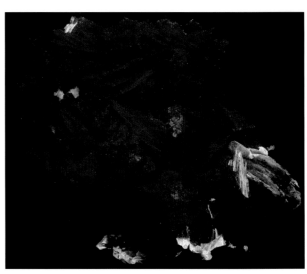

ALBITE: A superb plate of Albite crystals with Polylithionite and Leucophanite crystals from the Poudrette Quarry, Mont Saint-Hilaire, Quebec. There are also NF Serandite and Acmite crystals present. Albite, a sodium Feldspar, glows a rich, but not terribly bright, velvety red. The Polylithionite, a mica, glows yellow under SW, and Leucophanite glows a lilac purple color under SW and LW. 8 oz. 3.75" x 3" x 2". Value $35-40.

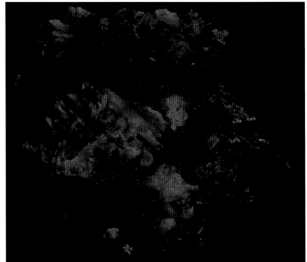

Same under LW UV.

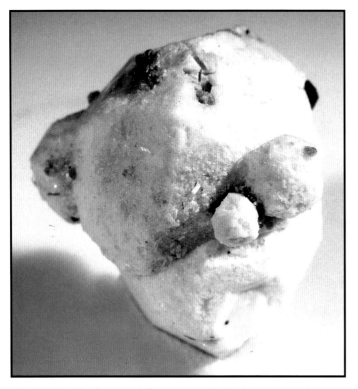

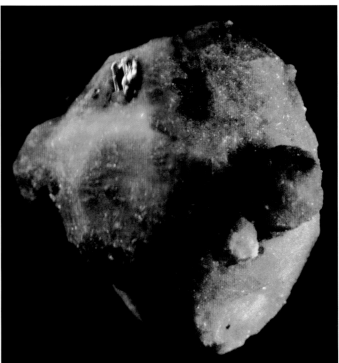

ANALCIME: Two fused Analcime crystals with NF Aegerine crystals and a small tuft of Polylithionite from Poudrette Quarry, Mont Saint-Hilaire, Quebec. Analcime is more often not fluorescent, but these crystals glow green (SW). .25 oz. 1 x 1 x .75". Value $15-20.

Same under SW UV.

ANALCIME: Three fused Analcime crystals with NF Aegerine crystals from Poudrette Quarry, Mont Saint-Hilaire, Quebec. These Analcime crystals glow yellow-orange (SW and LW). Analcime usually glows green from this location so this might actually be altered analcime, probably a pseudomorph of calcite in the shape of Analcime. .25 oz. 1 x .875" x .5". Value $18-22.

Same under SW UV.

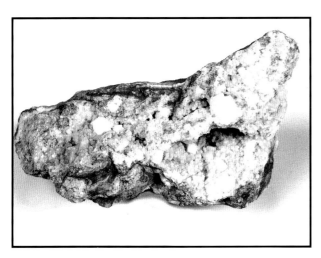

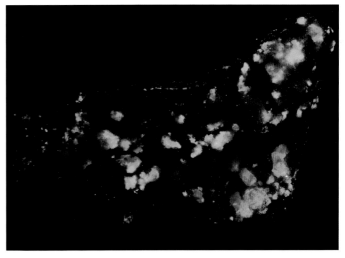

APOPHYLLITE: A group of white Apophyllite crystals growing in a vug. The Apophyllite glows Turquoise blue under SW. Not all the Apophyllite glows evenly, indicating that the activator is not evenly distributed throughout the Apophyllite. Believed to be from Ontario. 9 oz. 4" x 2.5" x 1.5". Value $15-20.

Same under SW UV.

CALCITE and AUGITE: A stone of Calcite containing NF Augite crystals from Elephant Lake, Ontario. The Calcite glows red (SW) and is not as bright as a Franklin Calcite. 8 oz. 3.5" x 2.75" x 2". Value $15-20.

Same under SW UV.

CALCITE and FLUORRICHTERITE: Calcite containing Fluorrichterite from Wilberforce, Ontario. The Calcite glows red-orange (SW). Fluorrichterite is a rare mineral, known from only this one location. It forms well shaped crystals that can have a pearly luster. With the Fluorrichterite, in the white re-crystallized calcite, are crystals of Biotite making this specimen especially nice. Fluorrichterite only received official name recognition in 1996. 10.5 oz. 4" x 3" x 1.5". Value $45-50.

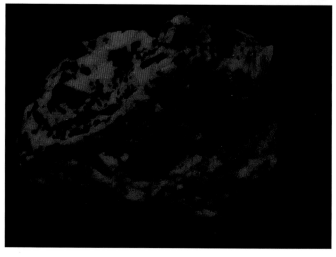

Same under SW UV.

CALCITE: A brightly fluorescent stone containing Calcite from Oka, Deux-Montagne County, Quebec. The Calcite glows bright orange-red. 8 oz. 3" x 2.5" x 2". Value $10-12.

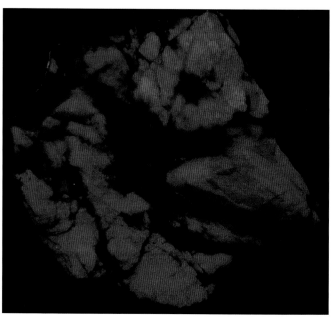

Same under SW UV.

CALCITE and HYDROZINCITE: Calcite with Hydrozincite from the now closed Frontenac Lead Mine in Frontenac County, Ontario. Calcite glows crimson red (SW), Hydrozincite glows blue-white (SW). 1 lb. 7 oz. 3" x 3" x 2.5". Value $30-35.

Same under SW UV.

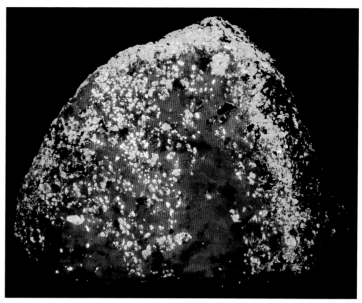

CALCITE and HYDROZINCITE: Calcite and Hydrozincite from Long Lake Zinc Mine, near Parham, Ontario. The Calcite glows red-orange (SW). The Hydrozincite glows blue-white (SW). 10.5 oz. 3" x 2.5" x 1.25". Value $20-25.

Same under SW UV.

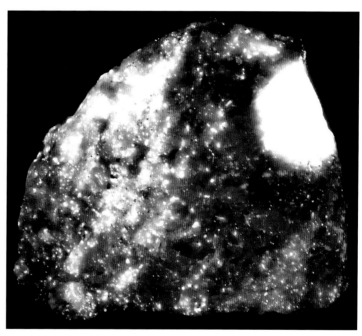

CALCITE with HUMITE and DIOPSIDE: A stone of Calcite with Humite (probably Chondrodite), and Diopside from Long Lake Zinc Mine, near Parham, Ontario. Humite glows yellow, Calcite glows red-orange (SW). The Diopside glow blue-green (SW). 6.5 oz. 3" x 2.25" x 1.5". Value $20-25.

Same under SW UV.

CALCITE with HUMITE and HYDROZINCITE: Calcite with Humite veins (probably Chondrodite), and Hydrozincite from Long Lake Zinc Mine, near Parham, Ontario. Humite glows yellow, Calcite glows red-orange (SW). The Hydrozincite is a haze of blue-white (SW). 9 oz. 3.75" x 2.5" x 1.25". Value $20-25.

Same under SW UV.

ELPIDITE and ALBITE: An attractive stem of tan Elpidite crystals with a small group of white Albite crystals from Poudrette Quarry, Mont Saint-Hilaire, Quebec. Much Elpidite is not fluorescent. Albite glows velvety red and this Elpidite glows yellow-green under SW. 1 oz. 1.75" x .5". Value $15-20.

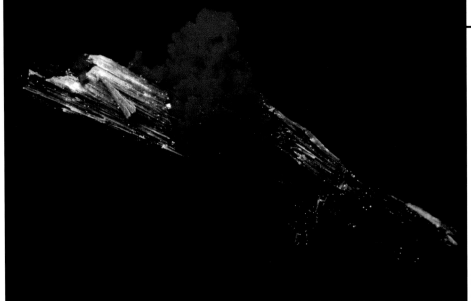

Same under SW UV.

ELPIDITE: Stems of tan Elpidite crystals with NF Aegerine crystals from Poudrette Quarry, Mont Saint-Hilaire, Quebec. Elpidite glows yellow-green under SW. .25 oz. 1 x .5". Value $12-15.

Same under SW UV.

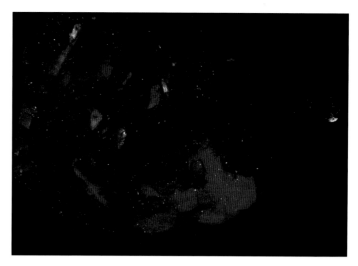

FLUORITE: A bed of NF Barite crystals with Fluorite from Rock Candy Mine, British Columbia. Not all Fluorite glows the same. Pieces from the same site can vary dramatically in fluorescence. This Fluorite glows purple (LW). 11.5 oz. 4.25" wide. Value $25-30.

Same under LW UV.

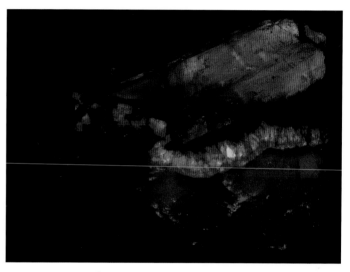

FLUORITE and CALCITE: From a very small find in Thunder Bay, Ontario, a stone containing fluorescent Calcite and veins of Fluorite. The Fluorite glow purple (LW). The Calcite glows red (LW and SW). 1 lb. 5 oz. 4.25" x 2.75" x 2.75. Value $22-30.

Same under LW UV.

FLUORITE and CALCITE: A stone containing Fluorite and Calcite from Bancroft, Ontario. The Fluorite glows purple (better under LW, but okay under SW) and the Calcite glows red-orange (SW). 1 lb. 10 oz. 4" x 3.75" x 2.5". Value $15-18.

Same under SW UV.

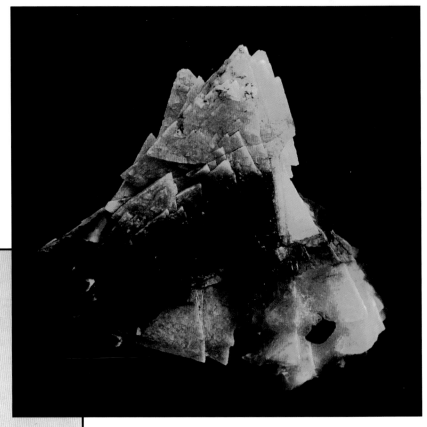

Same under SW UV.

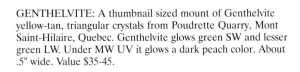

GENTHELVITE: A thumbnail sized mount of Genthelvite yellow-tan, triangular crystals from Poudrette Quarry, Mont Saint-Hilaire, Quebec. Genthelvite glows green SW and lesser green LW. Under MW UV it glows a dark peach color. About .5" wide. Value $35-45.

Same under MW UV. Note the completely different dark peach color that appears under MW.

144

Same under SW UV.

GENTHELVITE: Another thumbnail sized mount of Genthelvite yellow-tan, triangular crystals from Poudrette Quarry, Mont Saint-Hilaire, Quebec. About 3/8" wide. Value $30-35.

Same under MW UV. Note the completely different color that appears under MW.

HACKMANITE: Hackmanite from Bancroft. This is a beauty that glows pinkish red (LW) and seems to look like it has a fire within it rather than just a surface color. It bleaches white by sunlight but changes to a grape color if exposed to short-wave UV for a short period of time. 2 lbs. 12 oz. 5.75" x 4.75". Value $20-25.

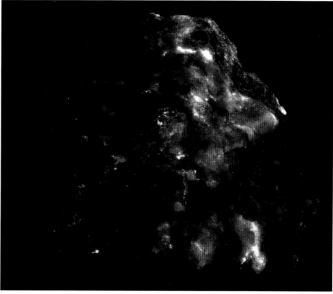

Same under LW UV.

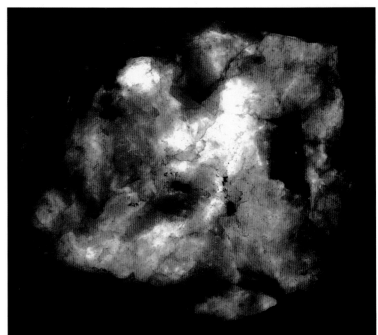

HACKMANITE: Hackmanite from Bancroft. Hackmanite is a variety of Sodalite that changes color (tenebrescence) after exposure to SW UV. This is a particularly brilliant example. It glows a bright orange under LW UV, as if there is fire within the rock. 13.5 oz. 2.5" x 2.5" x 2". Value $15-20.

Same under LW UV.

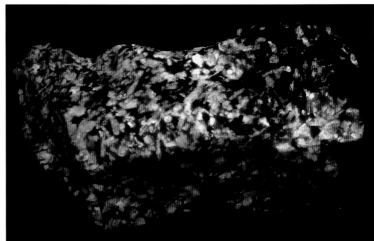

HACKMANITE: Hackmanite from Mont Saint-Hilaire. Glows pinkish red (SW) and mustard yellow (LW). Bleaches white by sunlight but changes to grape color if exposed to short-wave light. 8.5 oz. 4" x 2". Value $15-18.

Same under LW UV.

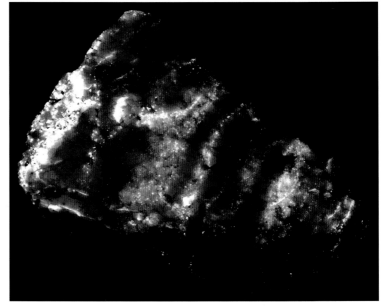

HUMITE, CALCITE, and ARAGONITE: A wonderfully banded stone of Humite, Calcite, and Aragonite from Long Lake Zinc Mine, near Parham, Ontario. Humite (probably Chondrodite) glows yellow, Calcite glows red-orange, Aragonite glows blue-white (SW). 1 lb. 1 oz. 4.5" x 3" x 1.75". Value $30-35.

Same under SW UV.

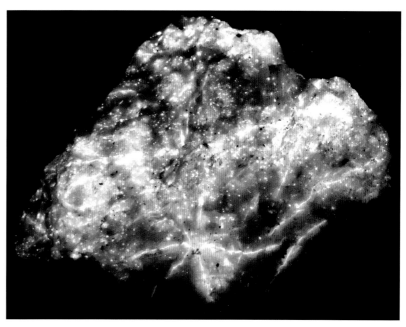

HUMITE with ARAGONITE and CALCITE: Another banded stone of Humite (probably Chondrodite) with great veins of Aragonite and patches of Calcite from Long Lake Zinc Mine, near Parham, Ontario. The Humite glows creamy yellow. The Aragonite glows two colors–peach and blue-white (SW) and creamy white and blue-white (LW). The Calcite glows red-orange (SW). 8 oz. 3.75" x 3" x 1.25". Value $30-35.

Same under SW UV.

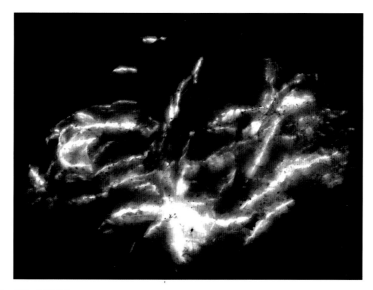

Same under LW UV.

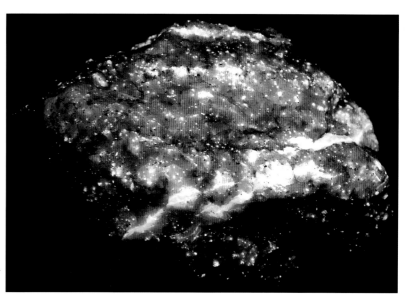

HUMITE with ARAGONITE, CALCITE, and DIOPSIDE: A four color stone of Calcite with a vein of Aragonite, Humite (probably Chondrodite), and Diopside from Long Lake Zinc Mine, near Parham, Ontario. Humite glows yellow, Calcite glows red-orange (SW). The spots of Diopside glow blue-green (SW). The Aragonite glows blue-white (SW) and creamy white (LW). 10 oz. 3.5" x 2.5" x 1.75". Value $30-35.

Same under SW UV.

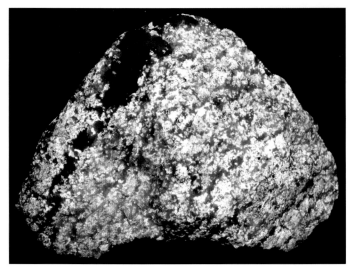

HUMITE with DIOPSIDE and CALCITE: A stone of Humite (probably Chondrodite), with Diopside and Calcite from Long Lake Zinc Mine, near Parham, Ontario. Humite glows yellow, Diopside glows blue-green (SW). Calcite glows red-orange (SW). 8 oz. 3" x 2.25" x 1.5". Value $20-25.

Same under SW UV.

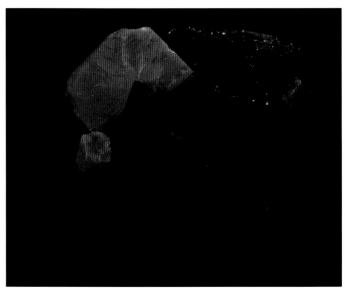

LEUCOPHANITE: Leucophanite crystals on Analcime with black NF Aegerine crystals from the Poudrette Quarry, Mont Saint-Hilaire, Quebec. Leucophanite glows a lilac purple color under SW and LW. 1.25" x 1". Value $30-35.

Same under SW UV.

LEUCOPHANITE and POLYLITHIONITE: Leucophanite and Polylithionite on Albite with reddish NF Rhodochrosite crystals from the Poudrette Quarry, Mont Saint-Hilaire, Quebec. Leucophanite glows a lilac purple color under SW and LW, Polylithionite glows light yellow under SW, and Albite glows velvety red under SW. 2 oz. 1.625" x 1.25" x 1". Value $30-35.

Same under SW UV.

NATROLITE: A Mont Saint-Hilaire grouping of Natrolite crystals. The Natrolite glows green. .5 oz. 1.5" x 1.25" x 1". Value $12-15.

Same under SW UV.

NATROLITE: A Mont Saint-Hilaire stone with a small cluster of Natrolite crystals. The Natrolite glows green. 4.5 oz. 3" x 2" x 2". Value $12-15.

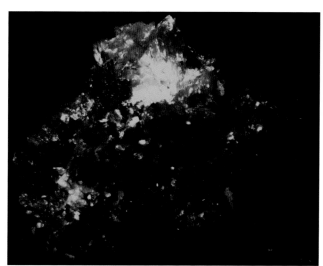

Same under SW UV.

PECTOLITE: A small stone with incredibly beautiful slender crystals of Pectolite from the Poudrette Quarry, Mont Saint-Hilaire, Quebec. The Pectolite glows orange-pink (LW, weaker under SW). .5 oz. 1.25" x 1.175". Value $25-30.

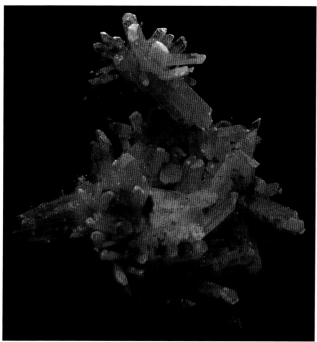

Same under LW UV.

149

POLYLITHIONITE: Polylithionite on Natrolite from Poudrette Quarry, Mont Saint -Hilaire, Quebec. A rare mineral of the Mica group (Lithium Mica). Not all Polylithionite fluoresces, but this example glows yellow (SW). 7 oz. 4" wide. Value $40-45.

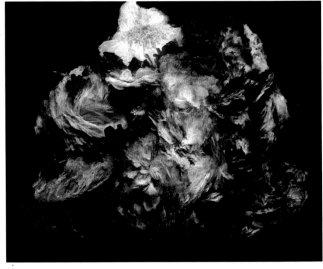

Same under SW UV.

POLYLITHIONITE and ALBITE: A superb bed of Polylithionite crystals with Albite crystals, Leucophanite crystals, and NF pink Serandite crystals from Poudrette Quarry, Mont Saint-Hilaire, Quebec. Polylithionite glows yellow (SW), Albite glows velvety red (SW), Leucophanite glows lilac pink under SW and LW. 7 oz. 4" x 3.5" x 2". Value $50-55.

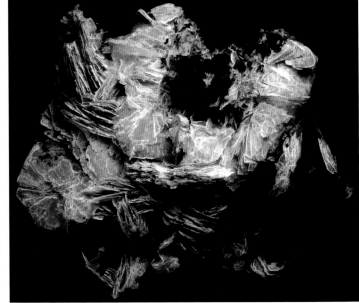

Same under SW UV.

RADIOACTIVE STONES: A group of eight mildly radioactive stones. Most contain Calcite that glows orange-red under SW. The radioactive elements show up under LW. They are (left to right – top row) Bytownite with Thorium from Oka; Natrolite (fluorescent green SW) with Thorium from Mont Saint-Hilaire; Sovite with Niobium from Oka; and Huttonite with Thorium from Oka. (left to right – bottom row) Bastnaesite with Cerium, Lanthanum, and Yittrium from Oka; Sodalite (which glows yellow-orange) with Thorium from MSH; Niocalite with Niobium from Oka; and Samarskite with Uranium and Niobium from Oka.

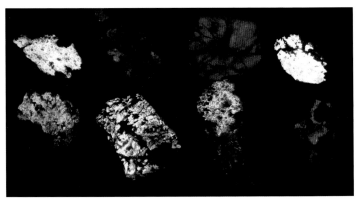

Same under LW UV.

SCAPOLITE: Light greenish tan Scapolite from Haliburton, Ontario. This Scapolite glows bright crimson red (SW). 7.5 oz. 3" x 2" x 1.75". Value $8-12.

Same under SW UV.

SCHEELITE: Scheelite from the Hollinger Gold Mine, Timmins, Ontario. Scheelite glows blue-white (SW). 1 lb. 10 oz. 4" x 3" x 2". Value $55-65.

Same under SW UV.

SELENITE: Superb honey colored Selenite crystal rose from the Red River Floodway, Winnipeg. Selenite glows green-gray (SW and LW) and has a strong blue-gray phosphorescence. These Canadian Selenite roses come from one place in Winnipeg, an ancient riverbed. The first collectors to dig this area originally dug hundreds, but the supply seems to be running out. Collectors look for perfect crystals and pay a premium for rocks with unbroken crystals. Sometimes the crystals are doubled and look like a duck's bill. Those are called "twinned" or "duck's bill." 6.5 oz. 4" x 2.5" wide. Value $75-85.

Same under SW UV.

151

SELENITE: Honey colored Selenite crystal rose from the Red River Floodway, Winnipeg. Selenite glows green-gray (SW and LW) and has a strong blue-gray phosphorescence. .25 oz. .5" x 1.75" wide. Value $5-6.

SODALITE: Massive Blue Sodalite from Bancroft Ontario. Most Sodalite glows orange (SW) and brighter orange (LW). Sodalite is a fairly common material, but the advanced collector looks for stones containing individual Sodalite crystals which are very hard to find. 1 lb. 4 oz. 5" across. Value $20-25.

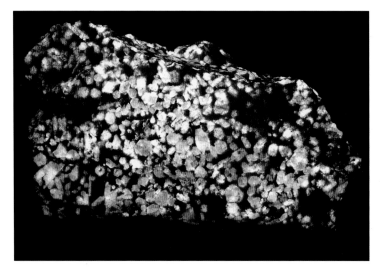

Same under LW UV.

SODALITE: A group of polished cabochons of Blue Sodalite from Bancroft Ontario. The Sodalite glows orange (SW) and brighter orange (LW). It is mildly tenebrescent (turns grape color on exposure to SW UV). Shown under regular light (regular light showing tenebrescence), and LW UV. Value $16-22 per pound unpolished.

Same under SW UV.

SODALITE: A group of polished cabochons of Blue Sodalite from Bancroft Ontario. The Sodalite glows orange (SW) and brighter orange (LW). It is mildly tenebrescent (turns grape color on exposure to SW UV). Shown under regular light (regular light showing tenebrescence), and LW UV. Value $16-22 per pound unpolished.

VLASOVITE: Vlasovite, Eudialite, Albite, and Calcite from the Mt. Kipawa Complex, Sheffield Lake, Villedieu Township, Quebec. Vlasovite, a rare mineral, glows yellow-white (SW) and peach (LW). The red Eudialite is NF. The Albite (Feldspar) glows velvety red (SW). The Calcite glows green (from a thorium activator) (SW). 6 oz. 3" wide. Value $40-55.

Same under SW UV.

WELOGANITE with SABINAITE: A stone with crystals of Weloganite, Sabinaite, Calcite, and Quartz from Francon Quarry, Montreal, Quebec. Sabinaite is only found at this quarry and at MSH. The Sabinaite, which glows blue-white, covers the background of the stone and you can see a few crystals growing out at the edges of the Calcite and Weloganite crystals. Weloganite glows yellow. The Calcite glows red-orange and the Quartz glows a weak yellow-white (SW). 4 oz. 2.5" x 2" x 1.5". Value $25-30.

WERNERITE: Wernerite, a name given to a massive form of Scapolite from Otter Lake, Grenville, Quebec. Wernerite glows bright yellow under LW and dull yellow under SW. Stones sold as Meionite or Marialite may also be called Wernerite. 12.5 oz. 5" wide. Value $10-15.

Same under SW UV.

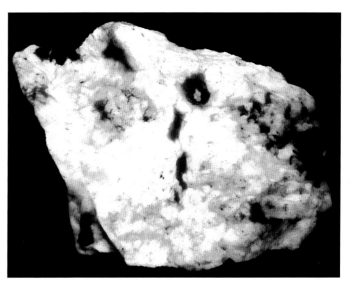

Same under LW UV.

Far left:
WERNERITE: A daylight yellow stone of Wernerite from the McGill Farm, Grenville, Ontario. This Wernerite glows an unusually bright yellow under LW. 3 oz. 2" x 2" x .75". Value $15-18.

Left:
Same under LW UV.

Far left:
ZIRCON: Light brown Zircon in Albite from Kipawa, Quebec. The Zircon glows tan (SW and lesser LW) and the Albite glows velvety red. .75" wide. Value $7-10.

Left:
Same under SW UV.

Greenland

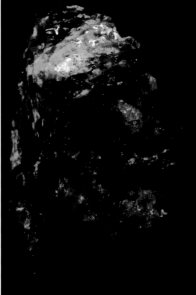

Same under SW UV.

HACKMANITE: (var. Sodalite), Hackmanite from Narsaq. It glows bright orange (LW) and a variety of colors under SW. The SW colors are green (Sodalite containing a uranyl activator), red-orange (Sodalite), and a purple-blue that is extremely phosphorescent (unknown). It is extremely tenebrescent and has turned a raspberry color. 3.5 oz. 2.5" x 2" x 1.5". Value $25-30.

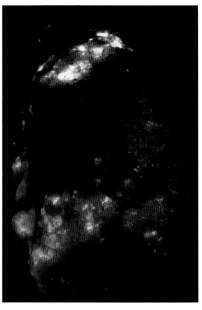

Same under LW UV.

154

HACKMANITE and SODALITE: Two bright LW stones from Greenland. On the left is an example of Hackmanite, a variety of Sodalite, from Narsaq. It glows bright orange (LW) and less bright orange (SW). It is extremely tenebrescent (turns raspberry color on a very short exposure to SW). 1.25 oz. 2" wide. On the right is Sodalite from Kvanefjeld, Ilimaussaq. It glows orange (SW) and bright orange (LW) This stone also contains Analcime which glows green (SW). 1.5" x1.5". Value (left) $30-35, (right) $15-18 (due to small size).

Same under SW UV.

Same under LW UV.

Daylight showing tenebrescence.

Far left:
POLYLITHIONITE:
Polylithionite (Lithium Mica) from Kangerlussaq, Ilimaussaq Complex. Polylithionite glows yellow. Most examples that come on the market seem to be small. 1.25 oz. 1.5" x 1.5" x 1.25. Value $30-35.

Left:
Same under SW UV.

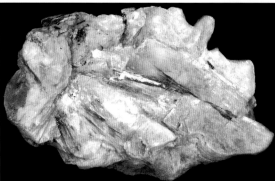

POLYLITHIONITE: Polylithionite from Kangerlussaq, Ilimaussaq Complex. Note the well formed crystal plates typical of the Kangerlussaq area. The Polylithionite glows bright greenish white under SW. 3 oz. 3" x 1.5" x 1". Value $50-60. *Photo courtesy of the Miner Shop.*

Same under SW UV.

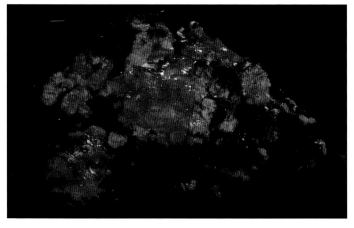

Same under SW UV.

SODALITE, TUGTUPITE, and MORE: An array of colors under SW cover this stone. It is from the Grass Plateau of the Tasaq Slope, Ilimaussaq Complex. The Sodalite glows orange (SW and LW), the Tugtupite glows bright red (SW), Chkalovite glows green (SW). There is an unidentified blue glowing material and a purple glowing material (SW). 9.75 oz. 4.5" x 2.25" x 1.75". Value $250-300.

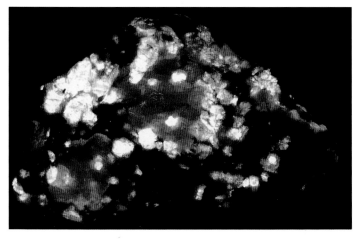

Same under LW UV.

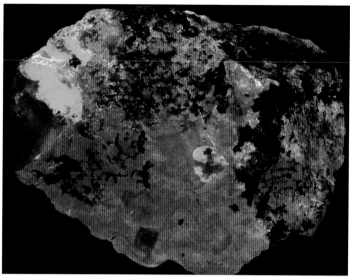

SODALITE: Sodalite from Tunulliarfik, Ilimaussaq Complex. This is a large rather gemmy chunk of Sodalite. It is very tenebrescent in some areas. The green areas are Ussingite and Chkalovite. 4 lb. 10 oz. 8 x 6". Value $300-325. *Photo courtesy of the Miner Shop.*

Same under SW UV.

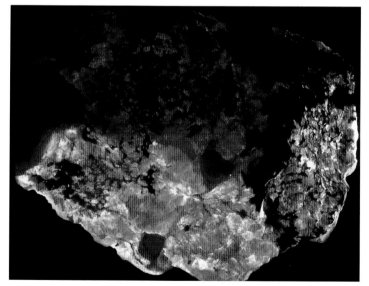

Same under LW UV.

Same showing tenebrescence

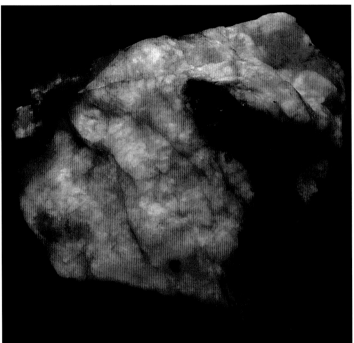

Same under SW UV.

TUGTULITE: Tugtulite from the Groen Outcrop, Tunulliarfik, Ilimaussaq Complex. A very unusual form of Tugtupite that is only found within one spot in the complex. It is a new mineral and seems to be composed of Sodalite and Tugtupite. Mark Cole has named it "Tugtulite" until a more formal name is determined. The Tugtulite glows a peachy color under SW, bright orange under LW, and white under MW (similar to the daylight photo). It is very tenebrescent and phosphorescent. 4 oz. 2.5" x 2.5" x 1". Value $100-125. *Photo courtesy of the Miner Shop.*

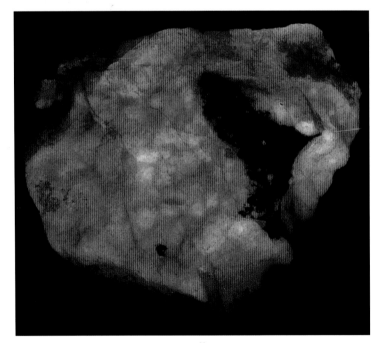

Same under LW UV.

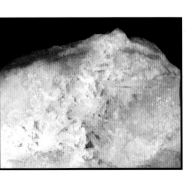

Same under MW UV

Same showing crystals in the rock.

TUGTUPITE: A group of polished and unpolished pieces of Tugtupite, a pink glassy crystal that fluoresces cherry red (SW) and lighter orange-red (LW). It sometimes bleaches out in sunlight and regains its red color when again exposed to SW. These are from Kvanefjeld, Ilímaussaq Massif, Greenland. Tugtupite is also available from the Tasaq slope, but it is a more porous, softer stone that, although it glows beautifully under SW UV, it does not make a very good gem stone for lapidary work. The diamond shaped cabochon is about 1.5" tall. Shown under regular light and SW UV. Value $2-4 per gram for unpolished lapidary quality, $40-50 a pound in non-lapidary quality.

Same under SW UV.

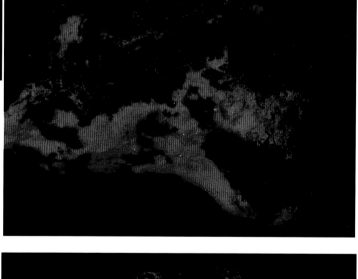

TUGTUPITE: A large stone containing bright gem quality red and white Tugtupite that fluoresces cherry red (SW), orange (LW), and is very phosphorescent. From Kvanefjeld, Ilimaussaq Massif, Greenland. 10.5 oz. 4.5" x 2.75" x 1.5". Value $450-500.

Same under LW UV.

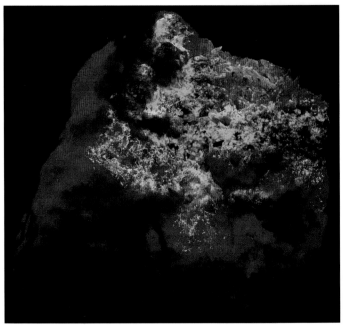

TUGTUPITE: An incredible stone of rare Tugtupite crystals. This is the only example of larger crystals found to date. From Tasaq Slopes, Ilimaussaq Massif, Greenland. The Tugtupite glows red (SW). 3 oz. 2" x 2" x 1.5". Value $300-325. *Photo courtesy of the Miner Shop.*

Same under SW UV.

Same under SW UV.

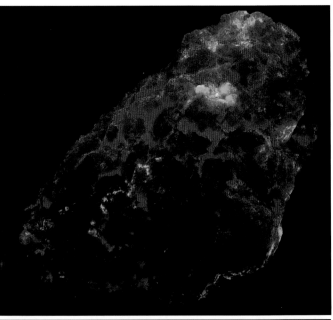

TUGTUPITE: Tugtupite from the Tasaq slopes, Ilimaussaq Complex. Veins of chalky Tugtupite in a matrix of Analcime. When there are vugs in the stone, there are often micro crystals in them. The Tugtupite glows a bright cherry red under SW and salmon orange under LW. 1 lb. 10 oz. 4" x 2". Value $200-225, *Photo courtesy of the Miner Shop.*

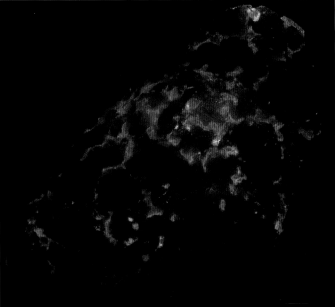

Same under LW UV.

Same under SW UV.

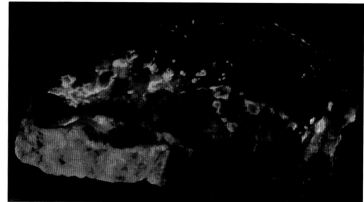

TUGTUPITE and ANALCIME: Tugtupite with Analcime from the Graes Plateau, Tasaq Slopes, Ilimaussaq Complex. The Tugtupite is in a matrix of Lujavrite (NF) and Analcime. The Analcime rarely fluoresces except certain specimens from one area within the complex. 1 lb. 2 oz. 7 x 3" x 2". Value $400-450. *Photo courtesy of the Miner Shop.*

Same under LW UV.

Same under SW UV.

USSINGITE and SODALITE: Ussingite and Sodalite from the Graes Plateau, Tasaq Slopes, Ilimaussaq Complex. The Sodalite glows with the typical bright orange and is tenebrescent. The Ussingite glows a bright green (the rarer color for this mineral). Other pieces of Ussingite can glow orange and can be mistaken for Sodalite. Under daylight, Ussingite usually has a purple color and a texture similar to Quartzite. Some Ussingite from the complex does not fluoresce at all. 1 lb. 7 oz. 5" x 4" x 2". Value $100-120. *Photo courtesy of the Miner Shop.*

Same under LW and SW UV together

China

Far left:
ARAGONITE: A dark stone containing a flower shaped crystalline growth of Aragonite from China. The Aragonite glows weak blue-white (SW). 5.5 oz. 2.5" x 2.25" x 1". Value $15-18.

Left:
Same under SW UV.

Far left:
FLUORITE: Blue Fluorite crystals with Pyrite and Quartz (NF) crystals, Yaogangxian, Sichuan Province, China. This Fluorite glows purple (LW). 2 oz. 2" x 1.5". Value $15-18.

Left:
Same under LW UV.

Far left:
FLUORITE: Light blue Fluorite crystals with Quartz (NF) crystals, Yaogangxian, Sichaun Province, China. Fluorite glows blue (LW). 2 oz. 1.75" x 1.5". Value $15-18.

Left:
Same under LW UV.

FLUORITE: Light purple Fluorite crystals with Quartz (NF) crystals, Yaogangxian, Sichaun Province, China. Fluorite glows purple (LW). .75 oz. 1.75" x 1.75". Value $12-15.

Same under LW UV.

FLUORITE: Almost colorless light blue Fluorite crystals with Quartz (NF) crystals, Yaogangxian, Sichuan Province, China. Fluorite glows purple (LW). 1.5 oz. 2.25" x 1.5". Value $15-20.

Same under LW UV.

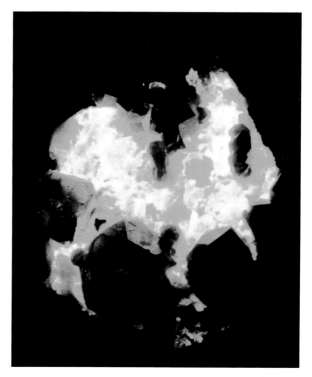

HYALITE: Garnets (NF) and Quartz (NF) on a bed of white Hyalite and Calcite from Sichuan Province, China. The Hyalite glows bright green (SW and LW). This is a great example of a tiny piece that is attractive in daylight and also has a fluorescent component. .1 oz. .75" across. Value $8-12.

Same under SW UV.

163

SCHEELITE: Large Scheelite crystals on Muscovite Mica from Mt. Xue Bao Ding, Ping Wu, Sichuan Province, China. Some of the biggest and most attractive Scheelite crystals have come out of China in the past few years. Scheelite glows blue-white (SW). 2 lb. 8 oz. 5.5" across. Value $175-200.

Same under SW UV.

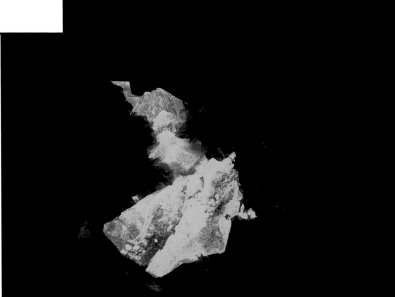

SCHEELITE: Medium sized Scheelite crystals on Muscovite Mica from Mt. Xue Bao Ding, Ping Wu, Sichuan Province, China. Scheelite glows blue-white (SW). 9 oz. 4.5" across. Value $80-95.

Same under SW UV.

SCHEELITE: Small Scheelite crystals on NF Quartz from Mt. Xue Bao Ding, Ping Wu, Sichuan Province, China. Scheelite glows blue-white (SW). 2.5 oz. 2.25" x 2.25" x .75". Value $30-35.

Same under SW UV.

WOLLASTONITE: White fibrous crystals of Wollastonite from China. This unusual Wollastonite glows mild yellow SW, peach and mild purple MW, and yellow, peach, and mild purple. 1 oz. 1.5" x 1.5" x .75". Value $25-30.

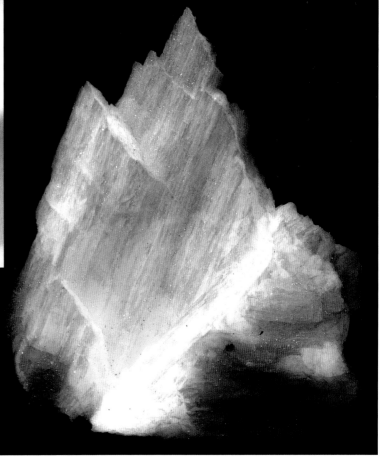

Same under LW or MW UV

Other Countries

BARATOVITE: A white stone with daylight pink radiating crystals of Baratovite and what looks like black blades of Aegerine (NF) from Dari-i-Pioz, Alayskiy Range, Tien Shan, Tajikistan (sometimes spelled "Tadzhikstan" or "Tadjikistan"). The Baratovite glows a brilliant light blue (SW). 2.75 oz. 2.25" x 1.5" x 1". Value $45-50.

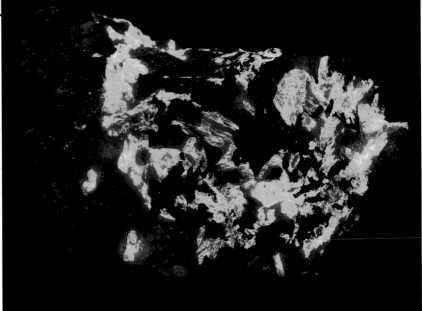

Same under SW UV.

CALCITE: A rock containing Chalcopyrite (NF black), Calcite, and Quartz from Huaron Mine, Ancash, Peru. The Calcite glows bright red (SW) and there is something in the quartz that glows greenish yellow (SW). A few fluorescent minerals have come out of Peru. 4.5 oz. 3.5" wide. Value $35-45.

Same under SW UV.

Left:
CALCITE: A dark stone containing fluorescent Calcite from Langban, Sweden. This Calcite glows fiery red. 8 oz. 2.5" x 1.75" x 1.5". Value $10-12.

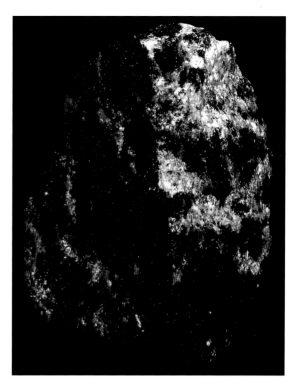

Same under SW UV.

CALCITE: Amber crystals of Calcite from Rotegria, Reggio Emilia, Italy. The Calcite glows white (SW) and has good phosphorescence. 8 oz. 3.25" x 3.25" x 1". Value $18-22.

Same under SW UV.

CALCITE: White crystals of Calcite from Bigadic, Turkey. The Calcite glows bright white (SW) and has great phosphorescence. 2.5 oz. 2.25" x 1.25" x 1". Value $18-20.

Same under SW UV.

CALCITE: Calcite from Eloford Quarry, Mendips, Somerset, England. This Calcite is very pretty under SW UV. It glows a mixture of blue-white and red-orange under SW, cream under LW and has a strong phosphorescence. 5.5 oz. 2.75" x 2" x 1.5". Value $20-25.

Same under LW UV.

CALCITE SPEARS FROM BRAZIL: A plate of small Calcite spears from Rio Del Sul, Brazil. The Calcite glows a beautiful pink-red (best under LW, but not bad under SW). .5 oz. 1.5" x 1.75" x .5". Value $12-18.

Same under LW UV.

CALCITE SPEARS FROM BRAZIL: A plate of Calcite spears from Rio Del Sul, Brazil. The Calcite glows a beautiful pink-red (best under LW, but not bad under SW). 2 oz. 2.5" x 1.75" x 1.5". Value $30-35.

Same under LW UV.

CALCITE and GYPSUM: Calcite and Gypsum crystals on Pyrite from N.B.H.C. Mine, Broken Hill, NSW, Australia. There are not a lot of fluorescent minerals currently found in Australia. The Calcite fluoresces red (SW) and the Gypsum fluoresces mild blue-white (SW). 3.75 oz. 3.25" wide. Value $45-50.

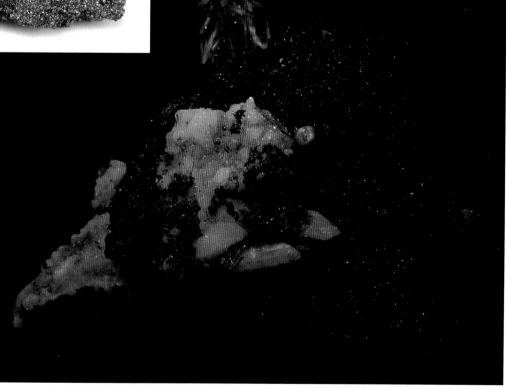

Same under SW UV.

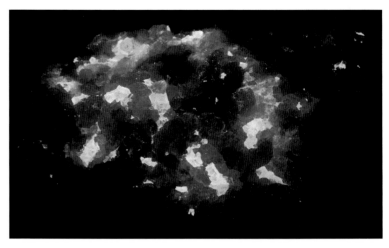

CALCITE on DATOLITE: A stone with yellow crystals of Calcite on a bed of Datolite crystals from Giannasi, Modena, Italy. The Calcite glows bright yellow-white (SW) and has good phosphorescence. The Datolite glows a weak yellow (showing here as blue) and there is an unknown mineral that glows weak pink. .5 oz. 2" x 1". Value $12-15.

Same under SW UV.

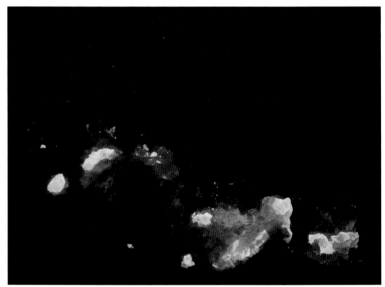

CALCITE on DATOLITE: Yellow crystals of Calcite on a bed of Datolite crystals from Giannasi, Modena, Italy. The Calcite glows bright yellow-white (SW) and has good phosphorescence. The Datolite glows a weak yellow and there is an unknown mineral that glows weak pink. 4 oz. 3" x 2" x 1.5". Value $15-18.

Same under SW UV.

CELESTITE on SULFUR: Celestite crystals on a bed of Sulfur crystals (NF yellow). Celestite glows blue white (SW). From Floristella Mine, Casteltermini, Sicily, Italy. This is a classic location for wonderful Sulfur crystals. 4 oz. 3" wide. Value $55-65.

Same under SW UV.

CELESTITE: Celestite crystals on a bed of Sulfur (NF yellow). It is similar to the Italian variety. Celestite glows blue-white (SW) and is from the Machow Mine, Poland. 4 oz. 2.25" wide. Value $30-35.

Same under SW UV.

CHABAZITE: Crystals of Chabazite from Quiraing, Skye County, Scotland. The Chabazite glows white. 1 lb. 4 oz. 4" x 3" x 2.75". Value $15-20.

Same under SW UV.

COLEMANITE: A stone with white crystals of Colemanite from Panderma, Turkey. The Colmanite glows white (SW and LW) and has great phosphorescence. 8 oz. 4.5" x 2.5" x 1.25". Value $25-30.

Same under LW or SW UV

COLEMANITE: White crystals of Colemanite from Bigadic, Turkey. The Colmanite glows bright blue-white (SW) and has great phosphorescence. 8.5 oz. 3" x 2.25" x 2". Value $25-30.

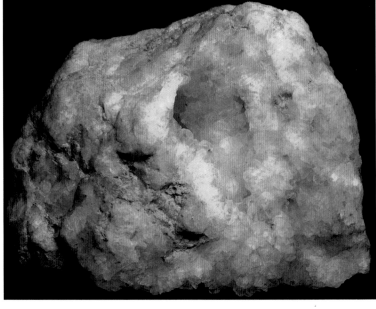

Same under SW UV.

FLUORAPATITE and TOURMALINE: A gem specimen of green Tourmaline crystals with Fluorapatite, Quartz, Mica, and Schorl from Shingas Valley, Gilgit, Pakistan. The Fluorapatite glows bright yellow-orange under SW. This piece is valued more for its aesthetic appeal and combination of minerals than for the glowing Apatite. 2.75" across. Value $80-100.

Same under SW UV.

FLUORITE: Yellow Fluorite from Aouli Mine, near Midett, Morocco. The crystals glow a purple color (LW) and creamy purple (SW). 6.5 oz. 3.5" x 2". Value $30-35.

Same under LW UV.

FLUORITE: Light purple Fluorite from the Blackdene Mine, Weardale, Durham County, England. This Weardale Fluorite from an old collection glows purple (LW and SW). It has exquisite clear crystals, some that are doubly terminated. Weardale is one of the classic locations for great fluorescent Fluorite crystals. 4 oz. 3.5" x 2". Value $80-95.

Same under LW UV.

FLUORITE: A spear of stone containing purple Fluorite from one of the mines in the district of Weardale, Durham County, England. This Fluorite glows an incredibly bright purple (LW and SW). The SW response is almost as good as the LW response. 1 lb. 1 oz. 6.25" x 2" x 1.75". Value $50-60.

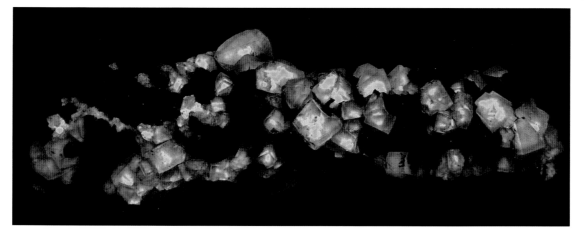

Same under LW UV.

FLUORITE: Green Fluorite from one of the mines in the district of Weardale, Durham County, England. This Fluorite glows purple (LW and SW). 5.5 oz. 4" x 1.75". Value $30-35.

Same under LW UV.

173

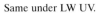

FLUORITE: Fluorite from the Rogerley Mine, Frosterly, Durham County, England. Rogerley Fluorite usually glows blue (LW and SW). 1.75 oz. 1.875" wide. Value $18-25.

HACKMANITE: An incredible example of a color changing Hackmanite from Badakhshan, Afghanistan. The violet color actually gets stronger (tenebrescence) and deeper when left in the sunlight and the color stays bright for weeks, if not months. Obviously, Afghanistan was releasing very few minerals over the last decade, but as the country has "loosened up" recently, some wonderful mineral examples are starting to appear. Currently, the prices are high, but they may come down a bit as more mineral treasures are discovered and get into the hands of mineral dealers. This beauty glows orange under LW and weak orange under SW. 15.5 oz. 5" x 3.75" x 1.5". Value $700-800. *From the Eric Weis collection.*

Same under LW UV.

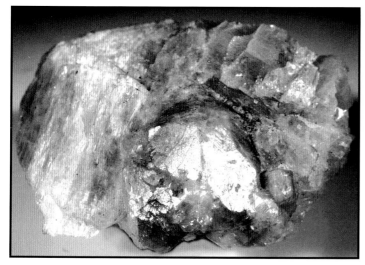

HACKMANITE: A crystal of color changing Hackmanite from Kokcha Tal, Badakhshan, Afghanistan. The crystal darkens to a raspberry color (tenebrescence) after exposure to SW UV. It glows orange under LW and has a strong phosphorescence. 2 oz. 2" x 1.75" x 1". Value $35-40.

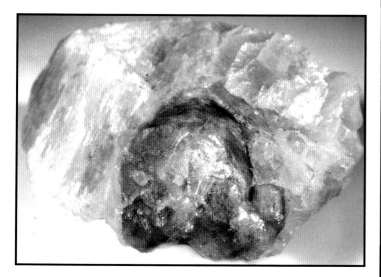

Same showing tenebrescence

Same under LW UV.

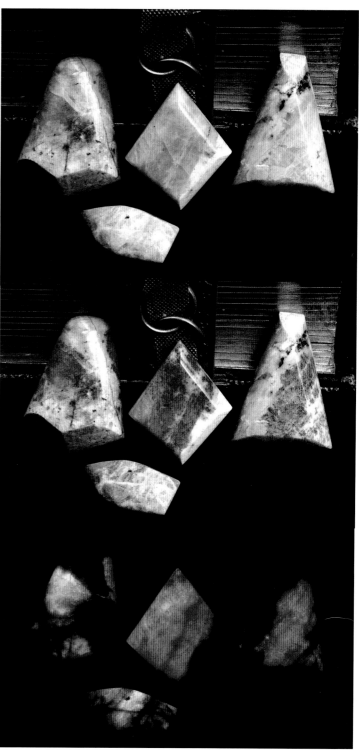

HACKMANITE: A group of polished cabochons of Hackmanite (color changing variety of Sodalite) with Natrolite, from the Kola Peninsula, Lovozero, Russia. Hackmanite fluoresces orange (LW). It is extremely tenebrescent (turns grape color on exposure to SW UV). Shown under regular light (regular light showing tenebrescence), and LW UV. Value $.30-.40 per gram unpolished.

175

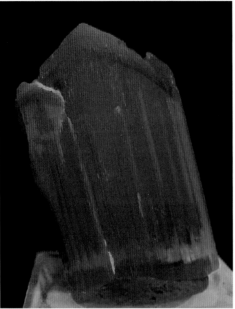

HIDDENITE: Hiddenite, a species of Spodumene, is a fibrous crystalline material. This example is from Gilgit, Pakistan. The Hiddenite glows pink (SW), orange (LW), and has an orange phosphorescence that lasts over ten minutes when the SW light is shut off. .5 oz. 1.125" x .75" x .25". Value $35-45. *Photos courtesy of GSL Rocks.*

Same under SW UV.

Same under LW UV.

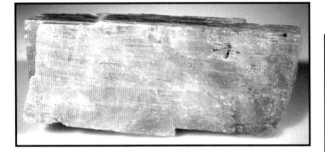

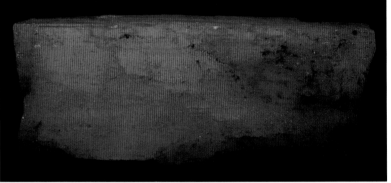

HIDDENITE: Hiddenite, a species of Spodumene, is a fibrous crystalline material that is often cut into gemstones. It loses its color in daylight and is sometimes called the "Evening Stone." This example is from Kunar Valley, Afghanistan. The green variety of Spodumene is called Hiddenite while the pinkish variety is usually called Kunzite. Hiddenite was first discovered in Hiddenite, Alexander County, North Carolina. The Hiddenite glows weak red (SW), orange (LW). 3.5 oz. 2.75" x 1" x 1". Value $16-18.

Same under LW UV.

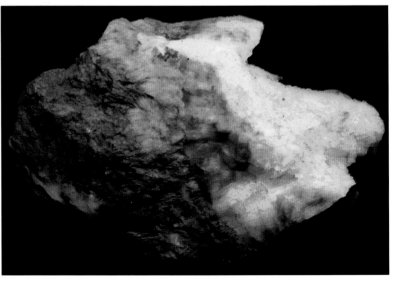

HYDROBORACITE: White crystals of Hydroboracite with Orpiment inclusions from Bigadic, Turkey. The Hydroboracite glows bright yellow-white (SW) and has great phosphorescence. The Orpiment glows a weak yellow-cream. 11 oz. 4.5" x 3" x 2". Value $30-35.

Same under SW UV.

LAPIS LAZULI: Egg shaped Lapis Lazuli from Afghanistan. I am told that this is the only fluorescent Lapis (although there is a fluorescent Lazurite from New York state). It glows light blue under SW and has sections that glow orange under LW. 3 oz. 1.75" tall. Value $35-45.

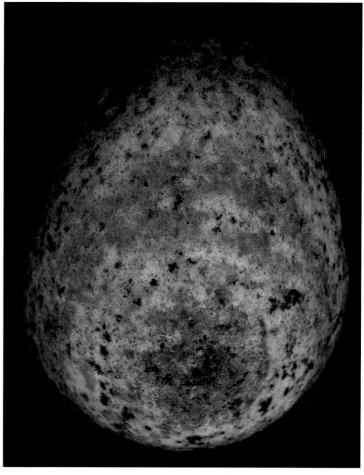

Same under SW UV.

MANGANOCALCITE: Crystals of Daylight light pink Manganocalcite from Pachapaque, Peru. The Manganocalcite glows pink-red (SW). 4 oz. 2.5" x 1.75" x 1.25". Value $10-15.

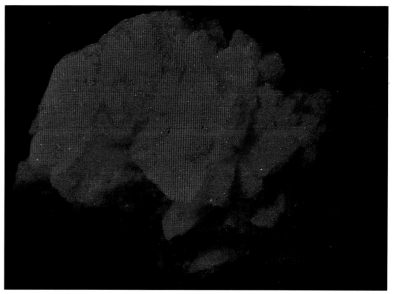

Same under SW UV.

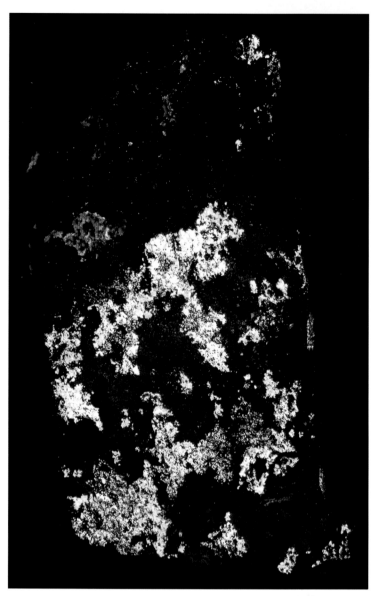

MARGAROSANITE: Platy Margarosanite with a touch of Calcite from Jakobsberg, Nordmark, Varmland, Sweden. This is very platy and looks like Hydrozincite since it appears as a surface coating (plates). Margarosanite is only found in two places–Franklin New Jersey and Varmland Sweden. Margarosanite glows sky blue (SW). The Calcite glows red-orange (SW). 9 oz. 3.5" tall. Value $50-55.

Same under SW UV.

POWELLITE: Powellite crystals with Heulandite (NF clear), Apophyllite (NF blue) and Stilbite (NF white). Powellite glows creamy white (SW). From Raigad, India. 10 oz. 6" wide. Value $35-40.

Same under SW UV.

178

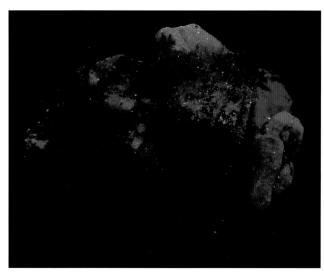

RUBY: Mysore Ruby from Mysore, India. Ruby glows a rich dark red (LW). Since the red is at the far end of the spectrum, it is difficult to see unless the viewing area is very dark. 1.5 oz. 1.5" x 1". Value $15-18.

Same under LW UV.

RUBY, APATITE, and PHLOGOPITE: Ruby in marble with Apatite and Phlogopite from the Kurakuram Mountains of Pakistan. This Ruby glows a bright rich red (LW and less intense under SW). The daylight Apatite glows blue-white (SW) and the Phlogopite Mica glows creamy yellow (SW). .25 oz. .75" x .5". Value $10-12.

Same under SW and LW UV combined.

RUBY with APATITE: Ruby in marble with Apatite from the Kurakuram Mountains of Pakistan. Ruby glows a rich red (LW and less intense under SW). The daylight Apatite glows blue-white (SW). .5 oz. 1" x .5". Value $8-10.

Same under SW and LW UV combined.

SCHEELITE: Scheelite crystals on matrix from Yxjoberget, Orebro, Sweden. Scheelite fluoresces bright white (SW). 3.5 oz. 2.5" wide. Value $15-20.

Same under SW UV.

SCHEELITE: A nice grouping of Scheelite crystals on matrix from Traveresella, Italy. This came out of an old collection and this site may no longer exist. Scheelite glows blue-white (SW). 12.5 oz. 4" x 2" x 2". Value $65-75.

Same under SW UV.

SCHEELITE: Scheelite crystals, the source of Tungsten, comes from Tae Hwa, Chung Ju, Chung Chong Pukdo, South Korea. Scheelite glows blue-white under SW. Scheelite from this location is rarely available on the mineral market. 2 oz. 1.75" x .875" x .5". Value $17-20.

Same under SW UV.

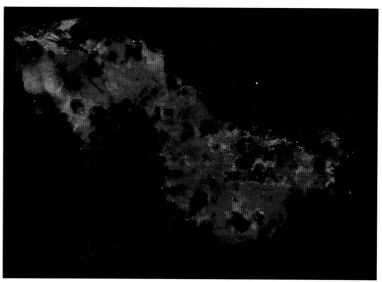

Same under LW UV.

SODALITE: A gray stone with a white patch of Sodalite. It is from the upper part of the Tuliok River, Kuibiuoi, Massif, Kola, Russia. The Sodalite glows two colors–blue and orange (LW) and it is very tenebrescent. After a five second exposure to SW UV, the Sodalite turns a dark grape color. There is probably another few unknown fluorescent minerals in the rock (orange speck, greenish area). 2.75 oz. 2.5" x 1.75" x 1.5". Value $15-18.

SODALITE: A large, daylight aqua blue crystal of Sodalite from Badakhshan, Afghanistan. This crystal glows orange under LW. 4 oz. 2.5" x 1.75" x 1.5". Value $300-325. *From the Greg Lesinski collection.*

Same under LW UV.

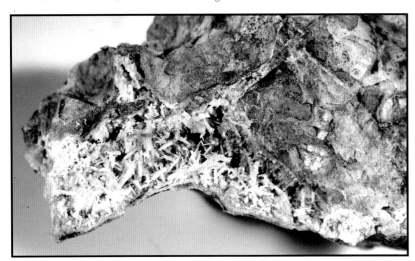

STRONTIANITE: A stone with seams filled with tiny white crystal spears of Strontianite from the province of Piagnolo di Vetto, Reggio Emilia, Italy. The Strontianite glows bright blue-white (SW), and has great phosphorescence. It glows tan (LW). This is the brightest response found in Strontianite which is a type of Aragonite. 1 oz. 1.75" x 1 x 1". Value $18-20.

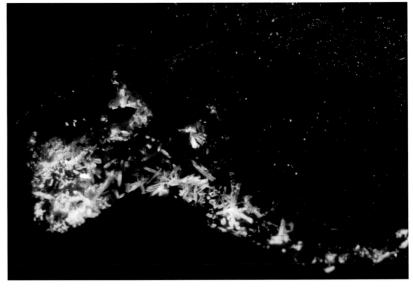

Same under SW UV.

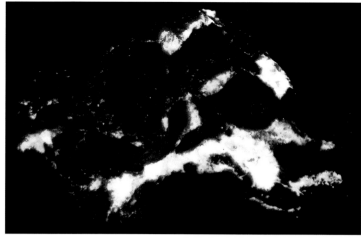

STRONTIANITE: Seams filled with very tiny white crystals of Strontianite from the province of Piagnolo di Vetto, Reggio Emilia Italy. The Strontianite glows bright blue-white (SW), has great phosphorescence. It glows tan (LW). This is the brightest response found in Strontianite which is a type of Aragonite. 1.25 oz. 2" x 1.5" x .75". Value $18-20.

Same under SW UV.

SVABITE: Svabite and Calcite from Langban, Varmland, Sweden. One side has a dense field of Svabite and the other side has fine veins of Svabite. This is a classic location for Svabite. The location also produces other interesting fluorescent minerals. Svabite is a Fluorapatite where the Arsenic content is greater than the Phosphorus content. 12 oz. 3.25" x 2.75" x 1.25". Value $40-50.

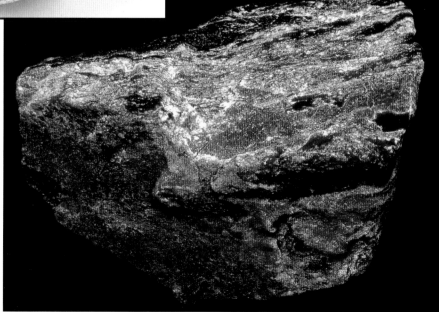

Same under SW UV.

UVITE and TALC: Brown Uvite crystals on Talc from Bradu Valley, Pakistan. Uvite glows brown-tan (SW), Talc glows white (SW). 11 oz. 4.25" x 2.5" x 1". Value $20-25.

Same under SW UV.

WILLEMITE from ZAMBIA: A wonderful stone containing lots of Willemite crystals from Star Zinc Mine, Broken Hill, Zambia, North-Western Rhodesia, South Africa. If this stone was from the Franklin, New Jersey area, it would cost many times this stone's value. The Willemite glows green and has a nice phosphorescence. 5.25 oz. 2" x 2" x 1.5". Value $50-55.

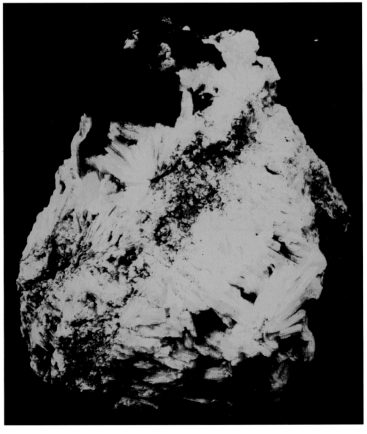

Same under SW UV.

material in pockets in a 15 foot long boulder. The symmetry of the second crystal recovered from the pocket (right) clearly was not hexagonal. I had the notion that the material was some type of beryllium silicate. To add to the confusion, I ran the Morin test for beryllium and it was positive. I later found out that I had detected less than one ppm beryllium. I had Bart run x-ray diffraction on both samples. The result was that both samples were identical and further, the x-ray pattern did not match anything in the ASTM x-ray files. Having had previous false alarms, I requested that Bart rerun the x-ray diffraction using quartz as an internal standard. The results were the same. Matters rested there until I read the guest editorial of Pete Dunn in the Mineralogical Record of November 1975 '"So you think you have a new mineral."' I sent a letter to the Smithsonian with all the information that I had on the material and the mineral became Zektzerite."* This Zektzerite glows blue-white (SW). The crystal on the left is about .4" high and the one on the right is about 1.5" high.

ZEKTZERITE: Zektzerite is restricted to the agpaitic granite of the Golden Horn batholith at Kangaroo Ridge, Okanogan County, Washington. It occurs both as an accessory rock forming mineral, particularly in the pegmatitic segregations and as euhedral crystals in vugs associated with microcline, rare smoky quartz crystals, zircon, gagarinite, arfvedsonite, okanoganite. The agpaitic granite is a sheet with gradational boundaries about 1000 feet thick occurring between 5500 to 6500 or 7000 feet above sea level in the eastern end of the batholith. The granite is recognized in the field by the presence of blue black amphiboles and, of course, the pocket contents. Virtually all the Zektzerite specimens recovered are from float boulders below the cliff band at about 6000 feet. In that respect, the occurrence is similar to the second recognized locality–the moraines of the Dari-i-Pioz. glacier in northern Tajikistan. (These pieces are from the collection of Jack Zektzer, the man for whom the mineral is named.) Jack tells a bit about the find: *"The first specimen was found by Bart Cannon in 1966. That specimen (left) has a 1 cm tabular pseudohexagonal crystal of very pale pink color mimicking a typical Morganite. This both Bart and I agreed was a beryl. There the matter rested until 1975 when I found more of the*

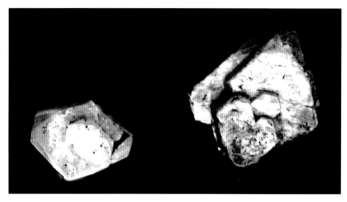

Same under SW UV.

ZEKTZERITE: Zektzerite with Neptunite in Microcline from Dari-i-Pioz. Massif (glacier) Valley, Garm Region, Tien-Shan, Tajikistan. This Zektzerite is usually found as grains rather than crystals. There are a few Russian rock dealers who specialize in fluorescent minerals from the former Soviet Union and who sell this mineral. This Tajikistan Zektzerite glows light blue (SW), Neptunite glows tan (SW), and Microcline glows red (SW). 1 oz. 1.75" x 1.25" wide. Value $35-45.

Same under SW UV.

Same under LW UV.

ZINCITE: An incredible yellowish-green crystal "tree" formed in the chimneys of Zinc smelters in Silesia, Poland. The crystals were found when they knocked down a hundred year old Zinc smelter and discovered that pure crystals of Zincite that had grown on the inside of the chimney. The Zincite glows an incredibly rich yellow-green (LW, less under SW). 3.5 oz. 3.25" x 1" x 1". When you can find them, they are usually found as individual crystals or small crystal groups This is an exceptionally nice piece. Value $250-300.

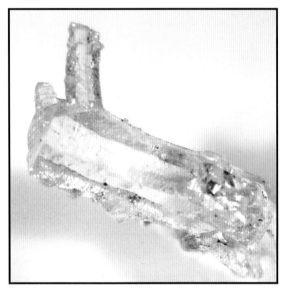

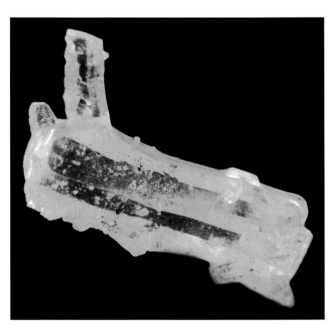

Same under SW UV.

ZINCITE: A small gemmy yellowish-green crystal formed in the chimneys of Zinc smelters in Silesia, Poland. The Zincite is man-made and glows an incredibly rich yellow-green (SW). .675". Value $4-5.

Same under SW UV.

ZIRCON: Zircon crystal from Mud Tank Carbonatite, Harts Range, Northern Territory, Australia. Zircon fluoresces golden tan (SW). 1.25 oz. 1.25" wide. Value $15-20.

Unknown Locations

Same under SW UV.

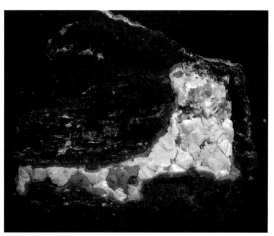

CALCITE: An attractive group of tan Calcite crystals growing in a vug with Chalcedony surrounding it. The Calcite glows tan under SW and LW. There is not a great deal of difference in the color under LW and SW. The Chalcedony glows white. From an unknown location. 1 lb. 1 oz. 5" x 4" x 3". Value $15-20.

Same under LW UV.

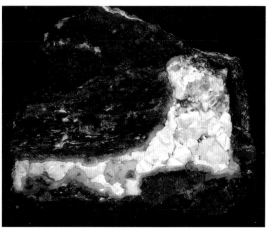

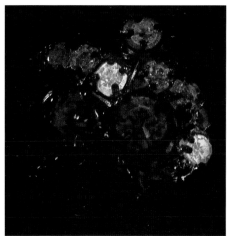

DIAMOND: This cocktail ring with a group of diamonds shows that some diamonds fluoresce under SW UV. The DeBeers diamond mine company spent years researching this fluorescence to try to help it find ways to differentiate man-made diamonds from natural diamonds. They found that the fluorescence of a natural diamond was not an accurate way to tell the two apart from each other. Two of the diamonds have a blue-gray response under SW.

SCHEELITE: Scheelite vein and specks in a pink rock (probably a Feldspar) from an unknown mine. It glows a bright blue-white under SW while the rest of the rock glows a velvet red. 4.5 oz. 3.25" x 1.5" x 1.5". Value $15-20.

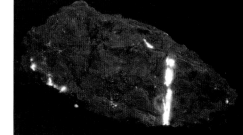

Same under SW UV.

Mineral Shows

FRANKLIN MINERAL SHOW: It is set-up time at the outdoor part of the late summer 2003 Franklin Mineral Show. This two day event is sponsored by the Franklin Ogdensburg Mineral Society and is the best place on earth to find fluorescent minerals. Dealers come from all over the country and offer great material. There is also an indoor section with a dark room containing some of the bigger fluorescent mineral dealers and a superb fluorescent mineral display.

FRANKLIN MINERAL SHOW: Kurt Hennig with his table of Franklin fluorescents and New Jersey Zeolites set up at the outdoor section of the Franklin late summer mineral show.

FRANKLIN MINERAL SHOW: Dru Wilbur, noted collector and geologist with his table of world-wide fluorescents set up at the outdoor section of the Franklin late summer mineral show.

SMALL LOCAL ROCK SHOW: These small local rock and gem shows sponsored by local mineral societies are often set up in parking lots or school gyms. Some wonderful material can be found there if you know what you are looking for. Often the material is from local sites and collections.

Miscellaneous Mine Collectibles

600 LEVEL: A sign from the Sterling Hill Mine in Ogdensburg, NJ. This was rescued from the "Old East Shaft" of the mine before the waters rose and cut off access to the lower levels. It dates to the 1920s.

NJ ZINC 25 YEAR PIN: A small gold and enamel twenty-five year pin given to a valued New Jersey Zinc Company employee. Value $18-22.

MINE SAFETY POSTER: From the Anaconda Company. 24" x 18". Value $15.

MINE SAFETY POSTER: From the Anaconda Company. 24" x 18". Value $15.

SHAFT DIRECTION: A 1940s sign from the Sterling Hill Mine in Ogdensburg, New Jersey indicating the direction of the shaft. This was rescued from the West Shaft area.

FRANKLIN FURNACE: Before Franklin, New Jersey was called Franklin, it was known as Franklin Furnace. This Franklin Furnace bottle came out of an old mine dump.

SAFETY EXIT DIRECTION: A 1940s sign from the Sterling Hill Mine in Ogdensburg, indicating the direction of the safety exit. This was rescued from the West Shaft area.

189

Resources

Collecting Groups, Information, and Museums

The Fluorescent Mineral Society. This is a great organization that publishes newsletters and links you with a group of people who will not laugh when you tell them you collect glowing rocks. It was started by Don Newsome, Thomas S. Warren, and a few other collectors in 1970-1971. It is a must-join organization for fluorescent mineral collectors. For information, write to Dr. Rodney Burroughs, P.O. Box 572694, Tarzana, CA 91357 or go to www.uvminerals.org. You can also order the popular books on fluorescent mineral collecting from the FMS.

The Franklin-Ogdensburg Mineral Society. This is the local New Jersey collector's organization that puts on two great rock shows each year. They publish a newsletter. Membership is $15.00 per year. Write to P.O. Box 146, Franklin, New Jersey 07416.

The Franklin Mineral Museum, 32 Evans Road, Franklin, New Jersey 07416. Open March (weekends only) then April 1 to December 1, Monday to Saturday 10 am to 4 pm, Sunday 12:30 pm to 4:30 pm. www.franklinmineralmuseum.com.

The Sterling Hill Mining Museum and Thomas S. Warren Museum of Fluorescence, 30 Plant St., Ogdensburg, New Jersey 07439. Open April 1 through November 30, 7 days a week, 10 am to 5 pm. Web site at www.sterlinghill.org.

Stuart Schneider's Fluorescent Mineral Museum Online at www.wordcraft.net.

The St. Lawrence Co. Rock and Mineral Club can be found at c/o Virginia Searles, 42 1/2 Maple Street, Potsdam, NY 13676, http://web.northnet.org/st.lawrence.co.mineral.club.

Franklin and Sterling Hill Minerals. Herb Yeates' web site is a superb source of information for New Jersey fluorescent minerals. www.simplethinking.com.

The Alkali-Nuts. The Mont Saint-Hilaire, Canada Fluorescent Mineral Group's web site is a wonderful source of information on MSH minerals. It is at www.saint-hilaire.ca.

Rock and Gem Magazine, 4880 Market St., Ventura, CA 93003-7783. A full color gem and mineral magazine with articles and information on every aspect of mineral collecting.

Mineral Dealers

Anderson Fluorescent Minerals is a dealer in fluorescent minerals. 1430 Vue Du Bay Ct., San Diego, CA 92109.

Excalibur Mineral Co. provides analytical service, rare minerals, books, supplies. 1000 North Division St., Peekskill, NY 10566, website at www.excaliburmineral.com.

Purple Passion Mine, Bill Gardner, 4608 W. Bluefield Ave., Glendale, AZ 85308 sells fluorescent minerals from the mine and carries a quality line of mineral lights. Email him at wggardner@aol.com.

GSL Rocks is a dealer in fluorescent minerals and mineral lights. Write Greg at 4726 Porter Center Rd, Lewiston, NY 14905. Email them at gslrocks@aol.com.

Tom Jokela is a good source to buy Canadian fluorescents at www.element51.com/fluorescents.htm.

Veronica Matthews Minerals, P.O. Box 588, Hammock Rd., Westbrook, CT 06498 is a dealer in fluorescent minerals.

For information on traveling to Greenland and collecting your own fluorescent minerals contact The MinerShop, 15583 SW 151st St., Miami, FL 33196. MinerShop, in conjunction with Jewel Stones of Greenland, offers guided Adventure Tours each summer season. Tours are limited to eight people per week and include trips to all the locations mentioned in this article. For more information visit http://www.minershop.com, or send an email to sales@minershop.com.

Benitoite, Neptunite, etc. in Natrolite is available from Steve Perry at steve@steveperrygems.com.

Polman Minerals is a dealer in fluorescent minerals. P.O. Box 93276, Phoenix, AZ 85070. Web site is www.polmanminerals.com or email at polmans@compuserve.com.

Rocko Minerals, Box 3A Route 3, Margaretville, NY 12455 is a dealer in fluorescent minerals. Email him at rocko@catskill.net.

Canadian Micro Mounts at Simkev Minerals. They have lots of tiny examples of rare MSH minerals. Email them at simkev@kos.net.

Soenke Stolze's fluorescent minerals for sale with a web site at www.systematic-minerals.com and email at stolze@systematic-minerals.com.

Charles B. Ward is a dealer in fluorescent minerals. 4071 NC 80, Bakersville, NC 28705.

Mineral Lights and Supplies

Buy the best light that you can afford. They are expensive, but they are the most important tool that a Fluorescent mineral collector can own. Check out several sources here and ask questions.

GSL Rocks is a dealer in reasonably priced 9 to 13 watt "Way Too Cool" mineral lights. Write them at 4726 Porter Center Rd, Lewiston, NY 14905. Email them at gslrocks@aol.com.

Mineral Labs. Supplies, lights, and other great stuff. Mineralab, 2860 Live Oak Dr. #G, Prescott, AZ 86305. Web site is www.mineralab.com.

MinResCo. A resource for minerals, lights, supplies, etc. Mineralogical Resource Co., 15840 East Alta Vista Way, San Jose, CA 95127. Web site at www.minresco.com or email them at xtls@minresco.com.

Raytech Industries makes a good series of mineral lights, including a nice portable model. Contact them at 475 Smith Road, Middletown, CT 06457. Web site is www.raytech-ind.com or email them at info@raytech-ind.com.

Lapidary supplies (at the best prices) at The Rock Peddler, 771 Boston Post Road East #180, Marlborough, MA 01752. Web site at www.rockpeddler.com or email at rockpeddler@attbi.com.

Spectronics Corp., 956 Brush Hollow Road, P.O. Box 483, Westbury, NY 11590. Website at www.spectroline.com or email at uvuv@aol.com.

UV Systems. Makers of the SuperBright™ Mineral lights (one of my favorites), UV Systems, 16605 127th SE, Renton, WA 98058. Website at www.uvsystems.com or email Don Newsome at uvsystems@aol.com.

UVLP, Inc. (Bruce Fine) is a new maker of a good series of reasonably priced mineral lights. Contact him at 105-150 Crowfoot Crescent NW, Ste. #603, Calgary Alberta T3G 3T2, Canada. Web site is www.uvlp.ca or email them at helpdesk@uvlp.ca.

UVP, Inc. makes a good series of mineral lights, including a nice portable model. Contact them at 2066 W.11th St., Upland, CA 91786. Web site is www.uvp.com or email them at uvp@uvp.com.

Bibliography

Horvath, Lazlo and Robert Gault, "Mont Saint-Hilaire," *The Mineralogical Record,* Vol. 21, #4, Tucson, AZ, 1990.

Palache, Charles, *The Minerals of Franklin and Sterling Hill Sussex New Jersey,* U.S. Government Printing Office, Washington, DC, 1935, 1960.

Pratt, M.E., *Report on the Diamond Joe Mining Property,* Arizona Department of Mines and Mineral Resources, 1938.

Robbins, Manuel, *Fluorescence, Gems and Minerals Under Ultraviolet Light,* Geoscience Press, Inc., Phoenix, AZ, 1994.

Robbins, Manuel, *The Collector's Book of Fluorescent Minerals,* Van Nostrand Reinhold Company, New York, NY, 1983.

The First Hundred Years of the New Jersey Zinc Company, New Jersey Zinc Co., New York, NY, 1948.

Warren, T., Gleason, S., Verbeek, E., Bostwick, R., *Ultraviolet Light and Fluorescent Minerals,* Thomas S. Warren c/o Williams Minerals, Rio, WV, 1995.

Franklin-Ogdensburg Mineral Society (FOMS), *The Picking Table,* the Journal of the FOMS.

The Fluorescent Mineral Society, Inc. (FMS), *UV Waves,* the Newsletter of the FMS.

Index